Dominic Dro **tic Direct** **Shakespeare's**
Globe Thea from 2006 to 2016. He is the author of *The
Full Room:* *A–Z of Contemporary Playwriting* and of *Will and Me:
How Shakes   are Took Over My Life*, whic won the inaugural Sheridan
Morley priz He reguarly contributes to the *Sunday Times* and other
publications.

'[Dromgoole's] love of language is contagious . . . the storytelling
segues into scholarship with extraordinary skill from the off as he
ricochets the modern world with a 400-year-old text'
The Times

'Entertaining, moving and informative'
Evening Standard

'This deeply humane, consistently enthralling acount of a theatrical
odyssey encompasses travelogue and literary criticism, theatre history
and introspective narrative, political commentary and philosophical
reflection with beguiling readability'
SIR STANLEY WELLS

'Erudite and fascinating . . . there's a real sense of the camaraderie and
sheer fun of assembling a company and, quite literally, putting the show
on wherever you can'
Observer

'A delightfully idiosyncratic account of the Globe's vagabond mission
to perform *Hamlet* in every country in the world . . . The joy of the
book is Dromgoole's gusto . . . the way he meanders from personal
anecdote to wider textual of cultural significance makes his book feel
like a shaggy-dog documentary that you just don't want to end ★★★★'
Daily Telegraph

'Exhilarating. The playing company's intrepid journey around the world
– performing Hamlet's own troubled journey – succeeds in making
the famili   uminating journey

Also by Dominic Dromgoole

The Full Room
Will and Me

HAMLET: GLOBE TO GLOBE

193,000 MILES
197 COUNTRIES
ONE PLAY

Dominic Dromgoole

CANONGATE

This paperback edition published in 2018 by Canongate Books

First published in Great Britain in 2017 by Canongate Books Ltd,
14 High Street, Edinburgh EH1 1TE

canongate.co.uk

1

Extract taken from *Station Island* © Estate of Seamus Heaney and
reprinted by permission of Faber and Faber Ltd

The moral right of the author has been asserted

British Library Cataloguing-in-Publication Data
A catalogue record for this book is available on
request from the British Library

ISBN 978 1 78211 692 9

Typeset in Bembo by Palimpsest Book Production Ltd,
Falkirk, Stirlingshire

Printed and bound in Great Britain by Clays Ltd, St Ives plc

MIX
Paper from
responsible sources
FSC
www.fsc.org
FSC® C018072

For the family who went all the way round,
For the family who stayed at home,
And for Sasha, Siofra, Grainne and Cara

Keep at a tangent.
When they make the circle wide, it's time to swim

out on your own and fill the element
with signatures on your own frequency,
echo soundings, searches, probes, allurements,

elver-gleams in the dark of the whole sea.

Seamus Heaney
Station Island

CONTENTS

INTRODUCTION

WE PLANNED WITH GUSTO AT the Globe. Some believe that away days should be focused affairs in blank overlit rooms, with PowerPoint presentations, brows so furrowed as to be carved in stone, and bullet points ricocheting off the walls. Others prefer firing middle management through forests on zipwires, or forcing upper management to humiliate themselves on assault courses. At the Globe, we took a different approach – good eating and gargantuan drinking.

2012 had been something of a landmark year. Inspired by the London Olympics, we put together a festival called Globe to Globe. It was a happy, simple and bold idea – to present within a six-week festival every one of Shakespeare's thirty-seven plays, each in a different language, each by a different company from overseas. We imagined that we would attract student companies and amateur groups, but as the idea spread, it captured the imagination in the way only stupid ideas can, and grew rapidly in scale. Everyone wanted to join in – apart from the French – and we were inundated with enthusiasm from all corners of the globe. We ended up with fifteen national theatre companies, shows from the most distinguished theatres in the world and some of its most distinctive artists. One country, South Sudan, formed a new national company to put on *Cymbeline*. The festival was all we could have hoped for, a generous eruption of humanity and art and dialogue.

Big ideas like that, once achieved, leave a vacuum. Having ridden in such a balloon of happiness and open perspective, it was hard to land on the ground again. So for a few months after the festival, we wandered around busy but with a listless sense of inactivity in the back of our minds.

We were on a two-day away day. The ostensible task was huge – to plan for a new theatre we were building, an indoor candlelit jewel to complement our outdoor citizens playhouse. It was due to open in twelve months' time. Building it, programming it, managing it, staffing it – everything was up in the air and had to be settled over two days. Day one was Heston Blumenthal's pub in Bray, followed by pints of gin in a shabby railway pub tucked in behind Paddington. Day two began pale and chastened, but settled into a very pleasant lunch in Scott's of Mayfair, a fastidiously minty place that raised its eyebrows above its smoothed hairline at the caravan of bicyclists and mothers with babies and scruffy technicians who tumbled in. We planned well in there and then repaired to a nearby hotel for cocktails.

If all this sounds a trifle louche, it was. So before any Colonel Bufton Tuftons or Comrade Mumble Grumbles reach for the 'how-dare-they-do-that-with-all-that-public-subsidy' attitude, it's probably worth mentioning that the Globe got no money from the government, nor from any major sponsors. We worked hard, and we earned all our own money. Although skating on thin financial ice led to a daunting level of high-wire tension, it also meant that, after much of the profit had been given to education, research and the building, we were free to spend the money that remained. Somewhere in that merry drinkathon, within a bleary mayhem of flirt and wind-up and raucous laughter, someone said,

'We need another big idea, something like the festival.' With barely a pause for thought, I said, 'Let's take *Hamlet* to every country in the world.'

Such ideas have a peculiar naturalness. They arrive as if they were already in the room. Because they need no explanation, people grab them quickly and enjoy elaborating on them. They're fertile ground for the contributions of others. Soon everyone was riffing on the idea and starting to work out the mechanics and logistics. Then, almost as soon, everyone was off the subject and back to flirting and winding-up and laughter. But the idea had a simple force which meant that it would stick.

It travelled.

★ ★ ★

Hamlet is a unique play in the canon of world drama. Loose, baggy, sometimes unwieldy, constructed from a known story and a previous play, its many details improvised from the pained and beautiful stuff within Shakespeare's soul, it ranges across a northern European landscape dominated by a gloomy castle and splashed by a cold sea crashing on rocks. It is a landscape struck by more flashes of lightning than any work of art could ever hope to be. Those flashes of lightning come from many directions – linguistic brilliance, psychological insight, political acuity, mythic resonance and simple family truth. Together they combine to create a statement about what it is to be human that has never been surpassed, both in the age it was written for and since.

It is hard to enumerate the number of directions from which it glances at you as you shift through life. The swirling mists of the Olivier film version were my first sustained contact. One of those television events from long ago when the nation sat together to share public culture. Quotes had been filling my ears from an early age. My parents were both Shakespeareans, my father in a public verse-quoting manner, my mother with greater privacy. There were profuse early readings, where bafflement would be disguised as mystic appreciation. As with many cultural artefacts we are dragged to at an early age, we feign excitement to satisfy the dragger, yet silently resent the difficulty. But buried in the experience, however resented it may be, some small kick of life, some small ignition in a part of ourselves we don't fully know, tells us we must return to witness it again. A silent promise is made for the future.

At a certain age, the play started to sing. Studying it with a mind less petrified by respect revealed its energies, its defiance and its exuberance. Performances could be relished rather than escaped. Hamlet the character began to take shape, not as a repository of cultural significance and oddly expressed wisdom, but as a sweet-natured and brilliant young man negotiating his way through a domestic and political nightmare. The language started to live with its own punk energy rather than the sonorous authority the Academy stifles it with. Much of the verse became necessary as solace. *Hamlet* has thrived in the public world, but its continuing life in the human heart is what has guaranteed its longevity.

I didn't understand the speech 'To be, or not to be . . .' when I first committed it to memory, and I'm not completely sure I understand it fully now. But it has lived in the larder of my memory for almost forty years, and can still be pulled from its musty recess to provide its familiar quantum of comfort. It offers no answers, nor any facile questions. It simply lets us know the same comforting message we offer our children when they cut themselves on the sharpness of the world. We tell them we suffered something similar at the same age. The fact we endured the same, a small act of sharing, washes away a little of the pain. In our worst despair, the fact that Hamlet has shared the like hurt or worse, and that his creator Shakespeare has expressed it with such a perfect dance of thought and word, tells us we are not alone in our sorrows.

Hamlet's journey through the play is specific, but within its broad pattern, and in his detailed responses to its various events, we appreciate a convulsion of the spirit we all know. It is Sartre's nausea and the juddering tears of the junkie begging on the street corner; it is the sobbing of the infant at the most basic injustice, and the articulate despair of the graduate shunted into a world which has neither plan for nor interest in them. It is the confusion we know at all ages – the manifest injustice of the world – that something capable of creating patterns of such beauty is so often inclined to moral ugliness. It is the state of perception we carry within us as a template for understanding our world, yet while grateful for its insights, we live in fear of its capacity, since if indulged it can overtake all other modes of understanding and plunge us into an enclosed state policed by the act of perception itself.

Overwhelmed by these thoughts in that scattered age between eighteen and twenty-five, it was then that *Hamlet* gripped me. Hungry for a path through that maze, Hamlet's story offered a movement towards the light. Towards the play's conclusion, as the young Prince walks towards a trap set by his stepfather, a trap he knows he will not survive, his friend Horatio advises him that he can walk away from his own fate. He replies:

> Not a whit, we defy augury: there's a special providence
> in the fall of a sparrow. If it be now, 'tis not to come; if

it be not to come, it will be now; if it be not now, yet
it will come: the readiness is all. Since no man has aught
of what he leaves, what is't to leave betimes? Let be.

Within a play of complicated expression, this section is an oasis of
simplicity. Beginning with the first, heavily accented 'if', there are
forty-two monosyllabic words in a row, with only one exception
– 'readiness'. This extended baldness of expression is exceptional
in Shakespeare. For me at that age, the simplicity of this language,
allied with the calm at its spirit's centre, its message of transcendent
acceptance of all the world had to offer, the good and the bad,
served as a mantra.

* * *

Translated into too many languages to count, and performed
more times than Shakespeare ate hot dinners, and cold ones, or
drew breath for that matter, *Hamlet* is one of those rare documents
that can be said to have brought the world closer together.
Audiences all over the planet have shared in its capacity to enlarge
the spectator's openness and desire to question. It has not only
shrunk space; it has also contracted time. Each person who watches
or hears it is telescoped back to the moment in 1601 when an
audience in the Globe first heard the opening words 'Who's
there?' Just as those first spectators share in every subsequent time
those words have begun an evening of queasily soulful entertainment. We all share in the suspended window of time within which
a play floats, experiencing our own night of only-happening-now
uniqueness and sharing the pleasure with the millions of others
who have heard the same words in other times and places.

In 1608, on board a ship called the *Dragon*, *Hamlet* was

performed by its crew off the coast of Sierra Leone for a group of visiting dignitaries. The crew remembered enough of the play from what they had seen at the Globe to shamble together a show. Within ten years of its first performance, groups of English actors, known collectively as the English Comedians, were performing it across northern Europe in abbreviated, action-packed adaptations. Since then it has played everywhere, in theatres, fields, caves, hovels and palaces.

It has tested thousands of actors and actresses, leaving some exhilarated with triumph and some desolate with failure, and all hungering for more. It has been recorded, televised and filmed over and over and over again. The performances of actors from Sarah Bernhardt to David Tennant, from Mel Gibson to Maxine Peake have been captured for posterity, and the sheer inclusiveness of that brief list says much about the play's openness to interpretation. It is recited in schoolrooms, quoted in boardrooms, mumbled by lovers, pondered on by sages, argued over by critics, passed on from parent to child, cursed by students, and wept over by spectators. In silence, it is stored in the heart as a fortifying secret by millions of us afraid of the bruising world. It is part of the fabric that surrounds us and sits within us. It has become, in large part, us.

* * *

In honour of the transcendent ubiquity of this play, on 23 April 2014, 450 years after the birth of Shakespeare, the Globe theatre, in response to a daft idea floated in a bar, set out on an artistic adventure almost as unique as the play we were honouring. To tour *Hamlet* to every country on earth. All 204. Or 197. Or however many were deemed to be countries at that particular moment. Unprecedented chutzpah and a healthy quantum of stupidity helped launch the mission. Beyond that, more practical factors made it possible. Over nine years, the Globe had formulated a style of touring as portable as the style in which actors travelled from the first Globe 400 years earlier. We had built up a network of international relationships with the Globe to Globe festival, which meant there wasn't a corner of the world where we could not phone and find a friend. But more importantly, technology had come to a point with air travel and information hyperlinking where it was now possible to move a theatre tour across the globe at a plausible speed and prepare satisfactorily for every arrival.

The marriage of globalisation and modernity sometimes seems to transfer little more than paranoia and violence. But we looked at the possibilities thrown up by that modernity, and instead of saying 'Why?', we thought 'Why not?' Why not use the potential of the world to transport not terror or commodities, but sixteen human souls, armed with hope, technique and strong shoes, their set packed into their luggage, the play wired into their memories, and present to every corner of the world, with a playful truth, the strangest and most beautiful play ever written. Why not?

Exactly two years later, on 23 April 2016, the 400th anniversary of Shakespeare's death, the same sixteen people returned to the Globe, having visited 190 countries and, via a series of performances in refugee camps, the peoples of 197 nations. They had played in amphitheatres, in bars, on roundabouts, in studios, on the shores of oceans, in front of thousands crammed into stadia, and in front of a handful of Romanian children in the rain.

At this moment, it would be appealing to adopt a deep voice, or its prose equivalent, and write: 'This book is the story of that journey.' But it would be misleading. The story of that journey can never be told: it is too big, too profuse. Each gig offered up so much material, so many intersections with politics, culture and history, that each visit could prompt a book. There were 200 of them. It might also be something of an impertinence, as I only visited twenty of the venues, and those who really carry the stories are the company – the twelve actors and the four stage managers. They made the whole journey. They all have remarkable stories to tell. Each of the twenty countries I visited felt like an injection of rich information for the imagination to work over. A theatre company has a special capacity to learn about an area, freely moving from shambolic shebeen to ambassador's drawing room. Each visit was short but never short on insights. There is much that a tortoise can witness that a swift will miss, but the opposite also has a certain weight of truth.

An exhaustive hoovering up of every detail would be beyond me, but I was fortunate enough to see much that amused and provoked. Always through the prism of *Hamlet*. Each country has thrown fresh light on the play, its large themes and its smaller nooks and crannies, just as this protean play has been able to throw new light on the world and its many faces. The tour changed my view of the play, the play changed my understanding of the tour, and both shifted my perspectives on the world and on myself. I have tried to set down some of this dialogue between the play and the world, to see how each illuminated the other.

This book will tell several stories, amongst others the story of *Hamlet* itself, of how this infinite masterpiece was born, how it grew into the world and how, with its generosity of spirit, it still helps us to understand our changing world. It will attempt to understand how the play has travelled so far and penetrated so deeply. At each moment, my response to the play shifted, with each insight bringing fresh confusion, each confusion fresh insight, and I try to mark those moments. I do so in the full knowledge that this is only watching a train covering a few stations on a long journey. *Hamlet* will never stand waiting for us; it will always demand fresh understanding. The moment of 'Aha! I've got it!' will never arrive, nor should it.

Everywhere the play visited, it encountered countries of vast difference, caught in contrasting historical and political moments. The performance cannot hold a mirror up to so many forms of nature, but Hamlet, with his restless desire to dream up a new sensibility, speaks to all people in any moment trying to create a better future out of the ashes of a world that breaks their heart. As such, our production spoke to many of the people who encountered it, and learnt from them. Together I hope these stories, and this conversation between Globe and globe, give a little insight into our world as it is now, and also of this extraordinary play which still shadows and mirrors and changes that world.

1

WHO'S THERE?

ACTUS PRIMUS SCOENA PRIMA
Enter Barnardo and Franciscus two centinels
Barnardo: Who's there?

THERE IS NO BETTER OPENING line – the simplicity, the affront of
it – 'Who's there?' It works purely on its own surface, a nervous
soldier on a battlement, in the dark and cold, asking with a shiver
who walks towards him. It starts the play at a thriller pace and
sets the blood tingling. We opened our production with the cast
milling around amongst the audience and belting out a rousing
song. It was interrupted the first time for a speech of welcome,
with music underscoring, and then a second time abruptly –
dead-stopping wandering, singing and music with a barked 'Who's
there?' The play was underway, swords were out, tension bristled
the air. The first two words are an instant challenge to the theatricality of the event. Unless the director is very eccentric (many
are), the old soldier – Barnardo – will be looking out front. The
question immediately includes and excludes everyone watching.
It makes them participatory because addressed, and shuts them

out because the soldier cannot see, cannot know them – 'Who's there?' Two syllables and immediate unease.

Top of the Frequently Asked Questions as we set out on this adventure was 'Why *Hamlet?*' We flirted with other titles, but in our bones knew we were circling around and always returning to *Hamlet.* We had done two small-scale tours of *Hamlet,* in 2011 and 2012, so were confident that it worked, though we did cast our eyes along the waterfront. *A Midsummer Night's Dream* has an unsurpassable flight and grace, but an actor squeezing into a tattered fairy costume a year down the road might have been disheartened; *Twelfth Night* is not robust enough of tone to survive the exigencies of touring; and *King Lear* is just too dark. *Romeo and Juliet* was a clear candidate because of its iconic status, but the play is structurally broken-backed. Packed with beautiful poetry and a searing story, it loses its way after the death of Mercutio and never quite regains it until the end. Carrying that Fourth Act around the world would have been dispiriting. Also, and this was the weightiest problem, *Romeo and Juliet* reveals its own meanings after a brief search. Six months in, and the company would have uncovered its secrets. They would have known what they were playing, which is fatal. If the tour was to be a valuable journey for the company, and thus for audiences, the play had to remain elusive. This was guaranteed with *Hamlet. Hamlet* is beautiful, a necessity, it is ram-packed with iconic moments which translate across cultures, a necessity, but most important of all it is mysterious, the greatest necessity.

The protean nature of the text was as important as its elusiveness. We were visiting a vast variety of cultures, of peoples caught at disparate political and historical moments. There is something about the kaleidoscope of possible responses to *Hamlet* which suited a journey of such rapid and extensive change. *Hamlet* can inspire and it can challenge; it can provoke and it can console; it can rebuke and it can comfort. We needed to travel with a story that could talk to people in all these ways. It also needed to talk with purpose. Not with a message, God help us, but with a voice that had energy and purpose in its pulse. *Hamlet* is often given an obscuring energy as prescribed by a Victorian idea of tragedy – ponderousness and pain suffocate it with a pillow of self-glorying glumness. We didn't do glum at the Globe – the sheer glee of the room would not allow it. *Hamlet* has a gleaming energy, and through its bright and shining leading man it has its eyes on the horizon of the future.

As well as talking with variety, and with purpose, it is most important that *Hamlet* talks openly. It is not a muttering play, a manipulative play, nor a dishonest play. In its heart, and through the soliloquies which stud its progress, it is open. The paradox of being freely open and freely mysterious is a Shakespearean paradox. The man in the corner at a party, all dark and silent and brooding, is nine times out of ten not a man of mystery; he's a man with not much to say. It is perfectly possible to be garrulous and to conceal. This play manages to be naked and invisible at the same time. A paradox contained within those opening words, 'Who's there?'

So having decided on the play, we had to work out how to do it. Then the question 'who's there?' developed a new pertinence. Who was there to help?

★ ★ ★

To focus our brains, we kicked off the same way we had our 2012 festival, by throwing a big breakfast for all of London's ambassadors. This served as a mark in the sand, a way of getting ourselves organised and a way of making connections. The plan was to introduce ourselves, explain our plan and plead for help. A hundred ambassadors in a room at nine o'clock in the morning is a bizarre sight. Because of the variety and the early hour, everyone exaggerates their own distinctiveness, playing up their national stereotypes. A South American ambassador threw about extravagant Latin charm; the French representative looked unimpressed; the Scandinavians were blonde and kind, looking after the shy wallflowers in the corner; the Russian representative looked suspicious; a representative from the Far East boggled us with their efficiency. The event started to look like an oversized xenophobic sitcom.

Tom Bird, our executive producer, a warm and scruffy presence, made a great speech, then we led everyone from our restaurant into the theatre and onto our stage. This was a calculated thrill: standing on the Globe's oak boards is a privilege and never failed to give a jolt of energy. I stood in front of a map of the world and talked everyone through the journey. With outstretched finger, I outlined our imagined route across a beautiful map set up on an old wooden easel. From Europe through North America, Central America and the Caribbean, South America, West Africa down to the South, then across to Australasia, all around the Pacific Islands, and then working slowly back from the Far East and finishing with East Africa before heading home. With a few detours to avoid war and epidemics, this was pretty much the route we ended up following. There was something antiquated, of course, about a man standing beside a map of the world and pointing out how we would chart a course through distant lands. It was an irony we were aware of and played up.

The morning was a success. It galvanised us into action, though less than a tenth of our eventual relationships would come from this route. Governments can be useful, and they can be a burden. We were at pains to point out, from the beginning and throughout, that we were not going anywhere to play to local dignitaries or to be an extension of a diplomatic garden-party circuit. That we wanted to meet people and to play to audiences of people. In this we were 95 per cent successful. The number of countries we travelled to where tickets were free and where the audience was generously inclusive was one of the joys of the enterprise. There were a handful of cases where we felt we were being exploited and manipulated by a government to serve a purpose, and we pushed back. But in the vast majority of cases, we encountered innocence and enthusiasm. So the breakfast worked, and set a number of global hares running for us to chase. Business cards were collected in prodigious numbers, and the phones started to buzz.

★ ★ ★

The next big challenge was to announce the project to the press. This was ever a delicate business, since the dangers were twofold. First, that they would ignore it completely; second, that they would seek out ways to ridicule the whole thing. Why this is their collective first instinct is beyond me, but there you go, we get the press we deserve. We knew that we needed an endorsement of some sort, from a source of unimpeachable integrity. We put out many virtue-seeking feelers and felt we were drawing a blank, then, just as we were about to send out a press release, an email came through:

The six simplest words in the English language are TO BE OR NOT TO BE. There is hardly a corner of the planet where these words have not been translated. Even in English, those who can't speak the language will at once recognise the sound and exclaim 'Shakespeare!' *Hamlet* is the most all-encompassing of Shakespeare's plays. Everyone, young or old, can today find an immediate identification with its characters, their pains and their interrogations. To take *Hamlet* in its original language around the world is a bold and dynamic project. It can bring a rich journey of discovery to new audiences everywhere.

This comes with every wish for all your projects.

Ever,
Peter

This was a boon. Peter Brook, the great director and visionary of internationalism, was the right person. He is a sage soul who has long since reached a place of international respect. His words were dropped into the press release, and out it went.

All on that front was going well, then two weeks before we went into rehearsals we were approached by the *Sunday Express* asking how we felt about going to North Korea. We explained that we were going to every country in the world, that everyone deserved *Hamlet*, and that North Korea was full of human beings. They started talking about how Kim Jong-un had killed his uncle and had him fed to the pigs. It was clear their agenda was set. The journalist was an intern working part-time there and (fair play to her) was the only person who had worked out there might be a story in this. We discovered that she had got a condemnation out of Amnesty International. I had been a fully paid-up and admiring member of Amnesty for many years and was miffed that they hadn't contacted us about it. I rang their press officer, who had made the statement to the freedom-fighters of the *Sunday Express*. He was quick to make his feelings clear: 'We believe North Korea is an oppressive regime, with no respect for human rights, and that it is wrong for you to stage *Hamlet* there.'

'Well, we see the point on human rights, but we are taking this show to every country in the world, and North Korea is a country—'

'You're doing what?'

'We're going to every country in the world.'

'Are you?'

'Yes, did you not know that?'

'No, I thought you were just going to North Korea.'

'Well, we're stupid, but we're not that stupid.'

'No, really, every country in the world? Wow, great idea.'

'Yes, that's the only reason we're going to North Korea. Does that change your opinion now you know why we're going?'

A long pause. Then . . .

'We believe North Korea is an oppressive regime, with no respect for human rights, and that it is wrong for you to stage *Hamlet* there.'

The story ran. It made a minor splash in itself, but it set a ball rolling that followed us around the world, and the North Korea question popped up with deadening frequency. We were able to hone our response early – that we were travelling to play to people; that we were not there to defend any regimes, we were there to defend *Hamlet*; and that we believed that every country was better off for the presence of *Hamlet*. This response became practised, maybe over-practised. It would have been great to say more. That aside from North Korea being a murderous and mad dictatorship, which is a given and a disgrace, it often seems that if it wasn't there, people would invent it, since it fulfils a function that the rest of the world needs. Every playground looks to find one kid to ostracise, every village needs to choose one family that it treats as beyond the pale.

* * *

Our first *Hamlet* tour, before we decided to go global, had begun in Margate in 2011. We had such fun doing it, and audiences lapped it up so greedily, we toured it again the next year, with a large section in the USA. No one ever felt it was definitively this or that, but it felt fit for purpose. The second tour I wasn't free to direct, so asked Bill Buckhurst, an actor transitioning to directing, and doing so well, to take the model I had created – same set, same text and same music – and to make it better. He went with the brightness and energy of our approach, and filled it with a greater urgency and need to tell itself. For the round-the-world tour, I asked Bill to work on it with me, so that we might have the best of both productions. Happily, he agreed.

Together with its designer, Jonathan Fensom, we had come up with a loose aesthetic that resembled a 1930s socially progressive touring company, like Joan Littlewood and Ewan MacColl's Theatre of Action outfit. Donning a cloak here or a hat there, the company could quickly acquire the shapes and silhouettes of Elizabethan clothing. Over the two previous tours, working with two composers, Laura Forrest-Hay and Bill Barclay, we had put together a suite of music and songs which helped define the evening. Warm folky songs to relax the air and dispel the Shakespeare/*Hamlet* fear; and utilising the skills of the actor-musicians, a bit of everything else – some fanfare music, some atmospheric scrapings for the Ghost, some keening violin work to skim across transitions, a gentle pipe tune to introduce Ophelia, drums to punch the urgency along. Everything played live, and everything in sight. No concealment at the Globe: a show was a show.

At the end, as in all Globe shows, an eruptive and joyous jig, choreographed by the jig-meister Siân Williams. Every show at the first Globe – even a tragedy – would end with a jig, where the whole company danced together. In the original Globe, they would interrupt the dance, and the comedian in the company would tell jokes. We didn't go that far, but we did enshrine the spirit of jigging. It is a wonderful way of cleansing the theatre after the emotion spent in it, of letting the air in the room shrug off any residual pain with good grace. In the jig for *Hamlet*, the dead bodies left sprawled across the stage – Gertrude, Claudius, Laertes and Hamlet – were one by one finger-clicked back to life, with an invitation to a dance. They rose to join. Many interpreted this as a message about bringing the dead back to life, but in fact it was just a solution to the perennial problem of how to get dead bodies off a stage. The jig started slow and then accelerated to a thigh-slapping, hand-clapping frenzy that never failed to raise a joyous cheer. These were the bare bones, and they were bare indeed, of the production we had made. At the end of the first half, we did the dumbshow which the text demands. It started with two of the actors lowering two planks to meet each other. Written on them was 'TWO PLANKS AND A PASSION', an old actor's phrase defining all you need to make theatre happen. That was the spirit of the show. Now we needed actors to flesh it out.

★ ★ ★

Casting was always going to be the biggest challenge. Peter Brook says that casting is 80 per cent of what he does, and he spends careful years doing it. He invites potential colleagues to hang out and befriends them, long before he thinks of offering them a role. We didn't have that amount of time but respected the care in the process. When people asked, I said we were looking for 'actor-astronauts', people of balance and strength who could float out in space for a couple of years. Actors who could keep themselves steady, take good care of each other and keep their minds on the task in front of them.

Everyone's definition of good actors is different. I favour those who bring energy to the room, who bring wit to the language, who have heart but don't show it off, and who are steadfastly and uniquely themselves. Many directors want actors who erase their individuality to conform to the director's idea of a syncopated uniformity. I like individuals. Uniformity on stage breaks my heart; it is not a suitable response to plays or a world full of dappled things.

Above all else, the actors must be kind. When we were casting at the Globe, we always enquired around about how an actor was to work with. The Globe was reliant on actors – not on directors or designers. Trust and goodwill, as well as quality, were paramount. Trust that your actor would show up on time, cover your back and give you what you needed on stage was at the heart of our work. The importance of trust, and goodwill, were maximised on this tour by the many other potential difficulties involved. We needed great actors, but beyond that we needed great people. Luckily, we got them.

There is a magical section – a montage – in the film *The Sting* when Paul Newman wanders around putting his old team of conmen back together. He surprises them in their present place of work, be it a bank or a bookies, and, appearing discreetly at the back of a crowd in their eyeline, touches his nose lightly or tips his hat to them. They immediately drop what they are doing, whatever it might be, to come and work with him. It is a witty visual hymn to the never-diminishing bonds of the team. The early part of our casting became a little like that, as we gathered together a core of trusted old friends. To share between them the senior roles – Claudius, Polonius, Gravedigger, Ghost, Priest, First Player and sundry old soldiers – we recruited three old friends who if not grizzled were battle hardened – John Dougall, Keith Bartlett, and the king of the Maori acting community, Rawiri Paratene. To play the several lines of younger men – Laertes, Marcellus, Horatio, Rosencrantz, Guildenstern, Osric and Fortinbras – there were two actors who had played already in our previous *Hamlet* tours of 2011 and 2012, Tommy Lawrence and Matt Romain, and another who had spent several summers with us, Beruce Khan. An actress who had played a previous tour, Miranda Foster, a thoroughbred, was keen to play Gertrude, the Player Queen and Second Gravedigger. Two further friends, actresses of enormous promise, Amanda Wilkin and Phoebe Fildes, came on board to play the Gertrude line, and the Ophelia line, and to cross gender lines as Rosencrantz, Guildenstern and Horatio. Four stage managers – Dave McEvoy, Adam Moore, Carrie Burnham and Becky Austin – miracles of industry and phlegm, were prepared and happy to put life on hold for a couple of years.

All these old allies had hard questions about the working of the tour, about the pay and the conditions and the security and the time off, which we answered. But given the length of the commitment, and the hole it would punch in their lives, the amount they took on trust was affirming. They knew it was an adventure, they trusted us, we tipped our hat to them, and they came on board. There was something magical in their leap into the dark, something close to the heart of being in the theatre. Running away to join the circus is a cliché, but it has an application beyond Pinocchio – freedom, movement and independence are its essence.

We had three more members of the squad to find – a further young actress, Jennifer Leong, who came recommended by a brilliant Cantonese company we had worked with from Hong Kong. And our two Hamlets. We explored a number of options in our heads for who to go after, but finally resolved that discovery would be the best route, to find young and new actors. Unknown quantities who would bring the excitement at being there and the openness that was at the heart of the show. We met a few, and were beginning to worry, when Ladi Emeruwa, an actor recently out of drama school, sent in a tape of himself doing a speech of Brutus. It was clear, and it was eloquent, and he was alive within the thought. He was soon on board. Naeem Hayat had played at the Globe in our Sam Wanamaker Festival, with a short chunk of *Richard III*. There was something indefinably compelling about him – he seemed to be able to sit in the middle of the maelstrom of the role and to be at the same time on a mountain looking down on it. We met him, he read beautifully, and he was in. The fact that both our Hamlets were not white, the fact that half the company were non-white, occasioned some comment but for us was as natural as walking into a brighter room.

All groups that set out on any journey in the cause of Shakespeare live in the shadow of one set of names. In the First Folio, in a loving act of remembering and claiming, one of the early pages is headed *The Names of the Principall Actors in all these Playes*. An act of remembering, because many of these actors had died by the time the Folio went to press, including the author, Shakespeare, and the company's brightest star, Burbage. An act of claiming, because the Folio was put together by two of that company, Heminges and Condell. Their loyalty for their old muckers breathes through the list. Those names – solid, yeoman English names, sturdy as the oak of the Globe – are: William Shakespeare, Richard Burbage, John Heminges, Augustine Phillips, William Kempe, Thomas Pope (unfortunately spelt Poope for posterity), George Bryan, Henry Condell, William Sly, Richard Cowly, John Lowin, Samuel Cross, Alexander Cook, William Ostler, Samuel Gilbourne, Robert Armin, Nathan Field, John Underwood, Nicholas Tooley, William Ecclestone, Joseph Taylor, Robert Benfield, Robert Gough, Richard Robinson, John Shanke, John Rice. A different England talks through that list – fields and woods and cooks and tailors and early churches and market crosses – and through those tough Anglo-Saxon consonants. These are not names from the upper classes either; these are from trade and from soil. The names that have adorned playbills and programmes ever since are many and various, but we were happy that our list of names reflected a modern and a changed England. In no particular order, they were Amanda Wilkin, Becky Austin, Beruce Khan, Keith Bartlett, Rawiri Paratene, John Dougall, Adam Moore, Ladi Emeruwa, Carrie Burnham, Jennifer Leong, Tommy Lawrence, Phoebe Fildes, Naeem Hayat, Dave McEvoy, Miranda Foster and Matt Romain. A different world, and worthy names to send out into it.

* * *

The meet-and-greet before the first day of rehearsals was aglow with excitement, the company and the Globe staff giddy with the future. With many of these large ideas, no one ever quite believes it is going to take place until you gather together in a large room and it becomes intimidatingly actual. The feeling of jumping off the cliff into the unknown promotes a sort of hysteria, like a children's birthday party after the lemonade has been guzzled. I do my bit with the world map and say some words. After most of the staff have gone, I invoke the old Russian habit of a moment of silence before a long journey. We sit in a circle, quiet in our thoughts and starting to register the size of what is ahead of us. Nothing particularly magical happens, but it is a sound way of expelling some of the hysteria and settling people back into themselves before rehearsals begin.

Five weeks later, and *only* five weeks to rehearse a host of different versions of the casting, plus a lot of music, plus a dumb-show and a jig, five weeks and we were ready to do our first performances at the Middle Temple. This ancient building, in the heart of legal London, was the room where the first recorded performance of *Twelfth Night* took place in 1602. We thought it a propitious place to preview the show before starting in the Globe. It proved tougher than we would have hoped. The room has a gravy brown-ness which makes it feel like acting in soup, the acoustic is rough, and we had to play in a very odd traverse shape, which made it hard to know where to pitch the play. The response from the audience was a bit ho-hum. This disheartened some of the company, who I think had assumed the quality of the show would automatically mirror the ambition of the endeavour. The one doesn't necessarily follow the other. However, I was heartened. The show was there, the story was told, and it had a gracious modesty in the world. Too great an immediate success would have induced a grandiosity, which would have been a nightmare to tour. 'See, see how great we are' is not an attitude to take on the road – it's not an attitude for anything really. We wouldn't want to, in that acerbic Dublin phrase, 'Give ourselves a big welcome'. The tread of the show along the road needed to be gentle and hopeful.

The next week we opened at the Globe, and the first performance on 23 April went through the roof. The first show of a Globe season always has a giddiness, and with the prospect of the journey beyond, it went into overdrive. Hysterical laughter, rounds of applause and a huge shout-out at the end. In truth, the show was still rocky, and the actors didn't quite know how to handle the enthusiasm sweeping the room. They played three more at the Globe and were able to wrestle it into shape. They were also able to store within themselves the nuclear-strength goodwill that the Globe is able to generate, a radioactive glow that would keep them warm for months ahead. The show was not perfect, but it worked. It told the story, it carried the language and delivered it, and it presented the life within the story. This is not always what people mean by theatre these days. There is a difference between a car that works, and an exploding car with balloons on it. A car that works ferries people from A to Z, conveying them from where they begin to a different place, and along the way it shows them scenery, whether beautiful, sad or strange. A lot of theatre these days seems to be watching a car festooned with balloons explode, then bursting into applause and waiting for a blogger to deconstruct the event. Having been taken nowhere. Our show didn't dazzle or explode, but it worked.

And it felt ready to wander.

* * *

The other question thrown up by those two words, 'Who's there?', is of course one of identity. That felt more pertinent than ever as we headed out into the world of 2014. We were walking into a world of awkward and uneasy identity. In the West there was a blaze of issues and confusions around identity politics. These sometimes seem like the invention of a crisis by those who have too much time to invent crises, and sometimes seem like the freshest political thinking in the world. Beyond the West, it seemed that everywhere was re-inventing itself, that the spread of lifestyle and choice and ideologies promulgated by the internet was eroding old distinctions. Beyond the ambassadors appearing at our break-fast and exaggerating their own differences, it felt like the broader population were starting to melt theirs, to share and to collaborate in creating new personal choices. There are minorities who cling all the more fiercely to their distinctive identities, white suprem-acists and Islamic jihadists most noticeably, but they often seem to cling to anachronisms so fiercely because they can see the tide flowing so ineluctably in the opposite direction.

Stephen Greenblatt in his brilliant *Renaissance Self-Fashioning* discusses the cultural moment both before and during Shakespeare's life when the idea of a 'self' began to be considered, and the modes within which it was influenced. While recognising that the Renaissance period experienced a change in social and psycho-logical structures, he throws a spotlight on how structures of power worked to impose forms of control on people as they were attempting to forge their own identities. In his pursuit of how identities are formed, he asks to what degree we are auton-omous in the fashioning of our selves, and to what degree we are in thrall to the social contexts which surround us. The writing of his book was informed by the pessimism of America as it recovered from the Vietnam War, from Watergate and from the overwhelming sense that government and the corporate powerful were attempting to control the nature of individuals' selves. His conclusion was that no matter how much control we think we have, our identities are formed through culture, its hierarchies, its systems and ideologies. Autonomy is denied: 'in all my texts and documents, there were, so far as I could tell, no moments of pure, unfettered subjectivity'.

How much more is this the case now? The internet, and particularly social media, often appears to be one big forum for bullying people into shapes. Personality itself sometimes seems to be little more than a fashion, an aggregation which changes daily of what it is to be cool and in the moment, an aggregation which changes with such swiftness that to swim within its swirling currents is a deadly business. The only law within this shifting norm is that you have to stay within it, however its styling may change from one moment to the next. And that anyone will be punished, and publicly, for stepping outside its crushing conformities. The speed with which the crowd punishes those who do not share those norms is terrifying, even though the very nature of self surely demands their rejection.

How positive it felt, then, to send Hamlet out into this environment, a young man, under pressure, frantically trying to forge a new identity in opposition to the context that surrounds him. To send him out into a world of queasily shifting identities, the hero of all heroes who worried most consistently over the ongoing creation of himself. Not to provide any answers but to keep asking the question, 'Who's there?'

2

HONOURING THE UPBEAT

HAMLET *Speak the speech, I pray you, as I pronounced it to you,*
trippingly on the tongue . . .

Act 3, Scene 2

'GOOD MORNING, MR PRESIDENT. WELCOME to the Globe!' I
say from the stage. From down in the yard, a confident, low and
strong 'Good morning!' comes back at me. Having played to no
shortage of prime ministers and presidents over two years of
journeying, we have now landed the Big Kahuna. The least-disappointing man in the world, Barack Obama, stands in the yard
of the Globe. He is on a quick visit to London, and to honour
Shakespeare's birthday and the 400th anniversary of his death he
is paying us a visit. It is the end of our tour, and before we start
a final weekend of performances we are giving a quick private
turn. A security cordon has shut down the whole of Southwark,
helicopters hover noisily above, and a liberal scattering of terrifying
men with big guns sets no one at their ease. But in the theatre
it is early spring and fresh, and the company are backing me with
music as I say briefly who we are and what we do. Then Matt

31

Romain tears into Hamlet's advice to the Players, delivered straight to President Obama:

> Speak the speech, I pray you, as I pronounced it to you, trippingly on the tongue: but if you mouth it, as many of your players do, I had as lief the town-crier spoke my lines. Nor do not saw the air too much with your hand, thus, but use all gently; for in the very torrent, tempest, and, as I may say, the whirlwind of passion, you must acquire and beget a temperance that may give it smooth-ness . . . Be not too tame neither, but let your own discretion be your tutor: suit the action to the word, the word to the action; with this special observance, that you o'erstep not the modesty of nature: for any thing so overdone is from the purpose of playing, whose end, both at the first and now, was and is, to hold, as 'twere, the mirror up to nature; to show virtue her own feature, scorn her own image, and the very age and body of the time his form and pressure.

The Hamlets have been instructed when they soliloquise to quash their fears and talk straight at the President, to give an impression of the Globe's direct communication. After the performance, he joins us on stage – as relaxed, warm and direct as one might imagine – and talks Shakespeare. I ask him if he has ever acted, and he comes straight back with 'Have I ever acted? I act every single day. Every time I go down to Congress, I'm acting. When I sit down with certain world leaders, I have to do a lot of acting.' It's done with laconic timing, and with a surprising frankness before a group of actors he has never met. I decide to test his humour.

'It's great that Matt delivered "Speak the speech" straight at you, because it's quite a lesson in oratory . . .'

'Yes, indeed, there were a few tips I could take from that,' he conceded.

'Well, let's face it, you certainly need them,' I deadpanned.

There was a spilt-second of glint in his eye, a flash of 'who the hell is this guy?', and then a big laugh. Whatever admiration we felt – off the scale already – flipped into overdrive. The President could take a tease.

★ ★ ★

These words, Hamlet's celebrated advice to the Players, delivered before they perform his lamentable play, are, of course, lessons in acting rather than oratory. They are the prayer offered up by every playwright on the eve of each first night since. They can be brutally compressed into 'Oh, please, stop acting and just say the fucking lines.' Ever since first spoken on the Globe stage by Richard Burbage in 1601, they have been the ultimate rule book, which generation after generation of actors since, have done their level best to ignore. These words imprinted on their minds, they have walked off in the opposite direction and carried on mouthing, sawing, whirlwinding, o'erstepping and overdoing as if their lives depended on it. People treat these injunctions as if they were specific to the sins of Elizabethan actors. They are not; they are a perennial. Rehearsals for the last four centuries have often been simply a matter of returning and returning to their wisdom.

At the heart of the speech is a *cri de coeur* for respect for the 'modesty of nature'. The world is not full of people trembling or gnashing their teeth; it is full of people being. Nor of people muttering and mumbling either, sitting on the back foot and undercutting the energy of others. It is naturalness that is wanted – the same apportioned and appropriate energy we give to life is what we want to see on stage. Holding 'the mirror up to nature' is often quoted as if it means being studiedly contemporary, reporting on the world and trying to emulate what newspapers do; it is not. It is about being judicious and true in the playing of people and relationships; it is about being unforced and unaffected in the speaking of language. If that is played true to humans in the world, the form and pressure of the time will naturally make itself felt.

How do you create a rehearsal room so these things can happen? First, you make the room sharp: not clever, not necessarily wise, but certainly sharp. A room that is dull of wit will lead to a dull show. The wit, the insight, the spark of thought and imagination that is in the room will appear on the stage. This does not mean casting people who have university degrees. Nothing wrong with them, but they are not a necessity. It means casting people with emotional intelligence, with street-smart wit, and with an understanding of how language works in the space between people. Fill a room up with smart people and the play gets smart. Fill it with dullards – even if they've all got firsts from top universities – and you're stuffed.

Before anything else, you read the play, sit round a table and make sure of one thing: that everyone understands every single word of each scene they are in. There is nothing more depressing than a stage of actors who have no idea what is coming out of other people's mouths, nor even sometimes their own. This happens not infrequently. The earliest stage of rehearsals is the moment to sort this out. As you go through the play, no one is allowed to say the overall meaning of this, or the gist of that; you precisely drill down on every line, every phrase and every word, and make sure they know its exact meaning. If we are to have any theatre of meaning, we do not need to learn how to mime bottles into babies, how to monocycle, or how to scream and shout; we need to be precise and clear about language. Language is what is remarkable about us, language is what makes us and our world, not our ability to wave our arms around in the air. Dancing is a joy, singing takes us to places we could not otherwise reach, but language and being human are an intertwined genetic code creating us and our world. When we start hearing that theatre is not about language, we are often dealing with people who secretly hate it.

To keep the room sharp, there are a few rules. First, everyone is allowed to be a fool, and no question is too stupid. If something is mysterious or unknown, no one should be frightened to admit it. We all have black holes of ignorance, and we should be open about them. But just as important, everyone should be allowed to be smart. No one should be frightened of being informative and generous with knowledge. We are plagued in our contemporary theatre with a fetishising of childishness and simplicity, a worshipping of ignorance. If someone has something of interest or value to say, all should want to hear it. Most important of all, the room needs to be relaxed, and not proud. It always helps if you have a few people who have worked together before, and their relaxed manner with each other can help others worry less about being formal. If I can call one of my old colleagues something unspeakably rude on day one, it usually relaxes the air. If they can call me the same, even better. You want a room to be kind, and to be respectful of each other's feelings, but never, never formal.

The moment when people get up from the table can be awkward. There is no solution beyond getting on with it. If the room has the right atmosphere, and if everyone feels free to try stuff out, to make mistakes and be brave, then the awkwardness passes. Making the room feel right is axiomatic. People have to allow each other space to be human and honest and foolish. Many things can help with this: a few daft stories to start the day, an attentiveness to listening, a little clowning about. Nothing relaxes the air more than laughter, and a room full of laughter is a healthy room. Tears should be able to flow freely but not indulgently. And a room needs a powerful communal bullshit detector. This starts with how people treat each other, and extends out into the work. If people start acting untruthfully, or phonily, or ostentatiously, you want the room rather than the director to let them know that it is wrong.

There was a unique technical problem with rehearsing this *Hamlet*. It ended up making it one of the most exciting times I have spent in a rehearsal room.

Our challenge was to rehearse not a team but a squad. To ensure that we always had cover, we had created a system where everyone was learning two, three, four, five, six or seven parts. This was in the full expectation that not everyone would last the full two years (it is still *impossible* to imagine the same sixteen people that left returned). We had two people to play Hamlet at the start (three by the end), three Ophelias, three Gertrudes, three Claudiuses, three Poloniuses, and by the conclusion of the tour six people who could play Horatio. We could do the play with eight, nine, ten, eleven or twelve actors. We set this up to provide cover and to spread the load of playing, and we soon realised it would be another way of keeping the play fresh. Not only would every venue be new, but also the combination of roles would surprise. In the first year of performance, the company only performed the same combination twice.

We created a carousel system, where we would rehearse a scene with one group of people, then at the end of one iteration, ask one actor to step out to be replaced by another; at the end of the next, a different actor would step out and be replaced, and so on. The scene would spin around the room, and people would jump on and off the bobbing horses. From the first, I said that everyone should be generous and selfish. If they saw someone making a choice on a line or thought that they liked, they should steal it; if they did something new, they should be prepared to give it away. Similarly, if they wanted to do something different, everyone working with them should accommodate it. The broad structure, clean and simple and driven by storytelling, was set by its directors; the details were very much up to the cast.

The work in the room became a fertile mix of imaginative commitment and critical judgement. In the moment they were in the scene, they were in it, alive to its feelings and imaginatively responding to its possibilities. The moment they were out, they were watching the same scene and assessing the truth or life of what their colleagues offered up. There were drawbacks: it was hard for the actors to gain the sheer grinding consistency which ceaseless repetition works into their bones. But the rewards were immense: it gave them an in-depth knowledge of the whole play, it gave them a mature perspective on what they were doing, and it created an atmosphere of parity and of generosity which made them a team. No one was leading the show, everyone was sharing, and all had to look out for each other. This set them up for the challenges ahead. It was also exhilarating to watch. Always the same, and always different, just as every rehearsal should be.

★ ★ ★

What sort of production was it to be? *Hamlet* is one of the most misconceived plays in performance history, its original intentions now obscured by the barnacles of 400 years of theory and presumption. How do you clean off all these misconceptions and try to return it to its original colours? When the Sistine Chapel was cleaned and revealed its primary freshness, many were upset that those nice faded colours, saturated in the smoke and dirt of history, had been lost. They found the renewed work disturbingly vibrant. Part of the Globe's remit was to reveal Shakespeare's plays with their original vitality, and for that it was always running into the conservatism of those who like a screen of history between themselves and a classic – just as they liked the musty grime on the Sistine Chapel.

The best way to avoid a misconception is to have no conception at all. There is such a glut of ideas about how to present particular plays, it is sometimes most radical to have no idea. This is hard for many to negotiate, since without a concept, or an argument, they have nothing to talk of afterwards but the play itself, a nudity which they find embarrassing to look at. Our job at the Globe was always to tell the story cleanly, to judge the relationships impartially, and to let the language do the work. To keep true to the modesty of nature. This approach requires oceans of technique and discipline and rigour, where most conceptual work requires puddles. Yet because the work is invisible – it chooses to be – most do not notice it. We ask hard questions about the relationships, about the world and about the language, and then we work our thoughts in discreetly, always ensuring that story and language is bright and clear.

Before becoming technical about language and the verse, it is vital to remember that this is a series of scenes that present life. Without dipping into naturalism, it is important to keep in front

of us Shakespeare's particular realism. This is not a realism based
on scenery, on sofas or drinks cabinets or kitchen sinks. It is a
realism based on actors coming out and establishing their own
reality. They believe that this is a cold rampart of a castle in
Denmark, so we can believe it too. The actor playing Hamlet has
to believe he is Hamlet so we can join him in the illusion. It is
bare-bones realism and has to be presented with absolute conviction. With nothing to back you up, you have to look behind you
and say 'this is a castle', and look out beyond the audience and
say 'that is Norway', and believe that both are true. If you can do
that, and grind the everyday truth of it into yourself, you can
convince an audience. *Fingunt simul creduntque*, said Tacitus – as
soon as they imagine, they believe. This is the bedrock of
Shakespeare's theatre – believe it, say it, and with the participation
of the audience it starts to come true.

The advantage here is that the scenes are written with a deft
but tungsten-strength verismo. Whether it is that first scene on
the battlements with its quick jerky questions and answers; or
the torrid swirls of give and take between mother and son in the
closet scene; or the awkwardness of the reluctant cleric officiating
over Ophelia's funeral; or the strained goodwill of the Players as
they are told how to act by an amateur – in each of these moments
and others, Shakespeare sketches a couple of quick lines and there
is life: this is his great art. These moments are mysterious and
unknowable as life is: they have all its meandering rhythms and
peculiar upbeats. Like a breathing still life or an artful photograph,
these scenes have that sense of life contained, of impermanence
briefly held. This requires truthful acting, alive to each moment
as it comes, not trying to force it into a scheme. Actors can be
eager for patterns to help decipher plays, and audiences as well.
It takes discipline to resist the inclination to fall into the seductive

falsehood of patterns, and to stay true to the wonderful incon-
sequentiality of life. But when every detail is animated, then we
start to warrant that life – not speeches, or ideas, or patterns – is
at the heart of the mystery of each play.

Our actors were up for this, and relished the responsibility. The
extra challenge was not just embodying the feeling of the scene,
but expressing it with nothing to help as a visual signifier. Without
scenery, their bodies had to do rampart, or throne room, or closet,
or graveyard. Each of them expressed with a different physical
energy: Ladi was a boxer briefly, and has some of that watchful-
ness; Rawiri is all buffo comedy and prop-forward, bull-like
energy; Miranda has a proscenium grace; Jen is a slip of a thing
and looks like a delicate blossom. It was impossible to force them
all to be the same, or to adopt a unified movement scheme,
without bleeding the democracy and humanity out of the event.
Each in their own way learnt how to occupy the empty space
and fill it with their own imagination. And thus, with theatre's
natural complicity, ours.

As well as the life of a play, it is important to seek out its wit.
This is not a matter of looking for laughs; it is finding the irony
and the comic sense of each particular play and releasing it. When
you get to know a new friend, you spend a little time winkling
out their humour, finding out what sparks the twinkle in their
eye (if you find nothing, then walk away); in the same way, you
look for what curls the smile of a play. There was not far to look
with *Hamlet*. No clown appears until the arrival of the Gravediggers,
but up to that point an abundance of humour has spilt from the
Prince himself. To a degree, he is the fool who is missing from
his own play.

His very first line, 'A little more than kin, and less than kind',
is a thousand things, but it is also a serviceable gag. It is clear

from his first engagements with Horatio, and Rosencrantz and Guildenstern, that their friendships are based on sparring wit and competitive funnies. Hamlet himself is a bright generous wit, throwaway pearls spilling out of him. Compare him with any of the other major tragic figures. A night of *Live at the Apollo* with a bill of Lear, Othello, Anthony, Coriolanus and Macbeth would be big on heckles and short on laughs. But Hamlet could hold his own. Especially if his wit is played as giveaway and involuntary as it should be. If it settles into mordancy or sarcasm, then you've got someone telling you he's the most intelligent person in the room, and we can all go home.

Humour ripples through the play. Polonius is a comic creation whose speeches have a not-entirely-under-the-character's-control Shavian irony. Rosencrantz and Guildenstern travel a darkly comic journey from two enthusiastic boobies on a free holiday, to the heart of a corroding state, and on to their eventual deaths. Hamlet gives some of the best comic advice ever delivered to the Players, so he is clearly not only fun in himself, but a student of comedy. The play within the play, or at least the lines that Hamlet has written with some clumsy moral lessons for his mother, are so eye-wateringly bad, their intention must be humorous.

When the clowns do arrive in the form of the Gravediggers, they have deliverable material and a deadpan vaudeville exchange with Hamlet worthy of a partnership that has worked long years round the provinces. When Hamlet is brought face to face with death, it is with the skull of a comedian. It is the death of laughter that he registers as the most switching irony:

> Alas, poor Yorrick! I knew him, Horatio: a fellow of
> infinite jest, of most excellent fancy: he hath borne me
> on his back a thousand times; and now . . . Here hung

those lips that I have kissed I know not how oft. Where
be your gibes now? Your gambols? Your songs? Your flashes
of merriment, that were wont to set the table on a roar?

It is a vivid and abiding image – a boy shrieking with laughter
charging around on the back of a clown. It is a laughter that has
gone now, but we know it was once there.

Even after this episode, the humour has not gone from the
play, since right at the death Shakespeare throws on the campest
and most ludicrous colour in the play, the flamboyant and futile
Osric. This is not an inexorable tonal drift towards death; this is
a sudden firework display of character comedy. At exactly the
wrong moment. Shakespeare doesn't just pull the rug of expectation away, he exposes the bottomless pit beneath it – the
Chekhovian existential pit that always opens up when you get
stuck with a weapons-grade bore.

Observing these things in rehearsal, delighting in the comic
invention and observation the actors brought to the room, was
not playing it for laughs, it was observing what is there, and
allowing it to breathe. It oxygenated the room and allowed us to
understand more of the play. It released the relationships and
hence some of the pain at its centre. It ran counter to an imposed
orthodoxy about how tragedies should be remorselessly tragic,
but the Globe, I'm glad to say, had always bucked that orthodoxy.
Happily, it had always been at war with all that Victorian crapola
about suffering being allied to virtue, seriousness being good for
you, and joy bad.

A year or so later, I was completely lost in Addis Ababa, a town
of swirling complexity which defies conventional map-reading. I
ended up walking along a motorway for a while, then speared off
into what I took to be a park. Somehow I found myself in the

presidential compound. Before I knew it, I was surrounded by dogs and men with guns, all shouting and barking with enthusiasm at the shambling foreigner. They saw me off. The compound, a sprawl of manicured acres, sat high on a hill looking out over a wide vista of tin slums, wooden sheds and half-built/half-broken blocks. Starving figures sat propped against the railings on the other side of the road. There was something obscene and desperate about the contrast. 'You have to laugh,' I thought aimlessly to myself, a bit of Somerset wisdom which has never left me. Just as I thought it, I looked up to see a roadside billboard garishly advertising 'The First Indigenous Laughter School in Africa'. It was presided over by the World Laughter Master, Belachew Girma, a man who has broken all known records for continuous laughter. Research revealed that he holds regular classes to teach people how to laugh continuously for hours on end. Ethiopia's very own Yorrick. I have thought of him every time since, whenever I encounter the po-faced sternness of those who say that tragedies must be tragedies and laughter can never walk through them.

The attitude is not just about laughter; it is more about spirit. Listen to the energy in that 'Speak the speech' exhortation. This is not a moany boy; it is an exhilarated fire of breathless anticipation falling out of a hot-wired brain. It is an instruction for acting generally, but also for this play in particular. It is a call for wit and brio – the French cavalry cry of 'À l'attaque!' In a 1960's arts programme, an unashamedly old-fashioned bit of television, Orson Welles and Peter O'Toole discuss *Hamlet*, quaffing whisky and chain-smoking cigarettes with sixties cool. While O'Toole proposes a textually underfunded theory that Gertrude is a lesbian, Welles propounds something more interesting. That the principal fact about Hamlet is that he is a 'genius'. Where Othello's central characteristic is that he is a black man in a white man's world,

King Lear's that he is a tyrant and a bad father, Anthony's an old soldier, Hamlet's is that he is a bona fide genius. A Mozartian prodigy of thought and feeling, out of step with his own world, who cannot help spilling thought and insight. It is a very Wellesian insight, but a true one, and a significant instruction for the whole play.

Central to the playing is the way we handle the verse. Much has been written, much spoken and much argued over in relation to how best to treat Shakespeare's verse. On the one hand there are the iambic fundamentalists, who believe passionately that every foot (two syllables) should be stressed the same way with a clean de-dum stress on the second syllable at all times, and that the end of every line should be given a light pause. At the other end of the spectrum are those who don't give a toss, and who mutter, shout and maul the verse in any way they like. Both are criminal, the latter deserving of a longer sentence. In the middle is our resident guru at the Globe, Giles Block, who believes that the stresses are flexible, that there is a form in the verse, and that observing that form, and its hidden music, is the best way to understand the intentions behind the thought.

A year later, and a long way from the Globe, I was sitting in a nomadic tent in Hargeisa, being taught the many forms of Somali verse. The highest literary poetry, as exemplified by their leading poet Hadrawi, is called Gabri, with a sophisticated metrical system and definite rules of scansion. There is another form for warriors on horses, a form that follows the movement of the horse; a poetry for putting up a house; one for women for weaving; another for taking camels to water; even a specific form for milking goats. Each form you can recite for hours on end to entertain and entrance yourself while you sink into the rhythm of words and work together. Some experts say of Shakespeare's iambic verse that it relates to footfall, and to our natural pace of walking; some that it has an intimate relationship with the heart-beat; and others with the pace at which we breathe. Whichever, what is plainly apparent, and made clear in the variety of Somali forms, is that there is a physiological relationship between verse and our bodies. It does not live only in our heads; it relates to how we move and how we live.

There are Somali forms for courtship, where potential lovers meet and recite to each other. They compete with rival lovers for who is the best within that verse form. They test companionship of soul and sex with potential partners through how well rhythms and inventiveness commingle. It was thrilling to hear these examples from a culture that is still genuinely oral, just as it was in Shakespeare's day. President Obama himself talked of the similarities between Shakespeare and rap, and how the new Broadway hit *Hamilton* by Lin-Manuel Miranda is Shakespearean in its verbal inventiveness and in its scope. Rap is a great indicator for Shakespeare in the freedom it affords. It has a matrix of musical rules, which are there not to inhibit, but to release. Rhyming in rap, as in Shakespeare, is there not to make people freeze, but to delight in language and its possibilities.

As far as possible, I remain a verse agnostic, not adhering to any particular system. What matters is that there is clarity and wholeness in the saying of the verse. That the energy is the sound of something flying swift and bright past you, fast as a kingfisher on a bright summer's day, that makes you want to follow it, join it and buckle yourself to it. The complexity in the language is something to be relished – it is forged from brightness and excitement.

Actors get that or they don't. Some can hear the pitch and the music of a play, almost as if they have a mystic sense, some clue to the red shift in the life of the writer which occasioned the particular music of the play. As if they can hear that event, whatever it was, and understand how energy is still rippling out from it. It is impossible to teach; it is something innate in the stomach of the actor. They can hear it from each other and imitate it as they would learn a song, but it can't be taught. John Dougall, whom I have worked with often, is an actor of this sort. I have usually cast him in the early scenes of a play, so that throughout rehearsals, at the read-through, when people first stand up, when they first do runs, at the dress and on the first night, he has hit the right groove and, like a tuning fork, set a tone and a pitch for others to follow.

I have a physical allergy to attending workshops of any kind, and almost go into anaphylactic shock at the prospect of running one. However, about halfway through the tour, I was bullied into doing one in Ethiopia at their National Theatre. I sat in a shabby room with broken windows with a group of actors, someone banging together wooden scaffolding outside and someone else plaiting together strings of red onions in a corner. The actors told me of their theatre, its history and traditions. I asked them to recite a little of their traditional verse. It was a joy to hear, exhaling a coffee richness in their mouths. The mode of delivery was one of separation from self and from each other. They went outside themselves to recite, looking at the floor or above people's heads. In the time available there was little to do, but they wanted to speak some Shakespeare, and they wanted to speak it in English. I gave them the briefest of talks on the iambic rhythm, and then we went through just two lines: 'To be, or not to be: that is the question: / Whether 'tis nobler in the mind to suffer . . .'

It was hard at first to get them to slough off the effect of having watched too many movies, and they clung to a casual modern idiom. I encouraged them not to force individual words too hard, nor to run words together with an affected casualness, but to find the gently propulsive forward-walking rhythm of each thought, and to express it from their mouths into the room. To observe and relish that steady path into a thought. Their thrill at handling the language was immediate, and the simplicity of those essential six syllables translated swiftly. I encouraged them to say it looking into each other's eyes, and to enjoy the bold ease of that. Again there were inhibitions. If you are not looking directly at someone, it is acting; if you are, it can feel like lying. They got over the other side of this and enjoyed the direct address, the clear engagement and the simple talking. There was a warm, happy energy in the room, and I noticed for the first time what lurks within the iambic rhythm – a hidden hope. As each gentle upturned stress occurred and passed from person to person, it pulsed a discreet energy into the speaker and listener, and beyond into the room. It gave a lift. I left the room in Addis Ababa with a better understanding of the nature of verse than I had achieved before. It is talking with invention, and with energy, and with a steady hope.

Just as each actor found their own way to make the scenes come alive, so they arrived at their own understanding of how to handle the verse. The seniors Keith, John and Miranda all had long years of Shakespeare with the RSC and others under their belts. The music was safely contained within them, so they could modulate delicately and freely within that music. Rawiri had much experience too, but a more declaratory style, which, together with his openness of face and heart, has a massive charm. Most of the young ones were finely tuned drama-school graduates who had an appetite for Shakespeare which was its own enchantment. There was a spectrum within their approach: Tommy has an easy conversational naturalness; Phoebe began as presenting a little more; Jen tended to the demure and the shy, and being the least experienced with the verse had the most to learn. But like any proper team of actors they lifted each other up. They watched each other and stole a little of this from him and copied a little of that from her. The last thing we wanted was an absolute consistency. A group of actors is not supposed to be a faceless unit; it is supposed to be a team of individuals, and by the end of rehearsals (thank the lord), a squad is what we had.

They needed to be. The conditions in which they made the play work over the next two years would have torn a fragile group to shreds and patches. I watched it in front of 200 ambassadors sitting at large desks in the UN; in front of a reluctant audience in Djibouti, with the waves of the Red Sea crashing loudly behind; to 2,000 restless students in an acoustic horror house in Phnom Penh; in a hotel ballroom in Hargeisa; in a tin shed in a Syrian refugee camp; and in a Roman amphitheatre in Amman. Everywhere they went, no matter the conditions, they tried to make the play come to life in front of whoever was watching. There were more extraordinary places I missed: 4,000 people crammed into a square outside a cathedral in Mérida, Yucatán; a roundabout in the rain in Bucharest; a bar in a Cameroon refugee camp; in a rock stadium before the crashing Pacific in Chile. Wherever they were, however impossible the conditions, or however speedy the set-up, they had each other, and they had the gentle support of each line of verse, its embedded rhythm tenderly placing a supporting palm on the base of their spines, the place where fear and exhaustion resides, and with the lightest touch it kept them upright and somehow kept them moving forward, into the story and towards the audience.

At one of the most difficult moments of the journey – one

actor very ill, another about to lose a close relation, another nursing a great friend towards a young death, a stage manager having lost his mother-in-law, Paris having just suffered the Bataclan massacre which made everyone nervous about home, and with everyone blitzed by exhaustion – the tour for a moment looked threadbare and fragile. Everyone was finding ways of coping, but it was clear that we were not flying on full tanks. I wrote to them:

> These are tough times. The play can help, your astonishing generosity to each other can help, the knowledge that you are doing something very special can help, the fact that beside all these personal heartbutts, and these more public tragedies, a lot of people are investing hope in what you are doing, that can help as well, but above all . . .
>
> Be kind to each other, and keep putting one foot in front of another.

That is what Shakespeare's plays teach us to do.

11 **Belarus**, Minsk   22 May 2014
    Janka Kupala National Academic Theatre
12 **Ukraine**, Kiev   24 May
    Mystetskyi Arsenal
13 **Moldova**, Chişinău   27 May
    National Teatrul 'Eugène Ionesco
14 **Romania**, Bucharest   30–31 May
    St Anthony Square
15 **Bulgaria**, Varna   3 June
    Stoyan Bachvarov Dramatic Theatre
16 **Macedonia**, Skopje   5 June
    Macedonian National Theatre
    Macedonia, Bitola   6 June
    Heraclea Lyncestis
17 **Albania**, Tirana   7 June
    Teatri Kombëtar
18 **Kosovo**, Pristina   10 June
    Teatri Kombëtar
19 **Montenegro**, Podgorica   12 June
    Montenegrin National Theatre
20 **Bosnia–Herzegovina**, Sarajevo   15 June
    National Theatre
21 **Croatia**, Zagreb   17 June
    Zagreb Youth Theatre
22 **Serbia**, Belgrade   18 June
    National Theatre in Belgrade
    Serbia, Čortanovci   19 June
    Vila Stankovic
23 **Hungary**, Budapest   21 June
    Margaret Island Open-Air Theatre
24 **Slovakia**, Bratislava   24 June
    Slovak National Theatre
25 **Czech Republic**, Prague   25–26 June
    Prague Castle
26 **Cyprus**, Limassol   5 July
    Kourion Amphitheatre

3

SETTING OUT THROUGH THE BALTICS

HAMLET *What players are they?*
ROSENCRANTZ *Even those you were wont to take delight in,*
  the tragedians of the city.

Act 2, Scene 2

STANDING ON AN OLD WOODEN jetty washed grey-green by the
sea in Ystad, in the south-eastern corner of Sweden. Murmurs
burble from a nearby restaurant sitting on rotting stilts above the
water, and small-town noises trickle towards the shore from the
miniature metropolis. The quiet of the Baltic in front and the
hills behind, as the sun goes down beyond them, is softly forceful.
It is broken by the rude throat-clearing of a ferry's foghorn as it
sweeps into the harbour. Another ferry emerging from the port
answers. They croak at each other cacophonously for a while.
Sweden to Poland, and Poland to Sweden. The passage cuts a line
across the Baltic Sea and the Hanseatic world, a stretch of water
long used for trade, for war, and for travelling actors. It is easy
to imagine from centuries past swifter and lighter vessels carrying
a cargo of new stories from the London stage.

A short walk behind me is a beautiful late nineteenth-century theatre, built in tidy proportion for the single-room plays of Ibsen and Strindberg. On first sight earlier that morning, I had thought it too domestic a space for the open expanse of our play, but the focus is so clean and the acoustic so simple, it proves a claustrophobic thrill to play, forcing up to the surface all the family poison, like an Ibsen three-acter. We are giving our fiercest and tightest performances thus far. Members of my office have flown out for the occasion. The logic behind this is sound: to stay connected with the company and to reward colleagues for their hard work. The result is hen/stag-night mayhem. I've stepped out for a little quiet, being not quite in mayhem mood, yet.

The sea and the ships remind me of the first stage of our *Hamlet* journey. Shortly after the premiere, the company left London on a suitable mode of transport. Gathering just beneath Tower Bridge on the Thames, surrounded by a couple of hundred well-wishers, the company boarded a small tall-boat and set off for Amsterdam. It was manned and helmed by taciturn Danish Captain Haddock lookie-likies. There was champagne and waving and hugging. A laconic Northern actor disconnected us from the jetty, threw the rope off and uttered a drily minimal 'Bye'. A boat bearing two television crews sped alongside for a while and then tailed off. Then there was silence. The high spirits gave way to a settled calm as the boat navigated its way down the Thames and out into the North Sea.

We awoke the next morning to a calm sea and moved forward wrapped in a caul of mist. People sat quiet and still on deckchairs, they lounged together in the netting, they climbed one by one up to the crow's nest as if it was an act of anointing. Later that afternoon, we found the coast of Holland and spent four hours negotiating our way through the broad Dutch canals and rivers, lulled by a North Sea quiet broken only by the putter of the ship's engine. In the evening, we pulled in behind the train station in Amsterdam. The expectation may have been of a 24-hour party, a sea-borne bacchanal, but the opposite had happened. A peaceful journey, untroubled by wind or wave, stillness moving through stillness, had bonded the company together in a silence more profound than any amount of exuberance could achieve.

Throughout our journeys, and in planning them, we talked of their correspondence to the first journeys that Shakespeare's plays had made as they sailed from London to take their chance in the world, carried in the memory of actors. The most celebrated instance of this early promulgation by water involves *Hamlet* and is problematic. It was the iconic performance of Hamlet on board the *Red Dragon* off the coast of Sierra Leone in 1608. According to the notebooks of their captain William Keeling, they performed *Hamlet* twice in the course of their journey around the globe between 1607 and 1610. The crew, many of whom had no doubt seen the show at the Globe, used the mnemonic capacity of their age and stitched a show together for a group of visiting dignitaries from the African mainland. The exoticism of this – at such a distance from home, and so soon after its premiere – leads many, including us, to blazon it as proof of the speed at which *Hamlet* moved into the world. We accept the internationalism of Shakespeare as a commonplace, but assume it's a modern development; in fact, it's as old as the plays themselves. Yet a historical shadow falls across the performance. The *Red Dragon* was one of the first ships of the East India Company. The juxtaposition of Shakespeare, the most pervasive soft-power influence of all time, with the great-great-grandfather of all psychopathic corporations is an uneasy one.

Many make much of the historical ripples set running by this incident. It throws up a slew of questions about whether Shakespeare is only the innocent fellow-traveller riding along beside the spreading blush of British pink colouring the world's map. But such thoughts rarely account for the parallel historical movement, which is the freedom with which these plays travelled elsewhere beyond the English Channel. Had Shakespeare's plays travelled only where the English language travelled, it might be justifiable to raise an eyebrow. But, in fact, *Hamlet* was quite quickly all over northern Europe. It was carried by actors.

Known collectively as the Comedians of England, these performers were a late sixteenth/early seventeenth-century phenomenon, with as many as 200 employed across the Continent. What drove them to seek pastures new? Sometimes they were simply told to – the Earl of Leicester's Men accompanied their patron on his progress through Utrecht, Leyden and The Hague in 1585, when the Earl was appointed commander of the English troops in the Netherlands. Frequently it was because they could make more money on the Continent. The economic instinct is a powerful one for an actor. There are almost always too many actors and too few jobs.

The kind of theatre presented in a German market square would have been distinct from what was presented at the Globe. The moniker 'Comedians of England' provides a clue as to their playing style. There is evidence the plays were substantially cut, and that broad farce, music and gymnastic feats were highlighted over delicate psychological acting. *Hamlet*, as we can surmise from contemporary accounts and from early translations, would probably have run at about an hour, with an extended dumbshow, and with incidents like the killing of Rosencrantz and Guildenstern played out in graphic fight sequences rather than reported. The kings of the companies were the clowns, who had to be bilingual so they could crack local jokes and bridge complicated narrative jumps with a little live storytelling. The resident Gdańsk clown went under the moniker Pickleherring, and a German one called himself Hans Stockfish, which tends to imply that German humour has been something of a historical constant.

We know the names of almost a hundred English actors working across Europe during this period, acting alone as house entertainer, travelling with companies, or joining local outfits throughout Scandinavia, the Lowlands, northern Germany, Austria, Bohemia and the Baltics. (France was left almost completely off the circuit, principally because of its Catholicism.) Amongst that list of actors are some distinguished names, including Ben Jonson and (from Shakespeare's company) Will Kempe, George Bryan and Thomas Pope. The last two both spent time working in Kronborg Castle in Elsinore, which is a substantial clue as to how Shakespeare knew so much about the tide-splashed rocks without and the cold stone gloom within. Many question how Shakespeare knew so much of the places he wrote about, while forgetting the most powerful transmitter of information in history – conversation. Bryan and Pope, having frozen the tips of their fingers off for a couple of years entertaining the Danish court, were probably never short of a memory or an anecdote, and it is little surprise that Shakespeare's evocation of the wind-whipped, forbidding grandeur of Elsinore is so accurate.

English actors were popular not for their delivery of text, but for the physicality of their performance. An Englishman, Fynes Moryson, travelling in Germany in 1618 remembered a group of English players, 'having neither a Complete number of Actors, nor any good Apparell, nor any ornament of the stage, yet the Germans, not understanding a word they said, flocked wonderfully to see their gestures and action'. English plays were popular because the London theatres of the time were play-factories, turning out thrilling history after lurid bloodbath after psychological thriller after rom-com-sex-farce. One of the first plays in German is *Der Bestrafte Brudermord* (The Brother Murder), a radically cut version of *Hamlet*, though essentially the same play. A German noble, Landgrave Maurice of Hesse-Cassel (they don't make titles like that any more), was so enamoured of the English theatre that he kept his own company of English performers. They toured under his patronage and played in a theatre he had specially built for them. Landgrave Maurice even travelled to London to commission new plays from English writers. This dashing and quixotic figure could be a neglected inspiration for Hamlet. We now see Prince Hamlet and his joy at the arrival of the Players in Denmark in a new light: the scenes around the play-within-a-play are not only a celebration of his ludic ingenuity, but also of his internationalism. When he welcomes the Players, for his contemporary audience he would not be an Englishman welcoming an English troupe, he would be a Dane welcoming an international troupe. Thus Hamlet becomes an early beacon of cosmopolitanism and a reflection of his own world.

Hamlet is a play full of a broad international awareness. Hamlet, a Dane, attends university at Wittenberg in what is now Germany. Laertes travels to find his fortune in Paris. Fortinbras travels from Norway to pass through Denmark on his way to fight in Poland. Hamlet is sent away in the Fourth Act to England, which is in a client relationship with Denmark. He escapes his fate there through the intercession of some pirates, and pirates are the first and last word in internationalism. This is not a narrow or insular play. It is in its geography a Hanseatic play, a league of countries surrounding the Baltic, held together by trade, by conquest, and for a short while by the touring chutzpah and ambition of English actors. We are following an old cultural drove road.

In about 1600, the first theatre was constructed in Poland. A former fencing school in what is now Gdańsk (then Danzig), it was converted to host professional players from London. A rectangular courtyard space open to the elements, modelled on the Fortune Theatre in Clerkenwell, it proved popular with the locals, and audiences flocked in. The traditional practice was for these English companies to petition the local mayor, requesting permission to play. Copies of these petitions to the mayor of Gdańsk are extant and provide evidence of the touring tradition. They are fawning in tone but shot through with the deal-making toughness of men who know their own worth. There are moans about the rain at recent performances, negotiations over ticket pricing, and accounts of having to improvise venues at the last minute when the plague would not allow access to the fencing school (our *Hamlet* tour had to skirt West Africa for similar reasons).

In a classic bid to reassure the burgomasters, they plead: 'Our entertainment will be so modest and polite that nobody will be offended by it; on the contrary, there will be all manner of instruction for everyday life to be gained.' It sounds like an application to the Arts Council stressing educational value. Permits were often refused, with forbidding words about how taxes weren't paid on the last visit, and sometimes granted, though accompanied with dire warnings about the fines that would follow excessive fly-posting. These petitions form a sweet testament to how little has changed over the intervening centuries: making and staging theatre is still an odd blend of flashy bombast, pragmatic horse-trading and naked begging.

Shakespeare and his colleagues' approach to the international market was a large part of the London theatre scene in the sixteenth and seventeenth centuries. Shakespeare's world was a genuinely European one, both in its ambitions for its work and in its audience at home. London was a city teeming with overseas visitors; Shakespeare himself boarded near the Blackfriars Theatre with a French family. Most of our knowledge of the layout of the Globe comes from a diary entry by a Swiss tourist, Thomas Platter, and a sketch of the Swan theatre by a Dutchman, Johannes de Witt. The Globe has always had a reciprocal relationship with the wider world, accepting audiences at home and travelling out to meet them.

* * *

It used to be taken as read that the early modern acting companies upped sticks and left London to go on the road because of the plague. That, and the rage and contempt of the city fathers. There's truth in both, but there is now ample evidence that touring carried on when the London theatres were open and healthy, and that companies ran an extensive touring programme alongside their building-based work.

Why tour? First, money. There was an audience of hungry citizens unable to come to London to be entertained. There were also wealthy parochial patrons eager to impress client networks and posh neighbours with shows they could sponsor and present. Money, and making it, is the most original practice of all. This is hard to credit in our day, full of shyly presented outreach programmes so stuffed with proof of virtue and condescending good works that mischief and fun (the motors of all good drama) hardly get a look in. Equally defeatist is our glum expectation that people deserve a medal for playing in 'the provinces', an expectation fuelled by a snobbish centralisation of artistic legitimacy. Within such contemporary contexts, it is impossible to get our heads around the confidence and desire with which these companies would travel. They didn't arrive timidly in the hope that an audience might show up, promising workshops and Q&As as an inducement; they kicked the door down, saying, 'We're here! Come and get it. We're going to shag some story into you.'

Touring was in these people's blood. For several hundred years, British theatre *was* touring. The fun palaces built in London in the 1570s and 1580s were Johnny-come-lately edifices. For centuries, British theatre had improvised stage realities, conjuring up Christian ritual in the courtyard of an inn, ancient Rome on booth stages in market squares, and English history at one end of a Guild Hall. Theatres were made not from wood and brick and plaster, but from the collaborating imagination and willpower of actors and audiences.

Shakespeare's own company, the Lord Chamberlain's Men, were a touring company long before they found a home. They frequently visited Stratford upon Avon, granted permission to perform by Shakespeare's father, John. The young Shakespeare would have been ushered to the front of the audience by his proud alderman father in Stratford's Guild Hall. Something in one of those performances, some stray gesture of magical unlocking, maybe an actor looking deep into his eyes with their perennial promiscuous connection, could have ignited the desire to make theatre within the young William. No matter that they would have been intoning some thumping old lump of Tudor poetry, the boy would have been hooked. There is speculation that his first experience of making theatre was after hitching a ride with a touring company and thrilling to the freedom of life on the road.

This is another central fact about touring. It is a blast. It is the single reason why touring began, continued and still continues. Theatre has become so defensive as a business, having to protect itself from the depredations of pundits and critics, always looking to find virtuous and socio-political reasons to justify its own existence, that it forgets to mention the principal reason why people get involved in the first place. It is the best time that you can have without drugs. Touring sharpens the pleasures that life in the theatre naturally affords – the sense of fleeting connection, of families created that are intense and short-lived, and all the more intense for their shortness. It also distils the outlaw pleasure of trucking into a place, painting the landscape around you in new and surprising colours, gifting a story, some laughter and some new thought to a community, and then getting out fast before the ties of responsibility, or the heavy hand of the law, catch up with you.

When Shakespeare has Hamlet welcome 'the tragedians of the city' into the narrative of his own world, he is setting off chimes for the audience, and in self-reflexive fashion for the author. The play they perform is clonky. Though 'The Murder of Gonzago/ Mousetrap' (with Hamlet's additions) is terrible by comparison with the real play, the freedom with which the Players blow through the cold stone world of Elsinore offers a glimpse for Hamlet and for us of a better way of life. They are free to come into the world with noise and joy; free to make frustratingly real connections with their phoney feelings, while Hamlet cannot connect with his own real ones; free to cock a snook at the court in a play that says much that is unsayable; free to speak truth to power. And then, crucially, free to go.

★ ★ ★

Back in Ystad, we were not exactly speaking truth to power, but we were honouring touring theatre traditions by getting very merry. A fierce show was followed by a hosted event at the theatre, turbo-charged by the audience's excitement. 'But I do not understand, it is just the play,' a Swedish theatre-maker burbled at me, 'it is just the play. It is so naked. It is so exciting. Just the play.' We had a similar effect at our first international gig in Amsterdam's Stadsschouwburg playhouse, a grand old theatre which houses the great Ivo van Hove's relentlessly experimental Toneelgroep company. You could sense the unease from the hyper-cultured audience as we began. Nursed and nurtured as they were on radical deconstructions and conceptual reworkings, the sheer nudity and bareness was a shock. For a while, you could sense their feeling that this was all a trick, and that at a certain point a huge amount of scenery would swoop in and make an elaborate point about war or gender or corruption in FIFA. Then you followed their growing realisation that this is what it is, and instead of worrying about having to have an attitude about something extraneous to the play itself, they were simply being asked to watch the play. You could almost sense a letting go of tension, a shoulder-dropping freedom as they realised that an attitude was not required, simply a head and a heart. Their relief was palpable, and in Amsterdam and in Ystad they rose in exhilaration at the end.

We repaired to our Spartan hotel, which we filled with Hellenistic delirium. It was early in the tour, and the company were all cautiously careful about each other's boundaries. There were no such worries between the company and the theatre staff, and boundaries were merrily crashed through. The scream of 'Jacuzzi!' went up, and everyone crowded into the one room with a functioning Jacuzzi and then all dived in. I didn't because I was tiring rapidly, and because younger actors have the most absurd bodies and comparisons are odious, so sloped off to pass out. The next morning offered the pleasure of watching extreme hangovers meeting a Nordic breakfast. Gherkins, pickles and coleslaws have a disorienting effect on delicate stomachs.

* * *

It was a determination of mine from the moment I arrived on Bankside that we would revive the first Globe's practice of going on the road. It was time for the Globe to spread the word beyond the polygonal enclosure of its own walls. We travelled first on a circuit around the United Kingdom, then reached out to Europe, then to the USA, and now, with *Hamlet*, were covering as much of the planet as we could.

Why did we risk the dignity of a loved institution with this new endeavour? First, we were filling a hole. Touring Shakespeare had been a continuous tradition since the plays were written. These plays were made for walking, not for sitting at home, but when we began our touring, the tradition was withering on the vine. Companies that had toured for decades had decided to dump that tradition and ditch their audiences, without leaving so much as a note on the kitchen table. The holes we were filling were not just cement municipal theatres that have to be filled with product; they were holes in the stomachs of people who had grown up with an appetite for the unique food Shakespeare provides.

Shakespeare wrote for the rough and simultaneously sophisti-cated instrument of the Globe, and towards the end of his life with an eye to the indoor theatres and the new storytelling and technological advantages they offered. But he also had a constant memory of the melodramatic pulse of the older forms of story-telling. The rough magic of touring companies was hard-wired into his understanding of theatre. He wanted to adapt and grow those energies, but he did not want to extinguish them. Shakespeare was never crudely dismissive of these forms. His affection for the hard-nosed pros who drift through *Hamlet* is palpable, as it is for the rude mechanicals in *Dream*, and for the absurdly pretentious presentation of the Nine Worthies in *Love's Labour's*. Nor, though an artist, was he as po-faced about being an artist as many of those who have reinterpreted him. He made his art out of mud and laughter.

There's a fashion in theatre now for creative elements to dub themselves theatre-makers. 'I'm not an interpreter of plays; I'm a theatre-maker,' they tell you rather shrilly. Fundamentally, this seems to mean they tell other people what to do, while they furrow their brows earnestly behind fashionable spectacles and practise some happening hand movements. Give them something to actually make — to sew, to clip together, to lift, to light, to attach — and they will break down in tears. Our touring shows had to be mountable and demountable within a couple of hours. Some of my sweetest moments in my time at the Globe were helping in that process. Then, when our stage management told me to go away because I was not helping, there was a similar pleasure in watching the economy of effort, the dexterity of hand and the skill of mind with which they completed their task. On beaches, in piazzas, in grand auditoria, in scruffy ones, they made a theatre each time. The simplicity of that, the purity in process, the truth in endless motion, is what our touring aimed to preserve.

Touring kept us honest. Our small-scale tours were the antidote to the institutional self-importance which being static can encase. If you are putting out chairs in a mud-sludged field, if you are improvising tickets for an insta-box-office from a book of raffle tickets, if you are dismantling a set as the rain pours down, it is hard to take yourself too seriously. However much you might try. We come into the theatre for the simple pleasure of giving joy and sharpening insight and honouring truth. It is easy to get diverted from that. We went on the road not only to risk our dignity, but actually to lose it. If you can't risk your dignity, you are lost as an artistic institution, and if you can't happily give it away, then you're lost as a theatre. There was something about doing this barebones, back-of-a-van, booth Shakespeare, at that moment and onwards, that served as a two-fingered salute to those who would build a moat around his work.

There is still a gatekeeper mentality in much of the Shakespeare world. Gestures, extravagant ones often, are made towards accessibility and openness and internationalism. When faced with the reality of that openness – a reality presented by the Globe with its twenty years of tickets at £5 catering to many millions – the high priests of the Shakespeare industry often run screaming back to their closed-shop conferences, burbling angrily about tourists and schoolchildren and the uneducated. Taking Shakespeare on the road was our best way of flying far from such exclusion. Taking *Hamlet* to the world was for us both a fact and a gesture: actually going to every country and metaphorically saying these plays were built for everyone.

The hares that Shakespeare set running 400 years ago still run, and, year on year, run further and wilder.

★ ★ ★

Four hundred years after Gdańsk opened its first theatre in the old fencing school, an enterprising group of visionaries, led by an ebullient academic, Jerzy Limon, built a new theatre on the same site. It was an impressive and expensive endeavour, and we were accorded the honour of being the first company to play the theatre with our *Hamlet*. A spectacular edifice on the edge of a beautiful town, it lacked the festivity one associates with a theatre. Built entirely of a forbidding and sombre black brick, and entirely featureless on the outside, undisturbed by signs or colour, it looked more like a holocaust memorial than a palace of fun. The inside was brighter, filled with startlingly blond wood. A cursory inspection revealed that no actors had been involved with its creation. From the stage, it was impossible to see almost a third of the seats, let alone be seen by them. There was a retractable roof, like Wimbledon – a brilliant idea – though there seemed to be an embargo on opening the roof if there had been any trace of wind over the preceding four months.

There was an opening ceremony the day before the first performance, attended by the President, the Prime Minister and a clutch of other dignitaries from Poland and abroad. Jerzy, who is one of the most charming and sweetest men in Europe, had come up with the lovely idea of our company presenting a petition to the Mayor of Gdańsk, as the Comedians of England had done 400 years before. We confected a speech from many of the ones we still have, with a few contemporary additions. Everyone was excited before the ceremony began. It didn't last.

The ceremony seemed to have been designed by committee, which was just about plausible, but appeared to be also executed by committee, which really wasn't. Speech followed long speech, and the sound system failed on a regular basis, so the audience, a large proportion of whom were not able to see what was happening, were treated to prolonged muttering by dignitaries. Video was as troubled as audio, and flickered to life uncertainly.

Prince Charles appeared on a screen, though sadly unaccompanied by sound, mouthing noiselessly his goodwill to the project. Various exotic acts appeared unsupported by much in the way of technology or knowledge of how the stage worked. Temporary relief was called when there was a bomb scare and everyone had to quit the theatre for an hour or so.

However, return was inevitable, and we were all shepherded back in. Our company were preparing to go on and present their petition when they noticed the stage filling up with smoke. They were reassured this was an effect and told to carry on. The stage was soon so full of dry ice that they quickly became uncertain as to where the audience was, or, more alarmingly, the edge of the stage. One of them nearly fell off and had to be held by a colleague. The dry ice had now spread to engulf much of the audience. It was hard to know how to start, but, no matter, they groped around in the smoke to find each other, and once able to present a united front, started shouting out their petition into a primordial fog. The Mayor of Gdańsk, for a reason unexplained, was being played by an English actor, Julian Glover, rather than by the Mayor of Gdańsk, who would seem to have had a better claim on the role. No matter; Julian made his way out of the audience, not without some difficulty through the smoke, to accept our company's petition.

Shortly thereafter came the much-heralded banquet: a chance for people to enjoy food and wine and celebrate the new theatre. They still wanted to show off some of their new technology, so the hydraulic system became a dumb waiter. Traps were pulled away magically, engines whirred into motion, and from below the stage appeared tables laden with tucker. To everyone's surprise, in the middle of the tables there was a naked lady painted gold. She was posed in what in yogic terms is described, I think, as the downward dog, and was wearing an impressive headdress. This we were told was Nefertiti come to bless the feast. She was surrounded by sandwiches, and sandwiches which had been made several hours before. The sight of a naked Nefertiti surrounded by sarnies, curling slightly at the edges, was too much for some of our company, who started to get a little hysterical.

The next day, our performance was something of a lost cause. The actors were game as ever, but the theatre felt like a new car, the sightlines were beyond hopeless for many, and the audience was full of people from the UK whom we do our best to avoid in London, let alone Gdańsk. They sat there with a sour incomprehension, wondering when something so simple was going to stop being so simple. Happily sitting on one end of the front row was Andrzei Wajda, the great Polish film director, and a personal hero, now sadly deceased. An impish 88-year-old, he beamed and gasped and chuckled his delight, and was full of a straightforward and acute appreciation afterwards. 'Shakespeare as it was, Shakespeare as it should be,' he said. We settled for that.

4

WORDS AND WALLS IN MITTELEUROPA

POLONIUS *What do you read, my lord?*
HAMLET *Words, words, words.*

Act 2, Scene 2

PRAGUE, AND THE NIGHT WAS chilling fast, amply threatened by bulging storm clouds rolling towards us across the central European plain. We were in a misshapen courtyard, cobbled together by history, a medieval turret in one corner, a dull communist block of concrete in another, a chic cafe beneath a spreading oak in a third. Seven hundred Czechs and a few British expats were waiting in excitement on plastic garden furniture, wrapped in blankets and polythene sheets. We had found our way there through curving byways, up and down the vertiginous slopes of Prague Castle, shaded by the baroque excess of St Vitus Cathedral. Everyone gazed towards a viciously overlit wall.

Having sloped and slipped through the fairy-tale windings of Prague, it was a strangely blockish site to be presented with. But there was something arresting about it. Crude arc lights hit the wall hard and heightened its irregularity, its bulges, and its unevenness. Its irregularity threw out questions. Why does this uniform plane of brick give way to these bursts of concrete? An architectural revision crudely achieved? A twentieth-century bomb dropped from the air? An antique cannon blast from the plain below? And why is this tier of piled-up sandstone capped by a higher tier of more perpendicular carved masonry? Had it been a garden wall that had then become a castle rampart? Had new stone suddenly become available, which was thought to be more robust? Beyond the questions, there was the pleasure of the sight itself. A lovely dance of greys, off-whites and fauns, all stitched together by the streaks of dirty brown, the rusty dribs and drabs that centuries of rain effect on stone. It felt possible in imagination to run one's fingers over its different surfaces. Smooth planed stone here, corrugated brick there, crumbly concrete above, stubbly rock below. A sensual pleasure achieved so completely by accident and history.

It was hard to look at the wall and not try to deduce what had happened in front of it. Prague is the ultimate Mitteleuropean crossroads of history where since Roman times and before, east and west and north and south have met and fucked or fought. Where chiefs and kings and emperors and despots have played 'I'm the king of the castle'. Prague has a pastel prettiness which surrounds the playing of that game with a gilded frame. It heightens the sense of man enacting history while having a knowing sense of its actual fiction. The towering castle-capped hills serve as a backdrop before which people stage their odd show. Sometimes history feels real, plugging away at life in an industrial town in a valley; sometimes it feels unreal, storming up or fleeing down the hills of Prague.

Beside me sat the Czech Republic's leading Shakespearean, a scholar who had translated every one of Shakespeare's plays into

Czech and whose versions were still respected and used. We had met at a reception earlier, and his enthusiasm for our arrival was humbling. A gentle courteous soul, he bore the scars of his country's complicated history with a light grace. It was impossible not to warm to him and not to feel embarrassed by his excitement at our being there. Warmth radiated from him as if Shakespeare had entered the room. It feels churlish in the circumstances to say that the Globe in London is only a little more real than any of the others in the world, and that our actors are not ordained with any special Shakespearean-ness; they are just hard-working pros who have done a lot.

He sat beside me, and I briefly apostrophised the wall in front of us. Thankfully he didn't treat me as mad, or laugh at me as a recreation of Brick Tamland in *Anchorman* – 'Wall! I love wall!' – but gently sketched in a little history.

'Much history has happened in front of this wall . . . much cruelty . . . before this piece [pointing to some air in front of one section] for 200 years people were executed, hung and er . . . quartered and drawn as you say . . . the crowds would gather where we are now sitting . . . in front of this section [waving at some more pregnant emptiness] there was a prison where for many years anyone who defied the king was imprisoned . . . there they would rot their way to a lonely death . . . up and down these stairs [following with his hand the ghost of a long disappeared stone staircase] several royals escaped the castle when it was under attack . . .'

Spectral figures hung from ropes and twisted in the air, cowered in the corners of dank rooms, or scurried along passageways, stuffing the crown jewels into the linings of their garments. Those were real ghosts, however daft that may sound, and here we were with our flesh-and-blood Ghost, as embodied by John Dougall, in his dusted-down royal coat, masquerading as an old Danish ghost, as written by an Englishman 400 years dead. And here was his tortured report of purgatory coming alive in front of 700 Czechs in 2016. Ghosts old and new, real and fake, imagined and re-imagined.

In front of that wall, the show took on a vivid reality new to itself. Tales of kings displaced, princes robbed of their inheritance, court intrigue and threatened revolutions can take on a phoniness in modern theatres. Here in this enclave of trapped history, their phoniness was evocative. Beyond the narrative resonance, the words started to fly. The stone walls of the courtyard clattered the words around, and rebounded them into a palpable concreteness. The actors thrilled to the acoustic and, while acting the story fiercely, gave the best spoken account of the play I had witnessed thus far. The audience leant into it, eager for the language. A breath-bated silence came over the courtyard as people relished the pleasure of each new thought.

The clouds which had threatened throughout the day, and which had tumbled ever closer like a rumbling Napoleonic army on the march, shrouded the castle in their ominous darkness at the end of the first half. Just as Claudius looked up to the heavens and prayed for forgiveness, his first admission of the crime he has committed, the skies opened with a loud rumble and tipped sheets of rain down. Everyone scrambled for cover – the company to a medieval dressing room. Our worried promoter flitted in and out telling us that Czech audiences never stay to watch in the rain and that we may lose our whole crowd. Then miraculously, after twenty minutes of rain like stair rods, the downpour stopped as abruptly as it had begun, and the army of clouds moved on to terrorise another part of central Europe. The audience all retook their dampened seats. The pre-storm electric

tension of the first half – a tension that always feels more clammily real in central Europe than anywhere else – gave way to a
starlit calm, and a lucidity. The words were as important as before,
but no longer freighted with the same cargo of pain; they floated
light and clear beneath the stars and the steeples. As Hamlet's
spirit lightened, and as he found his own way through to acceptance at the play's end, the atmospheric pressure seemed to concur.
Outdoor playing often provides these tonal shifts, without thought
or design. They throw new patterns across the play, and sometimes
reveal more clearly what was always there.

At the end, I turned to the scholar on my right. His eyes were
rich with withheld tears. 'Thank you for bringing these words
here. Thank you for the words.'

★ ★ ★

The words of *Hamlet* can seem like an intimidating smooth surface,
a forbidding carapace of polished perfection, full of headache-
inducing philosophic thought and studied aphorism. Modern
editions, until recently, have often claimed a spurious authority,
scaring the reader or student with their assertion that this is the
one true text – as authorised by this degree of scholarship, or by
that imprint. This is baloney. There is no right text.

There is no one text of *Hamlet*. We have inherited three, the
first commonly known as the Bad Quarto, published hurriedly
in 1603 without the knowledge or permission of its author. The
second, known uncomplicatedly as the Second Quarto, was
published in 1604. It is twice as long as the first and is closer to
the intentions of its author. It is still rife with oddities of translation from rehearsal room to page, and stuffed with errors from
the magnificent laziness of printers. Quartos are single editions

of plays, small enough to hold in the hand or slip into the pocket. The third text is one of the thirty-seven plays collected together by two of Shakespeare's fellow actors, Heminges and Condell, in the First Folio. The Folio is much too big for a pocket. The Folio version of *Hamlet* is marginally shorter than the Second Quarto and full of differences of detail – speeches cut, some rearranged, and a whole host of different words and punctuation.

The single most surprising fact about Shakespeare is that he never supervised the printing of his own plays. Other authors did; some, like his friend Ben Jonson, quite assiduously. His sonnets and his longer poems are carefully laid down and prefaced by dedications from the publisher. These seemed to matter to him; their relationship with posterity was precious. But *Hamlet*? *King Lear*? *Twelfth Night*? They were left to push their way into print through the brambles of early printing, and emerge with their clothing torn and their shins scratched. It's hard to say why, but knowing that Shakespeare himself was an actor and had to watch day after day as his plays were mangled, shredded and retold by actors, it must have been hard for him to think of a play as a fixed thing. Having heard his Ophelia stammer and riff freeform in her madness, having cringed at the clowns going gleefully off-piste, and having despaired at bombastic actors merrily importing speeches from other plays when they lost their way, he may have found the whole idea of locking these plays down for posterity laughable.

This liberating contingency of attitude has not been enough for many of history's editors, who have felt the need to smooth rough edges, to make the fierce experience into an argument, and the chaotic expressionism of the original into something tidier and more certain. This impulse to correct is most marked in the punctuation. All three early editions feature punctuation that can best be described as random and sometimes seemingly crazed. Parentheses, semi-colons, commas and a glut of colons stud the work. Frequently their application runs counter to the sense. Yet often it reveals strange new thoughts and fresh punches of emotional energy. The first punctuation has the eruptive energy and dislocated music that you find in contemporary writers such as David Mamet or Caryl Churchill. Yet editors for several centuries have re-punctuated the plays, marking Shakespeare's work just as they would that of a sloppy student, and bringing him closer to proper English. At the Globe and with *Hamlet*, for the punctuation we try to go back to the originals, most often the Folio, whose music is probably closest to the original intentions, and start from there as a base.

The text we were using on tour was informed for its detail by the Folio and for its structure by the First Quarto. There are several theories about how this crudely named Bad Quarto came into being. One is that someone heard the play in performance and recited it to a printer. This is hard to credit. The mnemonic capacity of your average Elizabethan was far in advance of ours, but this seems to be stretching it. The other is that it was recollected by the actor who first played Marcellus, a character of no great import from the First Act. This seems more trustworthy given most of Marcellus's lines are more soundly remembered against the other two editions than the other characters. Marcellus also becomes bizarrely ubiquitous towards the end of this version, when usually he is absent. It's hard not to imagine that the same actor might have doubled as Hamlet's mother. In this version, the elsewhere increasingly marginalised and morally complicated Gertrude starts behaving valiantly towards the end, forming an unlikely alliance with Horatio to help Hamlet. There may be an actor's moral vanity at work here.

My feeling about the first quarto was informed by the not so subtle clue presented on its frontispiece. It says unequivocally, 'As it hath been diverse times acted by his Highness servants in the City of London: as also in the two Universities of Cambridge and Oxford, and else-where.'This is a touring text.Touring for millennia meant one thing – shorter plays. Actors carry lines like baggage. They are heavy. Offer a group of actors a play of 4,000 lines to take on the road with a small company and their response is liable to be brutal and simple. Negotiations will then ensue – some sanctioned by the author, some private amongst the company – about how to cut and shape a quicker and briefer version.

As well as the frontispiece, there are other clues within the text. At the end, with Hamlet dead and Fortinbras having entered to take over the kingdom, Horatio is left to recount what has occurred. In versions two and three, he says:

> Give order that these bodies
> High on a stage be placed to the view,
> And let me speak to th'yet unknowing world,
> How these things came about.

In the First Quarto he says:

> Content your selves, I'll show to all, the ground,
> The first beginning of this Tragedy:
> Let there a scaffold be reared up in the market place,
> And let the State of the world be there.

The first references a theatre in a room, the second a stage more improvised and temporary. This act, setting up a stage in the market place, is a description of how touring companies operated

– the booth-stage mode – which we had adapted for our small-scale touring.

According with our knowledge of how touring plays were cut, there is an emphasis on story and on action in the First Quarto. There is a cruder, bolder energy. Claudius is more of a villain, less of a politician. He and others are drawn in primary colours; swathes of philosophical musing are excised; complex plot junctures barged through. There are melodramatic flourishes. At the end of Claudius's prayer for redemption in versions two and three, he says: 'My words fly up, my thoughts remain below: / Words without thoughts never to heaven go.' In the Bad Quarto, he appends the line 'No king on earth is safe if God's his foe', which we added, thus turning a couplet naughtily into a triplet. It's easy to imagine the last line being intoned with a fierce glare to awe the groundlings in the market place.

Many are dismissive of this sort of writing. It has to be said that there is some outright rubbish in this text. Where Hamlet's most famous line runs, in the other texts, 'To be, or not to be: that is the question', in the First Quarto it fairly bathetically concludes: 'To be or not to be: ay, there's the point'. Some people have tried to justify the directness of even this line, which is taking revisionism too far. It's just bad, too casual to support its appropriate weight of feeling. But there are glories in the First Quarto which contradict the theory that Shakespeare had nothing to do with it. At the end of the 'Speak the speech . . .' instruction to the Players, there is a passage to the comedians that contains some of Shakespeare's finest writing about comedy and about acting:

HAMLET Let those that play your clowns speak no more
than is set down for them. And then you have some again,

that keeps one suit of jests, as a man is known by one suit of apparel, and, gentlemen, quotes his jests down in their tables, before they come to the play, as thus, 'Cannot you stay till I eat my porridge?' and, 'You owe me a quarters wages', and 'Your beer is sour', and blabbering with his lips, and thus – when God knows, the warm Clown cannot make a jest unless by chance, as the blind man catches a hare: Masters, tell him of it. . .

This is a prescription against catchphrase comedy. The 'suit of jests' are comedians' stock gags, as senseless and as imperishable as those of the old radio comics, done with a set intonation and probably a facial contortion to boot. For centuries, these have tickled the audience within an inch of their lives, regardless of context or character, and driven authors to distraction. It's not hard to imagine Shakespeare's teeth-grinding rage when the Chekhovian delicacy of *Twelfth Night* is interrupted by a cry of 'Cannot you stay till I eat my porridge?' Or if the realpolitik tensions of *Julius Caesar* are broken by the clown camply intoning 'Your beer is sour'.

Hamlet tells them to avoid such nonsense, to stay in the play itself and stay alive to the moment, and then he delivers his zinger: 'the warm clown cannot make a jest unless by chance, as the blind man catches a hare'. This is an apt description of the greatest comedians at work, their ceaseless quest to be in the zone, the hot place of creativity. Or of an actor like Mark Rylance. Two of Mark's great credos are 'stay in the room and stay in the moment', alive to the possibilities of any creative interaction with the other people in the room – the audience. 'As a blind man catches a hare' is a peerless description of the actor's or any artist's twitching, attuned sensitivity to the movement of the world around him, and his or her sudden ability to seize the full poten tial in the air. To say this stuff has nothing to do with Shakespeare doesn't add up, yet this material appears nowhere else but in the First Quarto.

Yet, though the energy of that version, and its swift way with storytelling, informed the structure of our text, 95 per cent of its detail came from the other two editions. In the second and third versions, the sense is clearer, the music more assured and the characterisation more delicate and quicksilver. There are differences between the two later texts. Many have seen and argued a deliberate replanning done by Shakespeare, James Shapiro in *1599* most persuasively. But it is always hard to juxtapose Shakespeare and planning. The blind man can plan to catch a hare, but will finally rely on instinct. Shakespeare's pen scratched fast over the page, unslowed by heavy intentions or an excess of planning. We have little idea what played in front of his audiences, probably a beautiful muddle of author's intentions, actors' enhancement, actors' destruction, and the text floating uneasily between them all.

* * *

So a text that is not really a single text, but a bulging and receding interweaving of three different texts, crumbled a little by actors' egos and uncertainties, scumbled a lot by printers' eccentricities, and further distorted by the editorial conjecture of 400 years of textual study. Conjecture which has delved into every nook and cranny, with both scalpels and sledgehammers, knocking out chunks of speech here, excising wayward commas there. Further transformed by the tidal changes of intellectual fashion, which have reconfigured it radically in performance and often in print.

Yet still somehow a text solid and upstanding, and if not perfect, then why not all the better for that?

A Shakespeare text is not a fixed, definite entity; it is something liberally scarred by time, its bashed and beaten surface allowing you to touch a stippled combination of both it and what has been done to it by history. Similar to a wall built by centuries, collapsed and then rebuilt, finished and then started over again, some of its personality lurching angrily here, some fading shyly over there. How much more satisfying to the touch is that than an achieved and uniform surface?

5

MADNESS IN MEXICO CITY

HAMLET *How strange or odd soe'er I bear myself,*
As I perchance hereafter shall think meet
To put an antic disposition on . . .

Act 1, Scene 5

'DID YOU HAVE THE CHICKEN? Did you eat the chicken? OK, which of us had the chicken?'

Like refugees from a 1970s disaster movie, we quiz each other earnestly. We are an hour away from the start of our second show in Mexico City, and the company is crumbling like a castle under bombardment. Our designer, Jonathan, went down first, stricken by an all-possessing fever, with a sideline in comprehensive self-evacuation. He had struggled into our technical rehearsal the day before and lain prone for a couple of hours, raising his head feebly a few times before banging it heavily back down on the bench. He is now safe in his bedroom high above the Zócalo, the city's huge, heaving central square, and occasionally drags himself to the window to wave to us. Malu, one of the show's producers, lies flattened in the same hotel with a drip in her arm, the needle of which I'd replaced myself earlier, in the absence of anyone vaguely medical.

You can do a show without designers and producers; it is harder to bring one off without actors. With only an hour to go, Tommy, who is playing Horatio, has announced that he will not be appearing. He disappeared the night before, hasn't been seen since, and point-blank refuses to open his door. Noises have been erupting from his room, and they don't sound healthy. A long queue is already snaking around the makeshift theatre our hosts, the National Theatre of Mexico, have thrown up for us, and we are an actor down. The whole company has that febrile uncertainty that precedes a hefty burst of illness, that distant roar you sense within your body before the tsunami hits. Two nights ago, we had all sat together for a company meal high above the same square, eating the Mexican food, living the Mexican dream, and congratulating ourselves and each other for our all-round Mexican chillaxness. Now we are paying for it. Well, everyone who had the chicken is.

I improvise a quick plan and instruct the company, all too aquiver with anxiety to object. We will deal with the absence of Horatio by skipping the scenes in which he appears. At these moments, I will come on stage with a microphone and tell the missing bits of plot. The tide of fever is approaching fast, and I am starting to get a little messianic. 'Let's revive the old oral tradition,' I cry. 'Storytelling. Wey hey!'

'You don't speak Spanish,' someone objects. I look at them cussedly for being so all-round negative and unhelpful, then concede. 'Good point. I will bring this woman with me! She will translate!' I point at one of our Mexican production managers, whom I heard speaking reasonably good English earlier, and who is, well, close to hand. There are many other, much better, English speakers around, but they are not standing right next to me and thus disqualify themselves. My chosen translator looks terrified, never having been on stage before. The company look less than reassured.

The Zócalo is bang in the centre of Mexico City, and is the crucible that distils the essence of the whole diverse, confused and thrilling city. Largely consisting of seventeenth-century Spanish buildings, it has a grandiose splendour to outdo any European capital. But it's all a little wonky. The great Baroque monstrosity of a cathedral is slowly sinking down into the swampy marshland upon which the city floats. Almost right beside it is the freshly excavated Aztec pyramid of the Templo Mayor. The two religious edifices look like 400-year-old boxers, slugging it out for supremacy, the Christian church buckling at the knees and slowly sinking as the old Aztec temple rears triumphant from the ground.

When our Mexican hosts told us they were going to make a temporary theatre for us in the Zócalo after the style of an old Spanish *corral* courtyard theatre, we were thrilled – a great statement about public theatre to make in such a high-profile spot. It was only when we arrived at the stylish construction they had made out of scaffolding and cloth that we realised there was a fundamental problem: noise. The Zócalo is the noisiest place on earth. Four lanes of traffic circle the square, each driver feeling an irresistible compulsion to beep his horn as frequently as possible; every day sees a new political gathering at which *compañeros* proclaim they will fight to the death for their cause through speakers that can be heard in Honduras; each shop boasts its own sound system loudly touting the virtues of its wares; and in the early evening, everyone gathered in the square decides to blow a whistle, simply because they can. At any time of year, it would not be a great place to play *Hamlet* in an open-air venue. When our hosts announced there would be rock concerts every evening as well, we almost turned around and went home.

We decided to do the first show with microphones. We discussed the relative benefits of float mics, head mics and body mics, eventually erring on the side of the latter. Not a good move. These mics had a very limited field from which they could pick up sound, so when heads swung back and forth in the throes of articulation, the sound ebbed and flowed dramatically, deafening one moment – 'TO BE, OR . . .' – then an absent whisper – '. . . *not to be*' – then suddenly returning to top volume again – 'that is the QUESTION'. Worse, with the mics secreted within the heavy cloth of the company's costumes, every time they embraced each other they sounded like a bunch of grizzly bears enjoying a brutal orgy. Motivated by some group instinct for self-destruction, they all started hugging each other at every opportunity, thereby punctuating the show with regular outbreaks of ursine group sex. Worst, Miranda, who was playing Gertrude, was filled with Iberian *duende* and decided to strike her own chest whenever overcome with emotion. Which was often. Every time she did so, she hit her microphone and a minor thunderclap filled the auditorium. It was one of the most emphatic performances I have seen. A packed house had the decency not to laugh or throw things.

That was the first night. This is the second and, amazingly, it promises to be even more disastrous. The sun is lowering a great anvil of heat over the city, the noise level is high and rising (tonight we've opted for float mics), and the actors are forming urgent queues for the two plastic Portaloos backstage. Unfortunately, the long and sweetly excited line of audience members that circles the theatre runs alongside the queues for the loos, separated only by a low fence. It's difficult for any performer to maintain the necessary mystique while banging on a Portaloo demanding that the incumbent gets the fuck on with it.

Nevertheless, the usual glorious surge of optimism that prefaces every performance the world over, from primary-school nativity play to the glitziest opera, kicks in just as the show is about to begin. We walk out with a residual thin gleam of hope that all will be well. Madness. I stand there, microphone in hand, my appointed translator beside me. The outer edges of fever have arrived – colours are acquiring a lurid neon glow, and connections are becoming more magical than logical. My translator looks like she wants to cry.

'Good evening,' I say. 'Welcome to the Globe tour of *Hamlet*.'

Confident translation follows and a roar of joy erupts. This is great, I think. I explain that we are an actor down, but that the show must go on. The translation elicits sympathy and support from the audience. I explain that I will be appearing to bridge the missing bits with storytelling, and everyone seems ready to relish the game. This is going to be great, I tell myself. So I start:

'It was a cold, dark night in Denmark . . .'

Not bad, I think, and turn to the acting company arrayed behind me while the words are being translated, expecting looks of approval. Claudius's face has 'What in the name of fuckity fuck are you doing?' written all over it.

This throws me slightly, but I press on.

'And up high on the battlements . . .'

'Qué?' my translator mutters.

'Up high on the battlements,' I repeat forcefully.

'Qué? What is bateelmence?'

'Battlements. You know.' My febrile confusion is starting to max out. 'Battlements, edges of the castle, high edges of the castle.'

'Qué? High edges of the castle?'

'Yes, top bits, high margins of castle, where people walk about . . .'

All this is being played out amplified in front of 600 now slightly confused audience members, eager to see the famous Globe theatre perform Shakespeare. I look despairingly at the audience, who start to volunteer suggestions for what battlements might be in Mexican Spanish. I look back at the company, who are all wearing the rictus grins of the crew who know the captain is sinking the ship but can't admit it to the passengers. We eventually reach a consensus on the translation plebiscite with the audience, and I do the rest of my storytelling in the simplest English I can muster. I retreat from the stage throwing a 'best of luck' look at the company.

The rest of the evening is a matter of precision timing, as the company, all now succumbing to convulsions, try to judge whether they will be able to get in and out of a scene in time to satisfy their greater needs in the khazi. Then they have to calculate whether they will be able to get in and out of the toilet in time to attend to stage business. These are difficult calculations, with only two conveniences available. Actors are now starting to throw up as well, so buckets are brought ever closer to the stage to facilitate a quick feinted exit, a deft hurl, and then a return to the stage without missing a beat. Organisers, promoters and producers, including myself, are wandering around with that hopeless look of active concern assumed by those in impotent authority presiding over an unavoidable catastrophe.

As the venerable storyteller, my interruptions are becoming less and less frequent as my head starts to spin. And considerably less detailed. 'Someone tells Hamlet about an army' is my precis of the part of the Captain; 'Horatio says that Hamlet has come back', my pithy summation of the Fourth Act narrative pivot. The actors are possessed by a similar spirit of self-preserving censorship, excising chunks from scenes just so they can get to the end.

It is all a little too much: the heat crushing us in its vice-like grip, the panic and chaos backstage, the excitement of the crowd still inexplicably beaming towards us, the increasing eccentricity of the make-believe, the capacity of the Zócalo to transform its own noise and chaos into essence of rage and wildness, the fact that around us Mexico City is decked out in full Day of the Dead splendour. Everything is starting to melt: the swags of plastic sheeting into the scaffolding, the actors into the audience, English into Mexican, the play into reality, the speeches into the noise that fights them, all blurring into the dark-blue air that weighs heavily on the city – one big Mexican soup, its ingredients bubbling away and rearranging themselves into something strange and new.

★ ★ ★

Much as the disorienting, deliquescent evening is a product of particular circumstances, it is also a product of the play itself. *Hamlet* takes place in queasy mental territory, the tectonic plates of sanity shifting from the first scene. Bedlam itself was a magnetic presence in Shakespeare's world, sitting just outside the walls of the City of London, and drawing audiences to gawp at the behaviour of its patients. Many playwrights were lured by the spontaneous theatricality of the place, by its naked presentation of mental fragility, and the contingent nature of identity. The language of madness, set alongside the language of what purports to be sanity, undermines the security of an objective truth or value in words. Language, which can provide comfort as the source of healing, can also prove perilous as the gatekeeper to confusion. It can become the primary sponsor of madness, its endless strata and spirals driving both speakers and listeners from their senses.

Shakespeare dealt with madness more discreetly, and yet more profoundly, than his colleagues. In *Othello*, we see the collapse of a fortressed identity as the hero is undermined by Iago's facility with nuance and suggestion. In *King Lear*, we get a spectrum of different forms of madness: Edgar's feigned lunacy, with its linguistic bravura; the Fool's osmotic relationship with insanity, the thin membrane between sense and nonsense allowing just enough of the latter to pass into the former; and in Lear himself – Shakespeare's most pathetic demonstration of the consequences of the mind's slippage – memory, language, imagination, perception and passion are all at war with each other on a windswept battlefield devoid of familiar landmarks.

In *Hamlet*, madness lurks queasily under every smooth surface. The propelling motor of the play – Claudius's murder of his brother for love of his brother's wife – is an act of derangement. The court we meet at the beginning are disguising a covert unease with a display of confidence. Polonius positions himself as an amateur psychologist (he is sometimes played as such) and is eager to offer Gertrude his expert opinion: 'Your son is mad.' His daughter Ophelia is cursed with an excessively attuned sensibility. She lives at a dangerous level of perception from the outset, as evidenced by the sharpness of her recall of the moment Hamlet bursts in on her and the deep wound it leaves in her spirit.

> He took me by the wrist and held me hard;
> Then goes he to the length of all his arm;
> And, with his other hand thus o'er his brow,
> He falls to such perusal of my face

As he would draw it. Long stayed he so;
At last, a little shaking of mine arm
And thrice his head thus waving up and down,
He raised a sigh so piteous and profound
As it did seem to shatter all his bulk
And end his being: that done, he lets me go:
And, with his head over his shoulder turned,
He seemed to find his way without his eyes;
For out o' doors he went without their helps,
And, to the last, bended their light on me.

This passage, in its graphically precise detail, plays a double game, both indicating the nature of Hamlet's possession as he approaches Ophelia, yet also establishing, by the fierce lucidity of the reporting, the troubled mind of the reporter.

And destabilising the centre of the play, are a group of actors. The long stretch (almost a quarter of the play) dominated by the arrival and performance of the theatre company from London creates a liminal, uncertain reality that seems to infect the air of the play. The actors invoke Troy, and suddenly Troy is more real than Denmark. Elsinore's hold on its own materiality starts slipping, the court becomes intoxicated by the possibility of 'this play', and the play transports us to a place that both is and isn't the story we are already within. It creates a parallel world, coarse and clumsy, but nevertheless opening out the possibility of infinite others. Metatheatrical devices don't shore up reality, they throw it up in the air, where it scatters and falls reconfigured. The golden centre of this play is another play. The play is indeed the thing.

In any environment, whether an office or a family or a relationship or a theatre company, mental states can be contagious. Clarity, simplicity and confidence spread into the waters around them; confusion, complexity and insecurity muddy them. The Elsinore depicted in *Hamlet* is a pressure-cooker environment, where instability passes speedily from person to person. Ophelia has stepped outside the frame of her own portrait, yet tries with heart-rending courage to claw her way back in. She speaks in encoded riddles that mean everything to her but nothing to the others. But it is not just her. After Hamlet's exile to England, the focus narrows. This is common in Shakespeare's plays – a broad panorama reducing into a claustrophobic intensity – and this is true of the Fourth Act of *Hamlet*. When Ophelia rushes from character to character handing out rue and rosemary and columbine, it is not only the flowers she is dispersing, but also the burden of her excess of sensibility. No one is immune. Claudius disintegrates from a wise, sophisticated politician to a clumsy murderer. Laertes casts aside all niceties, social and religious, even before he jumps into his sister's grave. Families, political groupings, conspirators . . . All, if set on the wrong path, twist and contort each other into instability.

* * *

We were witnessing such volatility in Mexico, where notions of calm and cool had very much left the building. I looked across at Wills, our travelling production manager, a friend of great good sense and humour, and a man of awe-inspiring solidity and perspective (as well as bulk). Nothing phased him, he was our high-water mark of sangfroid. Until now. He just shook his head at me, mouthed 'no más', sat down heavily on a speaker and stared blankly out into the square beyond, sucker-punched by the extreme oddness of reality.

I had long since given up making my sporadic on stage appearances to 'help'. Instead, I watched in hallucinatory admiration as tonight's Hamlet decided to deal with Tommy's absence in the Fifth Act by saying not only all his own lines, but also all of Horatio's. For a fair old stretch, he simply talked to himself via an alter ego. He did it with skill and bright good cheer and a feverish, psychotropic certainty. Characters were melting into characters. Hamlet was standing sweaty with fever, babbling as two people, in a tongue foreign to his audience, on a makeshift stage, grasping helplessly for an equally makeshift identity. In many ways, he was himself again.

* * *

The madness in the play centres on the Prince himself – a man in a state of perilously contained agitation from the off. His first soliloquy ('O, that this too too solid flesh . . .') is an explosion of sewage, erupting onto the streets of himself from the gurgling catacombs beneath. From the moment he meets the ghost of his father, he knows his hold on himself is delicate (to put it mildly). He tells his trusted allies, with urgency, that he will soon put on an 'antic disposition', and that they are not to wonder at it. This opens up a quandary that has troubled people for four centuries: is Hamlet's madness real or feigned? Is he using it as a mask, or genuinely succumbing to it? The answer, as with most Shakespearean quandaries, is to avoid framing it as an either/or and to keep both possibilities open. Hamlet knows he is in psychological trouble, and knows he needs a disguise to conceal his pain. The solution is to create a mask that is both true and not true, to create a role that fits the self.

When Hamlet says he is 'mad in craft', he is speaking part of the truth; when Rosencrantz describes it as a 'crafty madness', he is doing the same; when Polonius says there is 'method in his madness', his is a genuine insight; when Gertrude says he is suffering from 'ecstasy', it is offered from a mother's understanding; when Hamlet asks that his mother and stepfather be told that he is but 'mad north-northwest', he is doing his best to describe a marginal state. Everyone is telling a version of the truth, all of which add up to a comprehensive, if chaotic, picture of a troubled mind, like a Cubist painting. For what is the truth with mental health but such an aggregation of different subjectivities? Which of us when looking at a friend or a loved one suffering from mental turmoil can say something simpler of them? Sanity plays endless games with its own definitions and leaves no one the wiser.

It is hard to gainsay Hamlet's own summary at the end of the play, when his mind is as stable as we find it, in front of Laertes and, more critically, his mother:

> Give me your pardon sir: I've done you wrong;
> But pardon't, as you are a gentleman.
> This presence knows, how I am punished
> With sore distraction. What I have done,
> That might your nature, honour and exception
> Roughly awake, I here proclaim was madness.

The caesura pause necessitated by the comma after 'This presence knows' is a pregnant one. It does not lead us to believe he is lying. This is not the moment in the play for manipulation.

Earlier he has said he was 'mad in craft', so both states can clearly coexist. Sometimes it is straightforward to tell when he is faking it. His joshing of Polonius and his cryptic responses to the old man's questions are clearly performative. Similarly, his carefree wildness and verbal exuberance in front of Claudius seems a mechanism to deal with an impossible situation. How else do you deal with having to co-habit with the murderer of your father? There's no book of etiquette for such things. Beyond his public face, there is a world of hypocrisy and linguistic falsity in the Polonius/Claudius generation that can only be met with the jabberings of the Joker.

The real moments of madness, the moments when, in his own words, 'Hamlet from himself be ta'en away' are easy to spot. Most of them, crucially, involve Ophelia. His first reported appearance to her is a vivid description of a mind absented. His explosion after he realises she has tricked him and starts raving 'Get thee to a nunnery' is so jangled and out of order it is clear he has fallen into a deep well of unwellness. This moment follows 'To be, or not to be . . .' and precedes 'Speak the speech . . .', two of the most articulate statements of expressed thought in dramatic history. The rapidity with which he collapses into the other self, the self revealed by madness, is the mark of someone in trouble beyond their own care. The third is over Ophelia's grave, when he can no longer bear to hear Laertes' expressions of grief. Having planned to hide himself, he bursts into the middle of the group, screaming like a demented rock star 'This is I, Hamlet the Dane!', before leaping into the grave to grapple with Laertes and scream abuse at him. This is a man with an alarming capacity for loss of self. In all three cases, the trigger is Ophelia, and love.

People can be loath to attach to a figure as cosmic as Hamlet a narrative as corny as a love story. His finely wrought sensibility has to be the result of something philosophic, something grand. But there is no reason why the corny and the cosmic cannot walk hand in hand. The evidence is clear. The letter he sends to Ophelia, which Polonius accuses of being stuffed with 'vile phrases', speaks of a love full of the innocence that always carries

the greatest freight of hurt. We know he has given her gifts, since
Ophelia's attempt to return them upsets him so deeply. And his
raving declaration over her grave, directed at Laertes,

> I loved Ophelia: forty thousand brothers
> Could not, with all their quantity of love,
> Make up my sum.

is hyperbolic, but true love and hyperbole are hardly exclusive.
Hamlet, in the jittery state he is in after the death of his father,
has returned to Elsinore and attached himself to the one person
who can fill the outsize hole within him. Nor does that love
have to be a reaction to a problem elsewhere. The heart is the
heart, and always its own boss. You can love and have crushes
wherever you like, you can make a thousand sensible choices, but
the heart is its own boss. It strikes without prescription. The love
for Ophelia is yet another factor piling weight upon Hamlet, all
that downwards pressure paradoxically catalysing his diamond-like
clarity of thought.

One of the most Hamletian figures I have known was the
playwright Sarah Kane, who took her life at the age of twenty-
eight, having produced a compact but astonishing body of work.
Often given to wearing a demonstrative black, at odds with her
own time – theatrically, politically and spiritually – and helplessly
over-exposed to the pain around her near and far, she stood
hovering off the pitch of the world on a wet day, much as Hamlet
does. As bright and free and joyous in moments as Hamlet can
be, a delight to drink with and a lover of infantile party games,
she was also incapable of setting herself apart from the world's
million cruelties, and had no choice but to go to war with them.
Yet what broke her, as much as anything, was love. Her loves

were total and titanic, consuming passions that obliterated all matter outside their own vivid and livid existence. When they didn't work out, as they could not, since the objects of her affection could never match her level of intensity, there was no consolation. Nowhere to turn. Stuck within that conundrum, the fact that she managed to celebrate love (in all her plays, but most noticeably in *Cleansed* and in *Crave*), love with its redeeming fierceness and its savage loyalty, says much for her courage as a person. But writing doesn't purge, it only stirs the pot, and there was no escape for her.

The loss of a parent is, of course, the other source of rocks in the rucksack. We know Hamlet is grieving from the start: he tells us so. His rebuke to the court about who is doing the best grieving smacks a little of competitive rage rather than sorrow, but the disorder of his thinking during the first soliloquy and his behaviour after the encounter with his father's ghost means there is no doubting the derangement caused by grief. Another manifestation of Hamlet's inner chaos occurs in the closet scene with his mother, after he has stabbed through the curtain and killed Polonius. That action, plus his loving recall of his real father, plus his horrified disgust at his mother sleeping with another man, plus his incomprehension at his mother's capacity to change herself, all contribute to a loss of self. Consumed by rage, he screams at his mother:

> A murderer and a villain;
> A slave that is not twentieth part the tithe
> Of your precedent lord –
> GERTRUDE No more!
> HAMLET A king of shreds and patches –

At that moment, when it feels his rage is about to bubble over into violence, the ghost of his father reappears, seemingly to protect his mother. There is a propensity for violence against women here, which is less than charming, but we can see the swirls and eddies of a spirit in grief, of a personality whose keystones and foundations have been ripped away. How can any of us expect to survive intact the loss of a parent?

Hamlet had always spoken to me most clearly when fresh from the poleaxing of lost love. What solution is there for that but work, and time, and booze, and walking the streets at night like some poor beast in the rain? When I was fresh from the poleaxing of a lost parent, my mother, an event that occasioned a ground-swell of wildernessing sorrow, I sank into a depression the like of which I had never anticipated. Sleeplessness, spiralling inwards, terror of the world, panic at events and responsibilities, all had introduced me to the brute reality of a state of which I had previously been sceptical. To my shame, I had always been dismissive of it in others, including Sarah Kane. 'Pull yourself together' was the shameful calibre of advice I offered. Until I myself was heartbutted by it.

Depression is a subject so thoroughly explored by others it seems impertinent to add to the pile of words already written. (It occasionally seems too thoroughly explored, but this is preferable to the stiff-upper-lip silence within which my generation grew up: rather a surfeit of understanding than a scarcity.) It would also seem a little impertinent, given that the moment I started talking to friends about it, it quickly became apparent I was only in the foothills of the condition; others risked themselves on far higher and more hazardous peaks. Competitive depression has given rise to a whole new form of one-upmanship. Anecdotes about mental deterioration are told with a wary eye, knowing that one can imminently be trumped by something more dramatic. Nothing sharpens the competitive instinct like comparing milligrammage of antidepressant – my 10mg a day turned out to be comically small in comparison with others' pharmacological mountaineering.

What I endured was foggy and mild beside the sharp plunges of Hamlet's condition. Shakespeare was a natural exaggerator, a compounder of what predecessors had only done by half. Plautus wrote the *Menaechmi* with one set of twins; Shakespeare stole the plot for *The Comedy of Errors* and made it two sets. Double the confusion, double the fun. In the source for *Hamlet*, the main character acts mad to achieve his ends; here he both acts mad and is mad. Why not pile on every conceivable stress, to take him to the very edge of that high rock, jutting precariously over the North Sea waves: a lost parent, a murdered parent, a political fortune lost, a betraying mother, a first love inexplicably cut off. Why not see whether anyone can survive all that, twisting in the lurching wind, and keep a grip on themselves? That Hamlet falters, that he does dip and surge out of himself, is inevitable and human. For all my milquetoast depression, I never came close to the flinging loss of self that afflicts Hamlet (thank God), but I am grateful the play is there as a paradigm to show what can happen at the brink.

It is not just anyone that these problems afflict, it is Hamlet, a young man of acuity and exquisite attunement. That is the further reach of Shakespeare's risk: he doesn't pile all these calamities on a dullard's head; he piles it on the man most susceptible to feel it. In many ways, the person least likely to survive it. The fact that he survives for as long as he does, doing us the favour of trying to articulate how it is to live it, increases our admiration for him. That paradox, the infliction of the greatest pain on the most sensitive human, begs the question close to the heart of the play. How are we to deal with the vast, illogical pain of the world? How, in the face of the world's desire to demonstrate its capacity for unnecessary torment, are we to react? Is madness not the only appropriate response? Hamlet is clearly far too exposed, just as Sarah was, but what is the correct amount of exposure? As Lear asks with a wrecking simplicity at the threshold of his own madness, when he thinks of those who have turned on him: 'Is there any cause in nature that makes these hard hearts?' Should we cauterise and harden our own hearts to protect ourselves better from the pain of love, from the pain of loss? Or should we open ourselves up as fully as possible, meeting pain with the vital sensitivity of a Hamlet? And thus expose ourselves to the foothills of depression in some cases, or to a plunging loss of self in others. What price pain, and what price its compensation – openness and wisdom?

* * *

The solutions to these questions weren't going to be found in the Zócalo that evening. Somehow, by a heroic triumph of will over common sense, we got to the end of the play. It was my birthday, St Crispin's Day, and driven by the same absurd sense of duty that got us through the show, we happy few repaired to a bar for what was supposed to be a party. Hardly anyone put a glass to their lips before we were all rushing back to the sanctuary of the hotel. I lay myself out on my bed, folded my arms across my chest like a recumbent knight on an old tomb, and waited for the waves to crash. Some lucid part of my brain was determined to stay present for this. It attacked my body first, legs and arms twitching gently, before surges of heat and cold expanded tremors into shakes and then full-on convulsions – arms, legs and torso hurling themselves into funny shapes like a cartoon character. 'Hello, I'm having a fit,' I thought. 'This is jolly.' It was one of the most cleanly out-of-body experiences of my life.

Shortly thereafter, the enjoyable weirdness gave way to the pure dullness of becoming an extension of the toilet, where every trip back to the bed is merely a pause before your master, the bowl, calls you back again. The early sprints became a grim, unending marathon, and disbelief grew at how an ostensibly finite problem could seem to stretch so endlessly onwards.

Sleep, wake, night and dawn folded in and out of each other in their uneasy wrestle, and somehow I became part of the new day. I quickly discovered that my psychodrama was being replicated in almost every other room. Distress calls were sent out to our Mexican promoters. Later that day, they appeared in numbers. They went from room to room, accompanied by a wizened, Yoda-like doctor. A figure of seemingly infinite wisdom, he asked peculiarly delicate and tender personal questions, most of which had nothing to do with our bodies. Having gained infinite trust, he then swiftly stabbed each of us in the arse with some cocktail of antibiotics, steroids and vitamins. It would be an exaggeration to say this did the trick, but his presence reassured and some form of normality returned.

With the whole company down, there was no way we could do a show that evening. We put an extra one on later, and somehow the company recovered sufficiently to do four shows in two days. I got out before that, a depleted figure, and was driven to the airport for an early flight by one of our producers. Still elastically attached to any passing convenience, I scrawled my signature on a contract and crawled onto a plane. Just before the plane was about to take off, my phone erupted with texts. A lovely gay woman I had met a couple of days ago, and who had helped us considerably, was making a late-breaking bid for me to donate some of my sperm. I assented enthusiastically in theory and prayed that the plane would take off soon.

Mexico is Mexico.

6

POLONIUS BY THE RED SEA

POLONIUS *Thus sir, do we that know the world, being men of*
reach
By indirections find directions forth . . .

Act 2, Scene 1

'ULLO, I AM ZE BREETISH Consul.'

My startled reaction revealed my prejudice. I didn't cover it well.

'You can't be. You're French!'

'Eet is a long stohry. Shall we 'ave a drink?'

We sat down. One by one the other members of the company came to join us, dressed in their evening casual best, and sat in a broad circle around this elegant, ageless man. Imported palm trees towered above us, and the heat of the day declined as a soft breeze blew in from the Red Sea. The consul spoke with a measured, steady calm, telling his own story, but also that of the statelet we were in, Djibouti. His tale was full of information, but for every five facts revealed, something in his delivery implied there were another fifteen concealed. He revealed a little about

Britain here, something of France there, some US history at one moment, some projections of Chinese influence in the next. Every time he did so, he seemed to open a door on a wealth of hidden knowledge, allowing a glimpse of a glistening horde of secrets, before deftly closing the door again, leaving us hungry for more. Demure, discreet but indiscreet, gently witty, old-school charming, his performance had a mesmeric quality.

Djibouti sits in a geopolitical cat's cradle all of its own. Right on the tip of the Horn of Africa, at the point where the Red Sea and the Indian Ocean meet, it is a place where world powers queasily coexist. With Yemen twenty-five miles distant across the Red Sea, Eritrea above, Ethiopia behind, Somalia below, this old French colony, not much bigger than the port at its tip, still retains a French military base, is home to the only US military base on African soil, and is the apple of China's eye as a port of entry to Africa. The inbound flight was full of American Navy Seals with scarily thick necks, bristling with the tension of those who know they are in the wrong place. What we had seen of the country spoke of power and little else. Blasted dune landscapes were punctuated by cranes and gargantuan concrete warehouses. Long expanses of flat dust elided invisibly into flat sheltered sea, so the supertankers looked as if they were moving through the desert. Flat dull dry dusty power, with little of the human evident.

The twelve-star hotel we were staying in, a gilded cage of luxury in a part of the world starved of it, was crawling with refugees from a Graham Greene novel. Financiers at the shadier end of the spectrum, arms dealers and diplomats floated through an environment where even the outdoors seemed air-conditioned. Most of them shared the pasty overweight ugliness of the over-rich and the under-earned. There was no shortage of Special Forces either. Really bad Special Forces. Not your discreet, blend-in-with-the-crowd, darkness-in-the-back-of-the-eye Special Forces. These were the macho, body-building, look-at-us-we're-Special-Forces type. They stood in the three infinity pools, crammed into eye-wateringly tight swimming trunks, staring at each other with their mouths open and occasionally flexing a pec. They seemed to like standing in threes, little triangles of nowhere-to-go mascu-linity. One of them I spotted absent-mindedly squeezing his own cock, which seemed telling. Fundamentally, every country with a substantial merchant navy parks these soldiers in this hotel in Djibouti, and then deploys them whenever a large ship passes down the strait as protection from Somalian pirates.

At the centre of all these competing interests, local, national and international, seemed to be our host. As the waves plashed gently on the artificially constructed beach, the view broken by more imported palm trees, we sat on wicker chairs on manicured phoney grass and listened to a deft and elegant lecture on the movement of power in the modern world. He threw up an exquisite cobweb, built from hints and allusions, subtle implications and wise inferences, which seemed to trap some of the mysteries of the world within its fine and glittering mesh. He was the lawyer for the hotel, for most of the government and, as his monologues spanned ever greater and finer filigree webs of influ-ence, seemingly for most of the important people in the world. He began his career from Paris representing Djiboutian rebels fighting for independence, when their principal freedom fighters were all incarcerated. When they won, he became, at a very young age, their de facto legal representative. As is true everywhere, last year's terrorist is often this year's president. So our host flipped at speed from being the radical representative of the beleaguered to being the legal advisor to the government. Partially resident in Djibouti for more than thirty years, over the intervening time his influence and his connections had spread wider and wider.

Now everyone wanted access to this tiny lump of earth parked critically at a geopolitical crossroads. The approach of each was different. The European Union had spent a couple of decades trying to revive a heritage colonial project, rebuilding one of the first African railways from Djibouti to Addis Ababa. Long years and about 30 million euros were spent doing feasibility studies, environmental-impact assessments and legacy papers. After all that extraneous care, they secured no local consent, interested no one in it, and nothing happened. Then the Chinese turned up and announced that they were going to build a railway right across the girdle of Africa, from Djibouti to Nigeria, that they were going to do it in two years and bugger the consequences. Everybody signed up, and it seemed to be going ahead.

It is curious how the blunt can-do attitude of the old colonial powers is still so effective in the modern world, and how incap-able of summoning up that spirit the old colonial powers are. I was reminded of an old Peter O'Toole legend. A friend shared a flat with both him and a painter in Earl's Court in their youth. The friend overheard the painter bringing a nurse home, and then his hours of futile attempts to seduce said nurse in his bedroom. He begged, pleaded, cajoled, commanded, wept – all to no avail. He tried jokes, songs, sad stories, heroic ones, long enigmatic silences. Eventually, he gave up and retired to the sofa in the sitting room. An hour later, my friend heard O'Toole shinning up the drainpipe, the front door of their digs being locked. The only access came through a window in the painter's bedroom. O'Toole was overheard clambering in. He spotted the nurse, and full of high spirits exclaimed, 'Good-oh! Fancy a fuck?' He received an exuberant 'Yes, please' by way of reply, and the rest of the night was filled with the noises of their happy love-making and cries of anguish from the painter on the sofa. Nothing beats confidence.

So there were the Chinese wanting access to East and Central Africa and the world, the Americans wanting to keep a security handle on where the oil was, and the Europeans trying to prove that they still deserved a place at the table. Beyond that there was every country which had parked a small military presence here to deal with the piracy problem, and was now wondering how else they could muddy the waters. Lurking in the background was everyone's paranoid concern about what the Russians might be up to. The morning we arrived, the Turkish President had left our hotel, so maybe the Ottoman Empire still had life left in it. A hundred years ago, the British would have claimed an important presence. Now all they had was a French Honorary Consul, and our *Hamlet*. The strait we were looking out on, twenty-five miles of water between us and Yemen, bears the Arabic name Bab-el-Mandeb, in French 'Porte des lamentations', and in English 'the gate of tears'. One of the earliest points of human migration, now four million barrels of oil move through it every day. Too much history, too much shifting influence, too much delicate diplomacy hovering over too much brutal weaponry for the mind to cope with. Or for this country to contain without some offering up of lamentations, and some spilling of tears.

At the centre of this matrix, or pretending to be, was our host, the Talleyrand of East Africa. Geography, history, politics, power and art – all seemed assumed within him. The French have an exquisite ability to assert, wherever they happen to be, a height of understanding and a depth of insight well above the mortal. All while keeping their trousers immaculately creased. The dapper and unruffled French *citoyen*, offering up a knowledgeable context and a disapproving raised nostril to whatever mess the world provides, is one of the enduring historical cockroaches, surviving and elegantly. Say what you like about the French, they know how to dance lightly. I have always been a sucker for this, floating away from encounters with the powerful thrilled by the sensation that I am now closer to the mystery of things. It is a large part of the daft mystique of government – boxes, dossiers, attaché cases, all supposedly enclosing the priestly knowledge which brings the chosen closer to the god of power. When each box probably contains no more than an apple and some aspirin.

Our host was a master of these arts, and he carried off an immaculate couple of hours. The only false note came towards the end. Having consistently told us how tired he was, having been a key player in the recent visit of the Turkish President, and how little time he had to help organise our performance, when I said that unfortunately we had to adjourn for dinner, he rather heavily hinted he would like to join us. Since we had company business to discuss, I didn't pick up on his need, but it didn't fit his master-of-the-universe poise. Need and poise aren't natural bedfellows.

★ ★ ★

Polonius, the father to Laertes and Ophelia, and chief fixer for Claudius, is as open to interpretation as any other part of this wilfully unmoored play. There are grounds for believing he was based on Cecil, the all-powerful adviser to Elizabeth I, who, together with his surrogate Walsingham, ran an extensive and frequently lethal intelligence service of his own. Cecil invented, or perfected, many of the stylings of intelligence work still used today – double-agents, triple-agents and agents provocateurs. When Polonius sends his servant Reynaldo to spy on his son, Laertes, in Paris, he tutors him in a cunning game of partial dishonesty to uncover more dangerous truths. He climaxes his seminar on snooping by stating the virtues of obliquity: 'By indirections find directions forth . . .' It is the mantra of diplomats, spymasters and power-brokers through the millennia.

In recent years, I have seen Polonius played as the brutal chief of a Stasi-like intelligence service; as an enquiring mind asking R.D. Laing-type questions in the search for psychological truth; as a clubbable British duffer whose wits are slowly slipping; and a whole rainbow of other colours. By and large, in our production we were playing him as a man over-promoted by a new ruler, so dizzy with his new influence and access to power that he fatally over-reaches himself.

However you play him, the chief delight for actor and for audience is the cadence of his voice. It is delicious, ripe and stuffed with excessive phrasing, full of the self-reference of the over-busy brain. Even within its lateral shifts and sudden switch-backs, it retains a stubborn musicality. When he discovers what he believes to be the reason for Hamlet's madness – his heart-break over the loss of Ophelia's love – Polonius spontaneously combusts with self-delight. His pleasure is that he has solved a secret, that he is at the epicentre of the mystery. With the King and Queen, when he reports his discovery, his nervousness sends his syntax into a whirlpool from which it appears he may never escape:

POLONIUS My liege, and madam, to expostulate
What majesty should be, what duty is,
Why day is day, night night, and time is time,
Were nothing but to waste night, day and time.
Therefore, since brevity is the soul of wit,

And tediousness the limbs and outward flourishes,
I will be brief: your noble son is mad:
Mad call I it; for, to define true madness,
What is't but to be nothing else but mad?
But let that go.
GERTRUDE More matter, with less art.
POLONIUS Madam, I swear I use no art at all.
That he is mad, 'tis true: 'tis true 'tis pity;
And pity 'tis 'tis true: a foolish figure;
But farewell it, for I will use no art.
Mad let us grant him, then: and now remains
That we find out the cause of this effect,
Or rather say, the cause of this defect,
For this effect defective comes by cause:
Thus it remains, and the remainder thus.
Perpend!

'Perpend!' is the despairing self-slap of the man trying to escape from the entrapping concentric rings of his own rhetoric. The circularity is maddening, not least to Gertrude, who upbraids him, but also delicious. Wherever we were in the world, audiences laughed with pleasure at this moment. Comically speaking, it was a banker moment. There was international recognition of the overly entitled windbag, of course, but the laughter was not cruel. There was huge affection, but also – delightfully – pleasure in the music of the language. Whether the audience spoke Mandarin, Swahili or Maori, the internal rhymes, the dancing fleet mono-syllables, the self-contradiction – it translated.

After he has told the King and Queen he believes Hamlet's love for Ophelia is the principal cause of his madness, he can't resist drawing things out:

And he, repulsed – a short tale to make –
Fell into a sadness, then into a fast,
Thence to a watch, thence into a weakness,
Thence to a lightness, and, by this declension,
Into the madness wherein now he raves,
And all we mourn for.

The pursuit of precision here, when describing something as ineffable as mental decline, is its own lovely joke. We can feel Polonius's approximation of the same confusion within his attempt to describe it. This is Polonius's music with a turbo-charge of adrenalin beneath it, but earlier we hear the same music at ease with itself. He advises his son Laertes shortly before he sets off to Paris and a long separation:

Yet here, Laertes! Aboard, aboard, for shame!
The wind sits in the shoulder of your sail,
And you are stay'd for. There – my blessing with thee!
And these few precepts in thy memory
See thou character. Give thy thoughts no tongue,
Nor any unproportioned thought his act.
Be thou familiar, but by no means vulgar.
Those friends thou hast, and their adoption tried,
Grapple them to thy soul with hoops of steel;
But do not dull thy palm with entertainment
Of each new-hatch'd, unfledged comrade. Beware
Of entrance to a quarrel, but being in,
Bear't that the opposed may beware of thee.
Give every man thy ear, but few thy voice;
Take each man's censure, but reserve thy judgment.
Costly thy habit as thy purse can buy,

But not express'd in fancy; rich, not gaudy;
For the apparel oft proclaims the man,
Neither a borrower nor a lender be;
For loan oft loses both itself and friend,
And borrowing dulls the edge of husbandry.
This above all: to thine own self be true,
And it must follow, as the night the day,
Thou canst not then be false to any man.
Farewell: my blessing season this in thee!

There are a host of contradictions in this passage. Much of the advice militates against itself; much of it seems so finely calibrated as to be an instruction in etiquette rather than morality; some of it seems to emanate from the style section of the papers, and after all of this instruction about how to be someone else in the father's image, it seems a mite contradictory to finish with 'to thine own self be true'. But there is good solid sense marbling through it as well, and who, in the painful moment of saying farewell to a child, when trying to flail some sense into the emotional winds around them, who hasn't sounded a bit stupid? The relations within the Polonius family are often played as poisoned, which leaves Ophelia and Laertes nowhere to go at the end of the play, so it is important there is an appropriate weight of feeling in these moments. Whatever the surrounds, what better, or better expressed, thing is there to say to anyone than 'to thine own self be true'?

Behind the contradictions, there is the confident balanced music of the man who can entrance a room, whether full of politicians or family members. When Shakespeare wants to write a nervous music, a confusion, a lack of articulacy, he does. People often mistake the fact that everyone speaks in verse for a belief that

they are all equally articulate. This is far from true. Blank verse
is an inimitable conduit for thought in the English language. This
means that thoughts can be jagged, drawn out, awkward or
confused. Hamlet's first soliloquy 'Solid flesh' is rigorously iambic,
while conveying the fragmented jumble of a crumbling mind.
When Shakespeare wants to write a confident music, he does,
and nowhere more elegantly than for Polonius. The seductive
beauty of cadence whether read on the page or heard in speech
is largely forgotten. To an English ear in Shakespeare's time,
cadence, whether heard in the luminous phrasing of a Lancelot
Andrewes in the pulpit, or in the arguments of the law courts of
a highly litigious age, or in the sack-soaked fruitcake wit of the
tavern, for that ear cadence was one of the great pleasures of life.
As with many of the verbal pleasures of Renaissance London, the
delight in cadence could trace much of its ancestry back to Rome,
and to Polonius's spiritual ancestor, Cicero.

Even with Shakespeare's fabled and misleading 'little Latin', he
would have had Cicero drummed into him several hours a day
for long years of his life. My hunch is that little made him happier.
Cicero's many volumes of letters, miscellanies and philosophical
writings offer a comprehensive portrait of a complicated and
changing mind, and a vivid image of the human wrangling of
the end of the Roman Republic. Beyond them the speeches,
transcribed with rigour by his amanuensis Tiro, offer a greater
pleasure. Not only do we hear the fresh unmediated sound of
Latin speech as it was spoken, but we also hear a genius of
language take the art of rhetoric to new heights. Cicero perfected
the syntactical rules within which we still live, and rules which,
when well learnt, unlock new systems and worlds of thought.
'Not only . . . but also . . .' itself is one of Cicero's favourites,
along with the tripling of decorative subclauses and a thousand

other tricks which he mastered, and which a fellow wordsmith like Shakespeare would have chortled and chuckled with happiness at encountering. Cicero's voice is sly, sarcastic, often small and petty in its judgements, but its music is breathtaking.

The word rhetoric implies something dry and stiff, a bone-dry bore orating slowly, but in Cicero's hands and those of his followers, it is something very different. It is jazz. The masters learn the rules, the chords, the sequences, the antiphonies and the harmonies, and then they let rip. In the process of letting rip, they get to places, musically and in thought, they did not know they could reach. This is what rhetoric is for. It is process not product. It is also the heart of Shakespeare's genius. Cicero spent years perfecting a skill-set, and then as a writer and as a speaker let himself loose. Shakespeare drenched himself in learning and in the world, and then floated free. Writing creates thought, thought does not create writing. The very process of sitting down with stylus and tablet, quill and parchment, typewriter and paper, keyboard and screen, the very physical process of scratching, scribbling, typing, inputting, the process releases ideas and insights which laugh to scorn all that planning and strategising struggle to achieve. Rhetoric, form and rhythm are ways and means of facilitating that release. Cicero's speeches are the finest exemplars of that, and although Cicero himself is only a small walk-on part in *Julius Caesar*, his influence is all over the work. Polonius in his glories, and in his shortcomings, seems an ironic testament to that.

Just like Polonius, Cicero was an arch worshipper of the smoke and mirrors of state. The Romans created a political system so baffling and peculiar that it makes particle physics look like noughts and crosses. Consuls, tribunes, pontiffs, governors, praetors and aediles – each represent patricians, people, provinces and priests within interlocking spheres of influence. The ways in which they interact with and contradict each other defies understanding. The aim seems to have been to create a system of power-sharing so opaque that anyone considering challenging it would retreat in the face of the inevitable migraines involved in trying to comprehend it. It also created a fertile ground for lawyers, and even more so for those capable of pretending to an understanding. Anyone who could bring off a general air of 'Ah yes, I would explain that but you would never understand it, wheels within wheels, old chap' could have a field day with the levers of power. If you could elevate that clubbable exclusivity to the aura of one of the very few initiated, if you could pretend a hieratic insight into the great mysteries, then complex politics starts to approach a quasi-mysticism. As Cicero managed to, and as Polonius rather less successfully aspires to.

'By indirections find directions forth' indeed. No matter that it is all unspeakable, Wizard of Oz, smoke and mirrors.

★ ★ ★

The show in Djibouti was not great. The setting could not have been more beautiful: an open stage with the waves of the Red Sea folding in behind, the sun going down before. But it was on the edge of the hotel compound, and the pleasures of this gilded cage were wearing thin. There had been little or no marketing, and with half an hour to go there was not much sign of an audience. I wandered around the cavernous marble-ceilinged hotel foyer picking up a few lost souls looking for the show, then positioned myself behind the airport-style security at the front door to steer the few people allowed in towards our temporary theatre. Thankfully a group of students arrived to give us some contact with the locality. When we settled, there were only about

120 people – a bewildering mix of a few ex-pats, some financiers from the hotel, a smattering of Special Forces, a sprinkling of Djiboutians and the students. The posh locals seemed more interested in the table of drinks than *Hamlet*, and seemed a little put out they had to watch the show; the students seemed keen to sneak behind the toilet and have a smoke or snog each other. Bizarrely the Special Forces contingent seemed quite into it.

Things got decidedly odder later. Our host was keen that we join him in his home after the show. He had issued the invitation during the monologue the day before, and had rung twice to confirm it. Having enjoyed his company, many of us were keen, and he hung around afterwards, being generous with compliments, and watching as we dismantled the set. We then set out in two vans and drove to a diplomatic area near the hotel, where we found large residence after large residence, each surrounded by a high white wall, each white wall enclosing palatial emptiness. The streets were deserted. No cars, no people. On a distant hill, we saw the city of Djibouti, a tumbling metropolis of houses and life. Here there was emptiness and silence. It was all manicured and elegant in the desert night air, but felt like a zombie film before the zombies show up. We swung through heavy iron gates into our host's residence, a cool white building set in a cool white compound. A string of buildings created a quad, on one side of which was his home, beyond his very own infinity pool, and beyond that a long private beach leading down to the sea. Paradise but again eerily empty.

Our host bounced from pillar to post with excitement. He scurried us through his home, showing us every room as if we were at the Ideal Home exhibition, pointing out with particular pride the pictures of himself with several large fish (always a danger sign), switching lights on, as if he had just moved in. He flicked the switch to illuminate the pool from underwater with the pleasure of a child showing off a toy. After he had shown us everything, he sat down and looked at us with a peculiar expectancy. As if it was our turn to start amusing him. Some odd silence gave the impression we were now supposed to burst into song, or start telling sad tales, or take our clothes off and start performing sex acts on each other.

What he seemed completely unprepared to do was to feed us or slake our thirst. A company of actors after a show has very powerful and simple needs. Food and drink. Nothing was forthcoming. When he began another monologue on geopolitics, expecting us to all sit and look entranced, I expressed rather forcibly the idea that food and drink were a little more than necessary. He looked a little cussed, then suggested that I went with him to the kitchen. He seemed to have a hard time finding it. When we eventually reached the kitchen, he said, 'Aha! Let's see what treasures we have in here', and walked straight into a laundry cupboard. Having located the fridge and the cellar between the two of us, I reassured him that I could take over from there and that he could return to the guests. I opened the capacious fridge to see – what else? – block after block after block of foie gras. Literally nothing else. I scoured the rest of the room for biscuits and returned to the throng with a mountain of foie gras and a few bottles of vintage champagne.

When I returned, he was entertaining everyone with a discourse about the difficulties of creating true democracy in Djibouti. With a small population with ancient regional and tribal differences, it is a delicate matter creating a system when a simple majority government can't reflect the vested interests of each group. As has been witnessed elsewhere in the region, and not that much further afield in Iraq, a first-past-the-post system can't guarantee

a place at the table for all the different ethnic and religious enti-
ties. The result is a power-sharing arrangement with representation
according to tribal numbers. This formula where everyone is given
a voice seems an elegant solution, and one which he had in part
authored.

He was proving persuasive and fascinating again, and the
company were feeling warmer with a lump of foie gras inside
them, and half a bottle of Lanson. But the strange confusion as
we had arrived, and the over-excitement at our presence, had
diminished his mystical authority not a little, and there was a
dangerous sense of humour floating around the group. We were
sitting around a marble-slab table beside the outdoor pool under
the stars, and mischief was tickling the air. Our host was telling
a long story about how a Spanish warship in the port had acci-
dentally fired off a missile headed for the diplomatic zone. As he
reached the moment where the missile shot off, he flung out his
hands and caught Amanda square in the tit. She said nothing, he
said nothing, sadly no one did, and a small titter of giggles started
to play between us. He then told a long story about the arrival
of something called the Kent in Djibouti. Unfortunately, he had
a very peculiar way of pronouncing the word Kent. For a while
we wondered if this was a product called Kent, the Duke of Kent,
or just someone he didn't like very much. It is very hard to
ascertain what it was without saying 'Keyunt' a lot. Which didn't
reduce the hysteria of the room. Eventually, we ascertained that
it was a ship called the *Kent*, but by this stage the room was close
to hilarity. I said that it was time for us to go to bed. Everyone
leapt up with alacrity.

He insisted on showing us the consulate. As we walked to it,
he kept slowing down whenever he got near a picture of himself
with a fish, and drawing breath ominously, before I hurried him

on. The consulate was sumptuous, dripping money and power and art to the appropriate degree, but escape was becoming important. Hysteria was growing but also an eerie sense of being locked in, incarcerated in the lovelessness and deadness of power. Just as we were heading for the vans of departure, I was walking abreast with Rawiri. We heard the ever-ebullient Keith behind us saying to our host, 'Tell you what, why don't you tell us your most exciting fishing story?' Fortunately, stage management saved the day and bundled us into vans. Our hysteria was spent as we drove back through the empty streets of the diplomatic area.

* * *

It often seems that if there were to be an eleventh commandment, it would be 'Thou shalt hate lawyers and politicians'. They run through popular culture emitting the same pleasant odours as bankers. Almost every story seems predisposed to bring them to a grisly end in art and life. Polonius's demise is in small part tragic, in large part comic. However fond of him we have become, to be stabbed to death behind a curtain and then have your body dragged around a castle in an attempt to find a hiding place lacks dignity. Cicero's life came to a squalid end. Having survived ceaseless shifts of power and the whims of various factions, the violent ugliness within authority caught up with him, and he was stabbed to death by a self-appointed militia. The Roman's end is rarely presented as a cause of great sorrow, more often as the becoming end for an ambitious shape-shifter. Both Polonius and Cicero love gossip, both love sitting in the middle of the matrix, reading the shifts of the wind, until their sense for its movement runs out, and it crushes them. Power is a 'massy wheel', and dancing attendance on it exacts a heavy price.

But it is a mistake to dismiss such figures, however easy a target. Cicero, within all his vicissitudes and shifting allegiances, did try to maintain the existence of the Roman Republic and to resist the inevitable arrival of the Roman Empire. Not too shabby a cause to die for. The Roman state for all its Gordian complexity did maintain a (just) functioning democracy for almost half a millennium, which is not bad going. The French are self-parodic with their diplomatic equivocation and their contrived hauteur, but who but the French could have achieved a gathering of opinions and a consensus as they did to effect a climate change deal at the end of 2015? They may dance lightly, but it takes a light touch to draw others into a dance.

The Poloniuses of this world, whether Cicero in the long distant past, Cecil in Elizabeth's court, or an honorary consul by the Red Sea in the present day, may grease the wheels in a way that we disdain, but they also keep the machine moving; they may equivocate a little too much, but sometimes we need a little equivocation; they may be a little economical with the *actualité*, but they also arbitrate, and someone has to arbitrate; they may talk nonsense and cause delay, but they also soften the blows of history a little. If we despise lawyers and politicians, what is the alternative? People of action and principle? God protect us from them.

The world of *Hamlet* gets darker after Polonius's death. For Ophelia and for Laertes catastrophically, and their grief is a measure of the emotional value of their father. In the world of the play, without Polonius's fussy, theatrical scheming, the door is opened for the harder-nosed brutality of Claudius. Much of the wit and the comforting human smallness is bled out of Elsinore with Polonius's passing. A domestic tragicomic atmosphere descends into brutal tragedy. The delightful cadence of Polonius's music falls out of the play's harmonics, and much humanity goes with it. There is little doubt Hamlet regrets his actions. When Claudius asks him immediately after the killing where Polonius is, Hamlet's response is whipsmart and automatic: 'In heaven.'

* * *

The United Nations is a long way from heaven, though probably close to Polonius's idea of Nirvana. It was our privilege to play there early in the progress of the tour – the first time a play had been performed in one of its grand chambers. We tried to get into the Security Council chamber but were blocked by the Russians – how UN is that? – so had to settle for the ECOSOC (the United Nations Economic and Social Council) chamber next door. We built a stage and performed to 200 ambassadors banked up behind desks decked out with flashing lights and national nameplates and microphones. Not the warmest environment to engage with, though thankfully there were 400 members of the public at the back. To add to the oddity, in the midst of all the ambassadors sat Kim Cattrall and Laurie Anderson, for a reason that no one could fathom. The British representative had told us to cut the show down to two hours, because no one would stay longer. We refused. He then told us to cut the interval, because everyone would leave. We refused. Happily they stayed, and applauded warmly at the end.

Functioning as a pressure-cooker meeting place for all the world's Poloniuses and wannabe Ciceros, the UN is not backwards in aggrandising its own mystique. It was built to pull all of the world's problems into the enclosing fog of its own smoke and mirrors. The process of getting inside was a protracted one of consultation, begging and form-filling. And a lot of waiting – the ultimate tool of power. All of that, the history of the place, and its mythification by television news, conspired to fill us with awe on approaching it.

An awe which the place itself rather sweetly fails to justify. The atmosphere is shabby earnest – tired carpets, old paint and sad 1950s optimism. The staff, from bored security men to Monica Lewinsky lookalike interns and over-zealous health and safety officers, all seem to accept they are participating in a comedy rather than a power play. A majestic Hepworth outside, a tapestry of *Guernica* within, ethnic artefacts at every turn – the sheer aesthetic quality of these objects seems to act as a rebuke to the shabbiness that encases them.

The United Nations was probably more effective at pulling off the trick of power and mystic arrogance before the lethal thugs of the Bush administration got it in their sights. The impression it conveyed to us was of a down-at-heel debating chamber filled with goodwill, but ill-equipped to deal with the brutalities of a freshly psychotic world. It made one feel nostalgic for its days of influence, and, because of its doddery frailty, made new sense of the value of the Poloniuses and the Ciceros. Rather them than the Cheneys and the Jihadi Johns. As a Palestinian said not so long ago, 'We are rather tired of living in the tragedies of Shakespeare. We would be very happy to spend some time in Chekhovian tragedy. Heartbreak and longing would do us just fine for a century or two.' The United Nations was built on the dream that the world could hold back, could swallow its rages and its injustices for a while and let those energies scatter to the winds while oratorical windbags filled the air with delicate rhetoric. It's a comical dream but better than many a tragic nightmare. The Ciceros and the Poloniuses are ridiculous, but you remove them at your peril.

★ ★ ★

We returned to Djibouti almost a year later in the tour. Something about the gilded luxury of the first visit had left a sour taste, and there was a desire to redeem it. Mr Grumpy Boots and Mrs Mardy Knickers back in the United Kingdom were always trying to fling the accusation of exclusivity at the endeavour, however distant from the truth it might be. We were only able to replace the sour taste with a sad one – such is the bitter comedy of our present world – since the opportunity came to return to Djibouti and play to more displaced people, this time Yemenis fleeing their civil war. A healthy crowd of several hundred gathered on the sands of the dunes and watched with affectless delight.

John was playing Polonius. His interpretation had morphed several times during the course of the tour, according to his changed understanding of the role, from stern authoritarian to confused fool to warm-hearted duffer. As the tour matured towards its end, his characterisation was now a lovely agglomeration of each. Impressive and scary and human in equal measure.

The audience loved him, and at the end they went wild for the jig, the music and the dancing soft-footing into the deep silence of the sand. The sight of John's Polonius dancing in the desert before a crowd of refugees, stiff collar and creased trousers in good order, head held proudly steady, his pomposity as absurd in this alien place as it possibly could be, yet all the more human and all the more beautiful for its daftness, was a steadfast tribute under a hot sun to the survival instincts of the Poloniuses of the world.

7

GOD ON A PACIFIC ISLAND

HAMLET *There's a divinity that shapes our ends,*
Rough-hew them how we will —

Act 5, Scene 2

MIDNIGHT IN DOWNTOWN TAIPEI, AND neon battles with dark-ness to create artificial day. Jen and I are on the street outside a curtained entrance, trying to wheedle our way into a club. After some arguments over ID and some haggling over money, we find ourselves walking into a large rectangular room wholly draped in heavy velvet. The doors behind us clang shut, and we look nervously around for a non-existent exit. Paranoia is trickling in until a sudden jolt shakes us and we clock that we're in a huge lift ascending slowly skywards. A second jolt and we arrive.

Friends who travelled in China in the mid 1980s had told me tales of discos defined by a stark sexlessness. They had danced awkwardly in white rooms lit with glaring strip lights, cans of Coke laid out neatly on metal tables, bubblegum pop shrieking out of Tannoys. Boys and girls, dressed respectably and shifting nervously from foot to foot, shrank from each other on separate sides of the room. This, they had been told, was the hottest scene in town. Well, things have moved on since. The lift doors in Taipei slide open to reveal monochrome pandemonium. Pulsating grids of white light cut expressive shapes on the matt-black walls. The bouncers – slender and smartly dressed – wear a cultivated look of deadpan violence. A bevy of underage girls, got up as some schoolgirl kung-fu fantasy direct from the brain of Quentin Tarantino, emanate a cheerful hunger for depravity. Cocaine seems to be obtained by a chit-signing system at the bar. Techno music thump thump thumps and booff booff booffs. There's excitement in the air, a sense of liberation and play – this is a reworking of the tropes of Western youth style, not a carbon copy. If I had to give it a moniker, I'd call it Festive Cool.

It is in this penthouse of industrial hedonism that I reconvene with the company after a couple of months' absence. The surprise on their faces at seeing me here, where I am a good twenty or thirty years older than most, is one of the pleasures of the trip so far. We hug and kiss and laugh at the unlikeliness. They are high on life – it is Naeem's birthday, and Taiwan is the first city they've seen in several weeks. They have just completed their longest and most arduous leg, hopping across the South Pacific islands. This is Ulysses' crew, fresh from gruelling Homeric adventures and determined to celebrate. We park ourselves on a banquette, and they circulate between there and the dance floor, the strobe flashes capturing them in jerky freeze-frame. On the banquette, whoever is taking a breather spills out tales of their recent travels in snatched, shouted fragments.

They have just come from Palau, a small island country in Micronesia, where, after much haggling over venues, a school hall had been secured and a princely audience of twenty-seven people assembled. Shortly before the show began, a grand Rolls-Royce drew up outside. Its tinted passenger window rolled down to reveal in the recesses a powerful-looking woman in dark glasses. Stage management approached with appropriate deference, only to be greeted by a barked 'Where is my money?'

'I'm sorry?'

'Where is my money? No money, no show!'

'Money for what?'

'To perform in my hall. $1,500 right now. I am the Queen of Palau. No money, no show!'

'Erm . . . we were told to pay the government!'

'You do not pay the government. You pay me now, or no show!'

She refused to leave her empowering backseat, so they continued to pacify her through the car window while frantically ringing London to find out what was going on. Dealing with the Queen of Palau is not something they train stage management for at drama school.

There are horror stories from the tiny buckaroo aeroplanes in which they've traversed the vast Pacific, many of which did not have the capacity to carry our excess baggage. This has meant the frequent non-appearance of the flight cases that carry costumes and props, and comprise most of the set. After one too many occasions where the company were cobbling together a show from only a third of the necessary components, while stage management tried to trace swords, chemises and painted props across the Pacific basin, a communal cry of 'Fuck it!' went up, and they resolved to abandon the cases and make the show up afresh in each new country. Local markets were scoured for cloth and scarves to denote character, and imagination was called on to transform unlikely objects into key plot elements – billiard cues apparently the best stand-ins for swords.

Cockroaches are a regular theme of the reportage – everyone has a cockroach story. In the silent dark of night, and the claustrophobia of small island life, many of the company have had little to distract them beyond counting and categorising the cockroaches assembled in their rooms. 'It was *this* big.' 'There were *this* many.' 'There were *three* on my pillow . . .' Cockroaches have infested the minds of the company as effectively and enduringly as they do the landscape. The king of the cockroach stories belongs to John. One morning, he had spruced himself up and headed down to breakfast in the company's less-than-salubrious hotel. On returning to his room, he found a large portion of the ceiling directly over his bed had collapsed. It had been worn down by the weight of months', years', decades' worth of cockroaches, which were now seething nightmarishly over the debris.

Besides these sordid anecdotes are happier tales of warm welcomes, and smartphone videos that capture brief, magical moments of contact. In Tuvalu, in a small space between the airport and the hotel, the company improvised a theatre for the day, and children watched them rehearse and perform with fascination. One pocket movie shows a gang of overjoyed four-year-olds dancing along in a frenzy of jerky happiness to the closing jig. Another shows a beautifully synchronised dance of welcome in a big sports hall in Kiribati. This form of greeting has been besmirched rather by its association with the image of visiting dignitaries sitting in besuited stiffness while indigenous people shake their bits and bobs at them. That's a shame, because what better way is there to greet people than with a dance? In Somaliland, I sat in a straw hut as people strutted out a rhythm before us, and felt unaccountably happy. Several of the company joined them and danced along. Maybe our leading parliamentarians should be encouraged to greet visitors at Heathrow with an exhibition of ballroom dancing.

A different kind of dancing swirls around the floor in Taipei. The Taiwanese dance together in clumps, the gathering together not sexual in intent, more simple joy at the individual merging into a tangled mass of bodies. Our company dance alone, Western style, or in couples. The difference is marked, and the fact we are different in other ways – the only white, black and brown faces in the room – adds to the festivity. Matt out of his own kindness finds a friend and brings him to our group. 'This is Xiu Ling,' he shouts. 'He doesn't have any friends here, so I've told him to come and join us.' 'Hello, Xiu Ling!' everyone shouts over the pounding noise. 'Isn't Matt nice, we all think.' Matt talks to him for about three minutes. Then he looks bored, dumps him and returns to the dance floor.

I'm too tired, too old and too leaden-footed to join the shifting throng and lower the temperature with my antique moves, so I sit still and the company yell more Pacific Island adventures into my ear. There are stories of sexual encounters in unlikely places ('drabbing', as the company have dubbed it), of snorkelling trips, of planes that bucked and lurched and tumbled like rodeo horses . . . But all the stories from the geographical swirl of the last few weeks seem to gather and converge around one place. One magnetic country draws the other stories together: Nauru.

At our ambassador's breakfast in the summer of 2013, one man had swept in late. Dressed in a Savile Row suit, a thin body propping up a lion's mane of hair, the classic British public-school jutting jaw, he looked quite the most important man in the room, surveying the crowd with a gaze of advanced entitlement. Was he a high-up at the UN, a Foreign Office bod, a director at the British Council? We approached him with trepidation.

'And where are you representing?' we asked gingerly.

'I,' he began with a thunderous confidence, and then faltered a little. 'I am the High Commissioner of Nauru.'

'Where?!' we chorused – the words 'Where is Nauru?' singing through our heads.

He looked a little crestfallen and pressed a brochure into our hands. This was the first I'd heard of this country, but the picture on the front of the brochure was pure enchantment. An aerial shot of a perfect disc of an island set in the deep blue of the Pacific. He explained that it was the smallest populated country in the world, an atoll briefly replete with wealth until Australia scooped out its central resource of guano to use for phosphate fertiliser and then deserted it once that resource was depleted. He told us that it was a beautiful place, that they would never have heard of *Hamlet* there, nor probably Shakespeare, nor most probably England.

Nauru became the focus of our sense of quest. This faraway place, foreign in landscape and culture, geographically inaccessible and a million miles away in mindset, became the symbol for the scope and ambition and otherness of our mission. 'We're even going to Nauru,' we'd say to people, and watch bafflement crease their faces. 'We're on the way to Nauru,' we'd tell ourselves as we started trying to define the scale of what we were doing. 'We've made it to Nauru,' we announced with a huzzah to the office, when pictures of the company dismounting from a small plane and walking towards a WELCOME TO NAURU poster digitally whooshed back to London. We've arrived in paradise, we thought to ourselves. From the stories I'm now hearing in Taipei, the truth was more muddied.

'Oh man, *Nauru*!' they shout into my ear. 'We couldn't get out of there fast enough.' 'Longest three days of my life.' A lot of the prevailing madness in the South Pacific leg seems to have coalesced in Nauru. The Australians, having stripped the island of its one natural resource, are now compounding the crime by exporting their most nutritionally void foodstuffs to Nauru markets. The grass fertilised by the plundered phosphates has fed cows and pigs, whose fatty offcuts return to Nauru in the form of nuggets and other processed lumps of protein. This has created not only an obesity problem, but also a pervasive listlessness – the sort of wholesale depletion of willpower and energy you see in any McDonald's on a weekday morning spread out across a whole island. As well as treating the island as a waste receptacle for its abattoirs, Australia uses it to detain and process refugees, who have made the long journey from Iran, Pakistan and Afghanistan. Some of our company had travelled to the detention centre on their day off and spoken to those held there. There will always be a chasm of logic and justice between a group of people who have chosen to charge round the planet enjoying mobility, variety and new cultural encounters, safe in their dreams of home, and those who have been compelled by a criminally unfair planet to set out on dangerous voyages in hope of a better future. But our company, with their generosity and tact, tried to bridge it by asking and listening.

Standing in the nightclub, I hear second-hand stories of boats that set sail full of people and docked half empty, whose passenger numbers were whittled away by hunger and violence and madness and suicide. These people had travelled through unimaginable horror stories, only to end up sitting on a disc of volcanic rock in the Pacific, while the Australian government turned a blind eye to their existence. On the island itself, there was tension and unease between the refugees and the indigenous population. A couple of years before, in an eruption of violence against the cruelty of their guards and the hopelessness of their fate, the detainees had rioted and burnt down part of the detention centre, the spiral of desperation leading them to destroy their own environment. In a year when the Mediterranean as well as the Indian Ocean was brimming with new narratives of migrant despair, it made the joy and the excitement of our travel look all the more like luxury. And hurled fresh questions at its purpose. What to do with the world's manifest cruelty and daftness and sorrow? How to respond? For the moment, there is nothing to do but listen to more stories.

On the company's second day in Nauru, simmering resentment had turned to naked aggression when opposition Nauruans lost patience with the government and attacked their own parliament building. Accusations of corruption involving Australia and the infamous guano were flying, and the company witnessed a jostle-off that culminated in a brief storming of the doors of the parliament. The following morning, they watched an opposition politician slamming the government on television. To their surprise, the same man was sitting on their plane leaving the island that afternoon. Take-off was delayed, then delayed again, and eventually several police officers boarded the plane and asked him to disembark. He refused. Things got heated rather quickly. Suddenly there was a technical problem with the plane, and everyone was asked to disembark. When they returned to their seats, the opposition politician had disappeared. A Rosencrantz and Guildenstern fate if ever there was one.

★ ★ ★

The weirdest story from the Nauru adventure is saved for last. In the world's smallest island nation, by some miracle of coincidence, the company had encountered a man who was attempting the same global journey as themselves. But this affable, well-set chap from the American Midwest was on a different mission. His aim was to walk through every country in the world bearing an enormous cross on his shoulders. It was a contemporary recreation of Christ's slow walk to Calvary. Handily, his cross has wheels. Aptly, his name is Keith Wheeler. Though the cross is impressive in stature, it is retractable enough to be taken on planes as hand luggage. His inspiration is the equally aptly named Arthur Blessitt. If you don't believe me, check out their websites.

Our Keith spoke to Mr Wheeler and discovered that he had been a student pole-vaulter at Arkansas State University when he'd had the calling. On Good Friday 1985, he swapped one pole for two and began his walk of more than 25,000 miles to 150 countries on all seven continents. He has been in jail forty times, been run over three times and left for dead twice. He said the only time he met any real antagonism was in Christian countries because he does not align himself to any particular branch of Christianity.

He was in Rwanda during the genocide and went into Iraq before the last war. Unable to gain a permit to enter Iraq, he carried his cross up to the Jordanian border, asked to meet Saddam, then went on his knees and prayed. The border guards after much kerfuffle and frantic phone calls allowed him through, and he had an hour-long meeting with Saddam. The company are impressed by his sincerity and his simplicity, and, though by no means an evangelical group, they respect, more than anyone probably, the scale of his achievement. In Nauru, he had been there during the rioting and had interceded just as it was getting heated. He claimed he walked into the crowd with his cross, started to pray and everyone calmed down.

Our company have different and personal reactions to religion.

Amanda's parents are both Anglican ministers, her mother a celebrated one, at one point tipped to be the first female bishop. Of Jamaican heritage, her mother runs a parish in Hackney and is a former chaplain to the Houses of Parliament, in which capacity she once spent all night sitting in silent vigil with the dead body of Margaret Thatcher. Matt's parents are both rabbis from the more liberal and progressive end of the Judaic faith, his mother one of the first female rabbis in England. Jen's background is culturally Buddhist, and her devoutness takes particular and unconventional forms.

Naeem is one of the most quietly yet determinedly spiritual people I've met. In rehearsals and on the road, I have frequently seen him react to difficult situations by dropping anchor in silence and stillness. When he has to absorb a new idea or circumstance, you can see him lower his internal temperature: as if he builds a high marble ceiling over his head and solid stone walls around him, shutting out the noise and heat of the world so that he can resolve its conflicts within the cool blue of his own private mosque. His parents are devout Muslims, so devout that sadly they have not allowed themselves to see the show and witness what their son Naeem is doing.

Once, over lunch in Djibouti, we discussed how religion informs each of our lives. The conversation was the kind of mishmash of belief and doubt and idiosyncrasy we have come to expect in our lapsarian world, where the fervent faith of previous generations has faded like the colours of frescoes in old chapels: 'My religion is a private thing, made up in my own way' . . . 'I use it to help find some sort of moral path through the world' . . . 'It gives me a sense of community' . . . 'I see God in everything' . . . 'I can't believe in the old structures' . . . I was as lost and as stumbling as the others. Agnosticism is conditioned by its own lack of articulacy; it has neither the brutal realism of atheism, nor the passionate certainties of religion. It operates in the no man's land where the mind searches for words that do not appear, to frame an image whose shape is shrouded in mist.

We sat there on the deck, the red sea gently bashing against the rocks below us, and talked about how this inarticulacy has plagued us all our lives. About how many of our sentences open with phrases of uncertainty: 'I don't know, but . . .' 'I have a sense of . . .' 'There is a feeling . . .' 'Something beyond our own ken . . .' The uncertainty frightens us, because it leaves a vacuum, but it also offers hope, because that vacuum needs to be filled. That absence provokes an appetite for the world, for all its surprises, and, most importantly, for love. A love that is ever on the wing, occasionally flying beside but more often caught on currents of air, floating away, leaving the gentle agnostic on the lookout once again. Love as a search, not a certainty. The agnostic's journey is always one of doubt, of openness, of confusion offered with humility to the world. It is in many ways, we hope, the journey we are making around the world, and the story of the play itself. *Hamlet* is a play for agnostics who are on the hunt for more. It is a play that resists certainty. Actively.

Christ wanders through *Hamlet* like the man with a cross pursuing a lonely Calvary around the world. He dances in and out of the play. There is a plethora of theories about the operation of Christianity and religion in the play – each theory a better reflection of the world it emerges from than the world it purports to explain. During eras that were keen to deploy Shakespeare as an extra buttress in that fortress called civilisation, *Hamlet* was a Christian play about a Christian chap whose head got a little turned but who found his way back to sanity again with some help from good old Christian clarity. What there is little doubt about, after Greenblatt's revelatory work on the question of purgatory in the play, is that the afterlife and ideas of proper and improper burial are the central source of much of its emotional heat. It is clear that the act of killing, whether of others or of the self, is framed in the context of its moral weight in the Christian world. It would be hard to contest, in a play whose central character has spent a substantial amount of time in Wittenberg, that the seizing muscular tension between Catholicism and Protestantism within which all of Europe was racked was not also a source of its restless energy.

Given all that, it still seems possible to overstate the presence of religion and Christ in the play. The soliloquies are clear thinking in a fog; they are not foggy thinking in a clear world. The afterlife is uncertain, as Hamlet outlines:

> Who would these fardels bear,
> To grunt and sweat under a weary life,
> But that the dread of something after death,
> The undiscovered country, from whose bourn
> No traveller returns . . .

(There is an inherent wobbliness in this statement, given that Hamlet is one of the few people who *has* met a traveller from that bourn: his own father. You do feel like shouting, 'What about the ghost then?' . . . But looking for cosmic consistency in Shakespeare is as daft as looking for it in the world.) There is something exquisitely unsure about the clumsiness of that 'something'. It is a word that questions rather than asserts. It is a wonderfully English word, as aptly used in its Anglo-Saxon vagueness here as in Wordsworth's 'Tintern Abbey' when he reaches for the sublime and can only find:

Of something far more deeply interfused
Whose dwelling is the light of setting suns,
And the round ocean and the living air,
And the blue sky, and in the mind of man . . .

In both, the word 'something' feels lumpy and contingent, emerging from a coarse, confused, secular world, from our loamy English earth, happy to reach for the heights but less than confident of its ability to touch them.

The messy human dynamics between characters also belie the idea of an infrastructure based on Christian certitude and stability. The love between Hamlet and Ophelia is a mortal love: it overpowers them both and destroys Ophelia. Religion offers no solace: the nunnery is elsewhere. Family dynamics are fraught and modelled on a pre-Christian pattern, with their conscious echoing of Aeschylus's *Oresteia*. Interactions between parents and children lay waste to everyone, and godliness does nothing to soothe, to mitigate, to heal. The play's politics are the machinations of human politics, monitoring internal dissent, squashing petty rebellions, jostling with other states for regional influence. The sanction of religion for these actions is sought, but more out of expediency than conviction. These are just people blundering around and across each other's blunderings. Even the Priest who appears seems, as with many of Shakespeare's friars and priests, more human than divine. We live now in a world full of people of terrifying religious certainty; none of them pop up in this play.

At the conclusion of the play, Hamlet does align his soul to a place of calm and quiet. He returns from his odd escapade with the pirates with a new strand in the twisted skein of his self: a religiously inflected determinism. Talking to his confidant Horatio about how he found himself back in Denmark, he says: 'There's a divinity that shapes our ends, / Rough-hew them how we will . . .'

This seems to settle the free will versus predestination argument pretty neatly. Later, we have his seraphic calm after he has accepted the challenge to fight Laertes: 'There's a special providence in the fall of a sparrow . . .' The fall of a sparrow is a reference to Matthew 10, 29–31: 'Are not two sparrows sold for a farthing, and one of them shall not fall on the ground without your father?' The biblical quotation, a weary soul finding sweet repose in providence, the final submission to a higher will, all seem to point in a certain direction – towards a nice undergraduate essay about a confused young man finally finding resolution through the religious language available to him.

But this is not the whole story. After Hamlet's return, he goes feral crazy at the sight of Laertes' outpouring of grief at Ophelia's grave; he cattily and viciously humiliates the court gadfly Osric; his pride manipulates him into accepting Laertes' challenge, and in the course of the fight he again loses self-control. The new-found religiosity, the Christian calm are there, of course, but they are wound tightly together with madness, depression, pride, aggression. Hamlet, and his creator Shakespeare, are too restless and protean to settle on a single thread. Hamlet incorporates religion within himself, he lives its richness and potential, but it does not consume the whole of him.

In the final, desolate, image of the play, as son, mother, step-father and Laertes lie twisted and bleeding on the floor of the court, as other freshly dead corpses lie in newly turned earth elsewhere, as the state teeters on the brink of collapse, and a foreign leader takes control, as all this loss stacks up, it is hard to see religion as much of a presence, let alone as an overpowering force. Christ is there, but not dominant – he is on the margins, flitting in and out of the play, as he flitted in and out of Shakespeare's world. As Arthur Blessitt and Keith Wheeler move through nations now, lonely figures wandering with a cross. Christ is driven to the edges of the play and the world, but he is still there.

* * *

It is almost morning in Taipei, and we are, as we have been in so many nightclubs, in so many cities, in so many countries, the last people to leave. The music is softer and the elaborate light shows have morphed into solid, white, go-home-now blankness. After their dystopian odyssey through the Pacific Islands, the company have spent all their stockpiled appetite for a big night out, and their excitement melts into exhaustion. The room, a few hours ago full of sex and noise and dance, and rich with stories old and new and yet to come, is empty as we step into the lift to depart into the dawn. The strangers all are gone.

65 **Portugal**, Lisbon   5 January 2015
Centro Cultural de Belem

66 **Algeria**, Algiers   7 January
The Algerian National Theatre Mahieddine Bachtarzi

67 **Tunisia**, Carthage   10 January
La Cathédrale Saint-Louis de Carthage

68 **Egypt**, Cairo   12 January
Bibliotheca Alexandrina

69 **Eritrea**, Asmara   15 January
Cinema Roma

70 **Sudan**, Khartoum   19 January
National Theatre

71 **Ethiopia**, Addis Ababa   22, 24 January
National Theatre of Ethiopia

72 **Dijbouti**, Djibouti City   26 January
Djibouti Palace Kempinski

73 **Somaliland**, Hargeisa   29 January
Ambassador Hotel, hosted by Hargeisa Cultural Center

74 **Kenya**, Nairobi   2 February
Oshwal Centre

75 **Uganda**, Kampala   4 February
Uganda National Cultural Centre

76 **Rwanda**, Butare   7 February
National University of Rwanda

77 **Burundi**, Bujumbura   9 February
King's Conference Centre

78 **Tanzania**, Dar es Salaam   12 February
The Little Theatre

8

MURDER AND THE RICE FIELDS

HAMLET . . . *now could I drink hot blood,*
And do such bitter business as the day
Would quake to look on.

Act 3, Scene 2

FOR A PLAY THAT IS supposed to be one of literature's most meditative and philosophical, *Hamlet* has a fairly impressive body-count. It's not quite in the *Terminator* class, but it's not a long way off *Titus Andronicus* either. The play begins on a tensely guarded battlement. Denmark is a country in a state of watchful nervousness – Fortinbras, the young tyro of neighbouring Norway, has 'sharked up a list of lawless resolutes' to recover lands lost by his father.

The back story for this unease is laid out after the first appearance of the Ghost. Hamlet's father, also called Hamlet, just seen in spectral form, had killed Fortinbras's father, also called Fortinbras, a generation ago – on the day of young Hamlet's birth – and thus gained for his nation a chunk of territory. The coincidence of the names can be confusing when first trying to figure out some dense exposition, but offers up a field day for psychoanalysts.

Factor in that Shakespeare's son who died young was called Hamnet, and the field day becomes an extended conference. Add the rumour that Shakespeare acted the part of the Ghost, Hamlet's father (shortly after his own father had died), and the conference spins out into a never-ending congress.

The killing of old Fortinbras is one of the many well-coiled springs which impel the play's trajectory. The second and principal killing is, of course, the murder of old Hamlet, the Ghost we have just seen. At first this is a mystery to us, though audiences then and now know that a spirit that walks the earth is not a happy one. We soon learn why, and the reason is presented with the melodramatic flourish of a popular barnstormer:

> GHOST I am thy father's spirit,
> Doom'd for a certain term to walk the night,
> And for the day confined to fast in fires,
> Till the foul crimes done in my days of nature
> Are burnt and purged away. But that I am forbid
> To tell the secrets of my prison house,
> I could a tale unfold whose lightest word
> Would harrow up thy soul; freeze thy young blood;
> Make thy two eyes, like stars, start from their spheres.
> O, if thou didst ever thy dear father love –
> HAMLET O God!
> GHOST Revenge his foul and most unnatural murder.
> HAMLET Murder!
> GHOST Murder most foul, as in the best it is;
> But this most foul, strange and unnatural.

The whole passage pivots around the word 'murder' with the architectural intent of the keystone being dropped into a complex arch. It pivots on the word just as a ballerina spinning a whirlwind pirouette spirals an unconscionable amount of pressure onto two toes. This murder kick-starts the narrative, and murder becomes the rocket fuel that powers the play along.

Of all Shakespeare's plays, *Hamlet* features the most impressive cull of its principal *dramatis personae*. Polonius is killed by Hamlet. Ophelia takes her own life in suicidal distress at her father's death and the disastrous love affair with Hamlet. Rosencrantz and Guildenstern have their heads lopped off by an English king we never see. Gertrude is inadvertently killed by Claudius's poison intended for Hamlet. Laertes is finished off by the poisoned tip of his own sword. Claudius is doubly done in by the sword's tip and his own poison. Hamlet is finished off by both these means too. When he intones 'the rest is silence', he appears to speak both for himself and for the other corpses strewing the stage.

Along the way we see the skull of a dead clown, amidst a field of other skulls, and we watch a Norwegian army cross the stage, off to commit senseless slaughter in Poland. The lightness and brightness of the play's thought, the flashes of its dancing wit, the wild spree of its improvised insight – all take place in front of a landscape of death.

Left alive, we have Horatio, a figure of unending goodwill, though more a witness than a protagonist, and Fortinbras, a soldier accustomed to fields of slaughter. He is able to survive the chaos and to give the audience some measure of its horror by his own disquiet: 'Such a sight as this / Becomes the field, but here shows much amiss.' It is a play that leaves few survivors.

The onslaught of action confounds the play's reputation as a philosophic treatise, and Hamlet himself is a long way from the 'procrastinator' of popular reputation – a myth given hefty emphasis by Olivier's film, which opened with the statement that it was 'the tragedy of a man who couldn't make up his mind'. In the second half of the drama, after the long period when he manages little more than putting on a play, he stabs Polonius through the arras, indirectly causes the death of Ophelia, and fixes a letter to dispatch his old friends Rosencrantz and Guildenstern. Without knowing what he is doing, he finishes off Laertes with his own poisoned sword, and knowing what he is doing, kills Claudius with sword and poison. In the space of about an hour of stage time, that is three acts of killing done in ignorance (the whole Polonius family), two intentional acts of killing done indirectly, and one done directly and knowingly and triumphantly. It is a wonder that in the course of this mayhem we retain such sympathy for him. It is hard to think of another Shakespeare protagonist who kills as many of those we have come to know and love as Hamlet. Yet when Horatio intones over his friend's freshly dead body,

> Now cracks a noble heart. Good night sweet prince:
> And flights of angels sing thee to thy rest!

we weep. Macbeth reveals the unfolding of a psychopath, and his chilling deadness to those around him is in a different realm, yet even he doesn't do as much damage to the main characters in the drama as Hamlet. Shakespeare has a capacity for sneaking things in under the radar, and the conclusion of this play, when we weep for the fate of a man who has caused so much destruction, is one of his most arresting paradoxes.

Once Hamlet begins to act, the mental cloud shrouding his perception, together with the speed of the drama, diminishes reflection on his moral choices. In the first half of the play, he is paralysed by questions; in the second half, with interruptions, he acts. 'To be, or not to be . . .' is a discourse on the rights or wrongs of self-slaughter. Its question of 'should I or shouldn't I?' is often misapplied to the other principal question of whether he should follow his father's instruction and kill Claudius. His struggle with the latter is less 'Should I or shouldn't I?' and more 'Why can't I?' It is less about moral choice than the summoning of willpower. From the moment the task is laid down by his father, he indulges in little moral analysis and a lot more self-castigation for not getting on with it. In another of Shakespeare's amoral manipulations of sympathy, we find ourselves willing him to get on with it, without counting the moral weight ourselves. The more he asks in exquisite language and with fierce truth, 'Why can't I kill this man?', the more we find ourselves thinking collectively, 'Yes, why can't we?', without asking whether it is right or not. We all become complicit.

At the conclusion of the Mousetrap play, when the court is in disarray, and he is cock-a-hoop with the success of his own plan, he finally speaks with the resolution of the authentic man of action:

> now could I drink hot blood,
> And do such bitter business as the day
> Would quake to look on.

Immediately after this, Shakespeare provides him with the ideal opportunity to follow through, when he passes the defenceless Claudius at prayer – 'Now might I do it'. He rushes towards Claudius sword in hand, 'Now I'll do it . . .' Then, mid-action, he pauses. Thus providing us with one of the play's most iconic plastic images, the young Prince, sword raised above the head of the praying King, pausing in the moment of murder. Someone about to kill, who has chosen not to.

The reasons he gives for stopping are legalistically religious. How can he kill this man at prayer, since that will send his soul straight to Heaven? What revenge would that be for the death of his father, whose soul was taken from his body in a moment of hedonistic ease, napping after a big lunch ('full of bread') without being confessed or having his soul cleansed? These reasons are serious, and in their own time fundamental to the repose of the eternal soul. In a largely secular country and a largely secular age, their currency is diminished. Yet the image still arrests. The man about to kill and choosing to stop.

We supplied other reasons. In the production, we experimented with Claudius giving a small gasp of remorse just as Hamlet arrives, so Hamlet is paused by a sudden burst of conscience. We pushed Hamlet closer, so it is the proximity that stops him, an alarming sense of the actuality of another's flesh. He smells the sweat coming off the King, he sees the vulnerability of the neck up close, and something animal stays his hand. This image is so strong and so securely layered into our cultural conscience because it is textured with so many ironies (the King who has killed and who wants to commune with Heaven and can't, unknowingly kneeling in front of the Prince who cannot kill), but also because it asks such important questions. In part, why do we kill, but also, more tellingly, why do we not kill? Why stop? Why not kill them all?

★ ★ ★

'Very flat Cambodia,' someone drawled in a Noel Coward voice as we descended from the air into Phnom Penh airport. The view was featureless, an unending plain surrounding the broad Mekong River, a flat brown marked out with agricultural rectangles. Even from on high, the brown seemed flecked with red, and the earth exuded a dark charisma relating back to its recent history of violence. Whether that red was real or supplied by a Western narrative soaked into the consciousness of my generation was hard to tell, but at that moment the scarlet clay made it real enough.

The Mekong River threads together three countries: Laos where it rises, Cambodia which it passes through, and Vietnam where the broad delta opens out into the sea; three countries caught collectively forty-odd years ago in a prolonged moment of insane state violence, a convulsion as historically senseless as any in the deranged annals of state warfare. The Vietnam War had a collection of pretexts: the end of colonialism, a proxy war for influence between the West and China, a clash of ideologies, a local turf war, and a test of America's superpower pride, but finally, as documented in many films and in much great writing, it just came down to grunts counting up their kills. The senselessness of this, a war without moral compass and simply encouraging soldiers to kill for the sake of killing, inflicted hideous damage on the landscape of Vietnam itself, spread destruction around it, and created a rottenness in the bones of all the participants wherever they hailed from. Vietnam suffered the brunt, but the hideous corollary suffered by its neighbouring countries was no side-show.

The Americans, as a precautionary measure, which took precautionary measures to a *reductio ad absurdum* all of their own, dropped as many munitions on neighbouring countries Cambodia and Laos as were dropped by all parties in the whole of the Second World War. The results were not only death on a horrifying scale, but also the destruction of social fabric and social cohesion, the sort of destruction which leaves the ground free for the worst to prosper in. Just as with Syria and Iraq, where shock and awe encountered social systems built slowly over decades and centuries and blew them to fragments. Whether healthy or unhealthy, these systems are better than nothing, since they provide checks and balances on the psychotic and the violent. Just as Bush and Blair's 'shock and awe' created the waste-ground within which the pathologies of Islamic State could flourish, so Nixon and Kissinger's brutal geopolitics created the soil to nurture the Khmer Rouge and Pol Pot. Social cohesion of whatever sort, gentle or toxic, takes generations to secure; bombs take several seconds to destroy it, and they leave little but chaos behind. Chaos, especially that created by violence, spawns monsters.

The Khmer Rouge rode into their capital Phnom Penh in 1975, shortly after the departure of Americans from the neighbouring capital Saigon. They drove in to the cheering of crowds lining the streets. Their leader Pol Pot and his cadre of colleagues had all studied in Paris and had become obsessed by the French Revolution. Something of the French predilection for purity and abstraction had driven slivers of mathematical coldness into their hearts. They resolved to go as far as they could with what they perceived to be the aims of Robespierre et al. Though with more thoroughness. Days after taking the capital city, the Khmer Rouge warned all the citizens to evacuate to the countryside, having spooked up a phoney American bombing raid. Once out in the country, they were never allowed back, as the political leadership attempted to turn the whole country into a nation of rice farmers. They declared this moment Year Zero, wiped history clean, and decided to start again and make a better world.

To make this easier, they attempted to eliminate anyone who might have other ideas. They went after not just the critics and the rebels, but anyone who could potentially become so. All the intellectuals, teachers and thinkers of any sort were wiped out.

There is an urban myth that at one point they resolved to kill anyone wearing spectacles, since spectacles were clearly a sign of intelligence. Though since anyone continuing to wear spectacles after that diktat can't have been that bright, it seems rather self-defeating. But it wasn't only intellect they resolved to destroy, it was also art in all forms. Art became an enemy. They didn't just try to cut off the head of the nation, they tried to destroy its capacity for imagination and for feeling. Of all of the scarring insanities of the twentieth century, Cambodia was one of the most chilling.

It was a horror show that only invasion could sort out, and the Vietnamese moved in to release the stranglehold which a fanatical government had over its own people. Though the Khmer Rouge were still leant political legitimacy by the recognition of the UN long after they had lost power, their international capital was worn down by the testimony of survivors, by the attention of investigative journalists, most notably John Pilger, and by a film, *The Killing Fields*.

Looking at the earth from the air, it wasn't hard to mentally score the fields with the scars of that past. Nor is it something that the Cambodians discourage. The tourist dollar is never going to be declined, and whatever brings it in helps. I spotted a tuk-tuk, a rickshaw with exhaust fumes. It had a panel on its side with a list of tourist attractions and the prices to get there. The first list was 'In the City', and coming in at Number Three below the Royal Palace and the National Museum, the Genocide Museum. The second list was 'Outside the City', and right at the top was the Killing Fields. Something about the nakedness of this commodification of genocide disturbed.

The uneasiness led to dark humour as we travelled to our venue. We only had thirty hours in the country, and as usual there was a determination to see as much as possible while there. Hands went up to indicate who wanted to visit the Killing Fields the next morning. People started noisily to sort their itineraries – sleep, show, big dinner, sleep, genocide museum. No sooner was it said than the company realised the dark absurdity of including a scene of murder within an itinerary. They riffed darkly on the idea – a wilfully light-hearted response to a travelling conundrum. How does anyone properly pay respect to the suffering of others?

It was not the first time the problem had arisen. With the same dark humour, the company talked back across the places they had visited where they had been brought face to face with man's capacity to inflict slaughter on man. Most recently, East Timor, where the Indonesians barged in in 1975 on a slim pretext and stayed for twenty-five years, decimating the population. There the company had visited the sight of the Santa Cruz massacre, the atrocity witnessed by Western media, the acknowledgement of which had begun the slow process of stopping people from looking the other way. In Rwanda, the company had to impro-vise an outdoor show when their indoor power failed, and gave a triumphant performance in a courtyard filled with thousands, some climbing trees and walls to watch. It was received exuber-antly, and, to the company's surprise, death was met with the same giddiness as humour and love. An academic travelling with them, researching the responses of audiences, asked a woman to explain why. She spoke of what it was like to live in a country still plucking human bones out of the earth, where they had all lost so many so close, and how death held less fear for them. Death was death, nothing special. In Ethiopia, there was another genocide museum, in another country where the geometry of an idea was forcibly pushed onto the bumps and curves of a country. These are explicit incidences in a world which often seems to be created out of genocide, where mass slaughter is the tool used to indent large shapes into the rock face of history. And where those countries that hide it the best – the UK, America and Australia – are far from the least guilty.

Arriving at the venue, one of the first questions asked by a technician was, 'Is this play about the Khmer Rouge?' He was pointing at a poster showing Hamlet holding Yorrick's skull. For many countries this image is an iconic reference to a play; here it is recent history. The Khmer Rouge created their own iconography of slaughter, scattering skulls across the land and piling them up in cairns which dotted the landscape. More practical concerns immediately distracted us as we negotiated how to survive one of the most eccentric venues we had encountered. It was a mammoth upturned bath, big enough to contain several thousand people, on a university campus, with a headmaster's lecture space at one end. It was not a space to perform a human and complex play.

The actors dashed back to their hotel, while I gave a talk at the university. Eighty or ninety bright and shining student faces gleamed at me in high expectation. I outlined the history of the Globe, then threw open the room to questions. They asked insistently, in a variety of forms, 'What can this play mean to us now?', 'What can it mean to Cambodia's history?' . . . I tried to answer, sensitive to the fact that their history was their history, and it would have been presumptuous of me, a know-nothing from elsewhere, to talk to them about how to heal their own wounds. Yet the appetite for meaning and clarification was a powerful presence in the room. This was not *Hamlet* the literary problem; this was *Hamlet* in a place still swathed in darkness and seeking hungrily for light.

There was little illumination looking likely back at the venue.

The show began to an audience of about 2,000, most students in for free. The room had the most infuriating acoustic, where if a member of the audience coughed it was abjectly deafening, but if the actors all stood at the front of the stage and screamed their heads off, no one could hear them. Blocking had to be re-assessed in such venues, and complex shapes flattened out into a line across the front of the stage; psychological nuance had to take a back seat to semaphoring hand movements, and textual music gave way to an Olympic shouting competition. Despite that, a sweltering pre-monsoon heat, and the atmospheric addition of bats which swooped through stage and auditorium, the actors wrestled the play and the space and the audience into a conversation. At the end, there was a hugely cheering reception, a roar of excited gratitude for giving the play.

Afterwards, we met some of Tommy's friends, who were working with an organisation called Cambodian Living Arts. Cambodia had long been a generous provider of arts and culture, especially of the arts that live happily on the cusp of private expression and public presence – music and dance and song. The Khmer Rouge put a devastating full stop to that tradition. Among the two million who died were 90 per cent of Cambodia's artists, singled out for execution. But some survived, amongst them a young Master Musician called Arn Chorn-Pond. In a children's labour camp, he learnt to play the *khim*, a Cambodian variant of the dulcimer, and one of the reasons he survived was that he would play it for the Khmer Rouge generals during mass executions. He later returned home, resolved to try to revive from the ashes as much and as many of the cultural traditions as existed, with the help of the few Master artists who had also survived. Through recording wherever he could, through teaching, and through passing the knowledge on in any way possible, the traditions were slowly coming back to life. Cambodian Living Arts were carefully regrowing a whole ecosystem which had been wiped out. In their own words:

> The arts play a defining role in the recovery and resilience of societies that have gone through the tragedy of war, genocide or armed conflict. Safeguarding the arts and the cultural values attached is fundamental to giving a sense of purpose, managing conflict-induced trauma and emancipating minds. In the current world situation of increasingly frequent and detrimental conflict, the arts have the power to build hope and foster self-determination.

Small hope from such fragmented but determined rebuildings. After the show, at a bright roadside cafe where we ate some delicious beef rumoured to be smeared with crack, some knobbly fried sweetcorn and a big bowl of curried frog, one of our promoters talked of her enchantment with the country, a little about the temples of Angkor Wat and their continuing capacity to amaze, but more about the landscape and its great annual conjuring trick. Once yearly, the rains come teeming down, and the clayey earth swiftly turns recklessly fecund, the reddish brown giving way to the most dazzling green, a dense and brilliant green as far as the eye can see.

* * *

Hamlet the play works on a double axis in relation to killing. One character, Hamlet, is spooled inexorably towards an act of murder, a thread reeled in ineluctably towards the strike of the act. Another character, Claudius, we watch unspooling away from his crime, his certainty and confidence unravelling as the play progresses. The moment in which Hamlet pauses before deciding not to kill Claudius is the moment, right in the golden section of the play, where the two axes intersect.

We cannot be certain that Claudius has done the deed for the first two acts of the play. We trust Hamlet, because he is the title character and because of the weight of words he hurls at us, but his overwrought imagination could be inventing villains everywhere. We have the report of the Ghost, but even in the play doubt is cast on its bona fides, since there is no certainty it is not a 'goblin damned' or some other such mischief-maker.

The first Claudius we meet is plausible, strong and cheerful. He is swift in the dispatch of government business, has an appealing common touch and seems tenderly considerate towards Hamlet. His words on the necessary deaths of fathers seem apposite. It seems hardly surprising that this confident and effective King would drive Hamlet to fury, since he is the antithesis of himself. Our suspicions are raised but not confirmed until Act 3 Scene 1. In lines which we eventually cut, he turns to us, after Polonius has spoken of how the face can dissemble what the heart feels, and in a swift and piercing aside says:

> O! 'tis too true;
> How smart a lash that speech doth give my conscience!
> The harlot's cheek, beautied with plastering art,
> Is not more ugly to the thing that helps it
> Than is my deed to my most painted word:
> O heavy burden.

The moment after he has said this, finally speaking his own truth, Hamlet is on, saying, 'To be, or not to be ...' Previously a shadow of suspicion had hung over this sunshine King, now he is occluded in darkness, and our knowledge of his crime colours his subsequent actions. Soon his edges are fraying. His relationship with Gertrude, confident and passionate at the beginning, grows fragile. His judgement, assured at the beginning, starts to look shaky. Carrying through Polonius's idea of spying on Hamlet and Ophelia is a crass and paranoid move. The idea of the play never seems welcome to him, and he arrives a hesitant spectator. What unfolds before him, the depiction of the act of killing his brother first in dumbshow and second in crude verse, is the manifestation of the nightmare of everyone carrying a burden of sin. Its manifestation in public is every ruler's nightmare. He leaps on to the stage, screaming, 'Give me some light!' The smooth politician of the first scene is now the autocrat babbling for relief from his bad dreams. We see him shortly after trying to jitter his way towards a solution with Rosencrantz, Guildenstern and Polonius. Then he is left alone, we imagine in a small chapel, and we watch as he tries to confess his crime before us, and shrive his soul.

What follows is one of the most active soliloquies in Shakespeare. It is the compelling theatre of a man wrestling with his own conscience, a man attempting to cleanse his own soul, to expunge his own history. Thankfully, most of us know little or nothing of killing, though it haunts our worst nightmares, the ceaseless running and running from a crime, and we absorb it empathetically from imaginative acts like Dostoevsky's recreation of the fevered self-torture of Raskolnikov. Seldom in literature has the sense of a human conscience tearing at its own enshrouding flesh been made more clammily real than here:

CLAUDIUS O, my offence is rank it smells to heaven;
It hath the primal eldest curse upon't,

A brother's murder. Pray can I not,
Though inclination be as sharp as will:
My stronger guilt defeats my strong intent;
And, like a man to double business bound,
I stand in pause where I shall first begin,
And both neglect. But, O, what form of prayer
Can serve my turn? 'Forgive me my foul murder'?
That cannot be, since I am still possessed
Of those effects for which I did the murder
My crown, mine own ambition, and my Queen.
Try what repentance can: what can it not?
Yet what can it when one can not repent?
O wretched state! O bosom black as death!
O limed soul, that, struggling to be free,
Art more engaged! Help, angels! Make assay!
Bow, stubborn knees; and, heart with strings of steel,
Be soft as sinews of the newborn babe!
All may be well.

'Help, angels! Make assay!' is not a gentle plea; it is a roar of need, the roar of someone who has lost their way, calling on any and every agency that might help to lend aid. It is at this moment that Hamlet appears unseen, and it is this Claudius, tormented by a sense of sin not abstract but clutching at him, pleading to a god that may or may not be actual, it is this figure that he cannot put to death. The young man trying to wrestle his sweet and pained imagination towards an act of killing, the older trying to wrestle his way away from it. Something about this symmetry makes it an artistic necessity that Hamlet does not kill, that the two people are static, stuck in confusion and unable to resolve themselves. One man reeling towards murder, the other away from it. Hamlet leaves the stage, and Claudius, unaware of the danger he has been in, looks to us and speaks nakedly of his failure to atone:

> My words fly up, my thoughts remain below:
> Words without thoughts never to heaven go.

For Claudius, for the murderer, nothing can atone and nothing can salve. From here on in, he becomes an increasingly desiccated figure, his hope and his humanity hollowed out by the weight of his sin. His paranoia and his desire to control become desperate, he threatens Hamlet physically to extort information from him, he sends him to England with secret instructions that he should be executed there, and he lies to Gertrude. This relationship, so sexually alive and powerful at the beginning, now seems sere and tedious. Claudius himself talks with a deadened flatness of the inevitable loss of love in any relationship:

> I know love is begun by time,
> And that I see, in passages of proof,
> Time qualifies the spark and fire of it.
> There lives within the very flame of love
> A kind of wick or snuff that will abate it;

On Hamlet's return, having faced down Laertes with the last vestiges of his old kingly authority, Claudius employs Laertes to help kill Hamlet with a plot that is improvised and squalid. His enthusiasm for it has all the grubby sniggering excitement of the small-time criminal. The commanding voice of the beginning is now the nervous paranoid snigger of the end. His plot falls apart as it is bound to, taking Gertrude, Laertes and himself with it. There is still a little life force left in him at the end, a belated scream for help just so he can keep going, akin to Saddam Hussein's spat out 'Fuck you!' to his executioner just before he fell the length of the rope that snapped his neck. Having been stabbed with the poison-tipped sword, and been forced to drink his own poison, Claudius cries out, 'O, yet defend me, friends; I am but hurt.'

This is a desolate end, the journey away from murder a comfortless path. The nausea in the soul of Claudius separates him from truth, from his closest loved one, from all others, and before long from his own self. Hamlet's reluctance to kill is given extra cause by the parallel narrative of Claudius. The story of Claudius exemplifies the identity whirlwind that is unleashed by such a crime.

Murder is brought into the heart of the play. Hamlet's initial reluctance to commit it being followed by mayhem on an almost deranged scale; Claudius's act of fratricide leading to a search for repentance, which once it fails causes the destruction of his own moral sense. The taking of a life is shown to be a poison uniquely of itself, which poisons everything around it.

* * *

Pol Pot died on the run. He had been holed up near the Thai border for two decades holding onto a nominal power and watching his following winnow away through desertion or through his own acts of paranoid murder. His own military had turned on him, and just before he was handed over to the government, he died in his sleep, some say through suicide, some through murder, whichever way through poison. This was denied in the anti-eulogy of his captor, Ta Mok. 'Pol Pot has died like a ripe papaya. No one killed him, no one poisoned him. Now he's finished, he has no power, he has no rights, he is no more than cow shit. Cow shit is more important than him. We can use it for fertiliser.'

Whether he suffered agonies of conscience is open to question. Whether all who have blood on their hands have the same passionate desire to rid themselves of blood's taint as Shakespeare's haunted murderers is again hard to imagine. The three people I have known who have taken human life seemed in one case to be properly haunted, in another to have made a sound accommodation, and in another not really to give much of a hoot. Depressingly I imagine the same spectrum is more generally applicable. Some struggle towards the taking of life, some just do it, some suffer the agonies of the damned afterwards, some sleep soundly. In that sense, *Hamlet* is set in an idealised context – it is not the savage landscape of Macbeth's Scotland or Lear's Dark Ages England, where life is comparatively cheap – this is a world where life has value, and the taking of it matters.

* * *

The morning after the show, incidents crowded in to bring these questions into sharp relief. I was sitting in the courtyard of our hotel, at a raised table made from a slab of marble, drinking sludgy and sharp coffee to sting me into life. I started receiving messages on my tablet. One was from Keith. He has an old friend who, as Keith travelled the world, was undertaking a parallel tour de force – drawing a cartoon for each country. His one for Cambodia was sharp and fierce. It showed a diminished Hamlet standing behind a river of skulls, crying feebly and faintly 'Yorrick, Yorrick, Yorrick' into the air above them. A mordant caption said 'The show went all right' above them. Another message was from a Globe colleague who was marking my final year in the job by sending me a quote every day. This one was from King John:

> There is no sure foundation set on blood,
> No certain life achieved by others' death.

Another message, a tweet to the company from a member of the audience, said briefly and pertinently all that we could want to hear from a citizen of a country which was slowly rebuilding a theatre tradition: 'I laughed. I felt pain. I lived. My first play and I could not have asked for more.'

Shortly after these three messages intersected, our two Hamlets, Ladi and Naeem, together with Matt, returned from their trip to the Killing Fields. They had the awkward and touching air of people who did not know how to arrange a face; the baffled look of children at a funeral who want to ask their parents how to behave. And who, in the instant before they ask the question, perceive suddenly, with a perfect lostness, that their parents are in deeper trouble than they themselves. I have worn the same face myself many times, and have seen it in those I love. It always pierces. A place where compassion lives but does not yet know a language, it is the confused place where morality begins. Matt described what they had seen: the scattered bones, the piled-up skulls, the tree against which babies and infants were hammered to breaking, the speakers which played cheerful Asian folk music as the torture continued. He spoke as if it was faraway, with that self-protective distance which stops people from crumpling.

I had been reading on evolutionary history on the way out, a book which oscillated sharply between providing comfort and provoking fear. On the comfort side, it posited that one of the primary reasons for our evolutionary progress was the fragility of our babies. Large brains led to us standing up and getting bipedal; being bipedal meant narrow hips on our mothers; narrow hips and large brains meant babies born early and fragile. Much of our social organisation was built from the necessity to build protective conclaves around vulnerable babies. On the fear side, there was our capacity for slaughter, acts of mass killing which required the same social organisation as protecting an infant. Slaughter of horses and other animals corralled as herds into enclaves where they could be hacked into food; slaughter of other members of the species homo, neanderthals foremost and most savagely, to clear the way for our own triumphant and blood-stained uniqueness. Finally, slaughter of our own family, *homo sapiens*, for what we don't know. Territory? Pleasure? Habit? Maybe both are true, and that is who we are, lost between a tender care for babies and a rapacious capacity for slaughter; an ingrained respect for life, especially that of the most vulnerable, set against a pathological and senseless capacity for destruction. *Hamlet* offers no answers, of course; that was never Shakespeare's path – art resists geometry as automatically as a country does – and Hamlet and Claudius are in no way exemplary. But maybe in the absence of solutions, Shakespeare, living happily as ever in the middle of an insoluble crux, simply asks us to respect the struggle to understand, and the struggle to improve. The struggle is all. The play lives uneasily on its own question, 'To be, or not to be . . .' Maybe asking the question persistently is the best we can ask of ourselves.

We bussed up for the journey out to the airport, where we would part: myself for London and home, the company going on to Laos and Vietnam, and more of the same richness of experience. The Phnom Penh we drove through was busting with life, markets flinging forth colour, roads packed with weaving movement, cafes crammed with men sitting on deckchairs watching football on one telly and soft porn on another, pavements thick with encounter and bustle. Whatever was done to this country – and for a small country more horrendous damage was done to it proportionately than to almost any other – whatever was done, life had surged back with all its irresistible bright comedy.

For that irrepressible stir back to life we must be grateful: grateful for the return of music and dance to a country that almost lost it; grateful that Hamlet pauses in that instant before killing Claudius; grateful even for the conscience of Claudius; and for the confused, compass-resetting look on the boys' faces after their trip to the Killing Fields; grateful for the ultimate meaninglessness of man's killing and cruelty in the face of our capacity to refresh and renew; and above all grateful for the deep and dazzling green which bursts recklessly forth when the rains come.

9

SOLILOQUIES IN THE ANDES

HAMLET *Now I am alone.*
O, what a rogue and peasant slave am I!

Act 2, Scene 2

QUITO, ECUADOR, A CITY ON a high plateau floating between two volcanoes, where the high altitude renders everything DayGlo sharp. In the middle of the city, there is a park dominated by outsized acacia, cedar and eucalyptus, with grass so luminescently green it looks freshly spray-painted. Small crowds of two or three hundred, all indigenous (not a mestizo in sight), gathered in spaces between the trees and formed themselves into large ovals with a clear space in the middle. As I crossed the park, I heard ripples of laughter and light spreading from these groups. I approached and nudged my way through the wall of bodies, two or three people thick, to see what was in the centre.

All the attention, the lit-up faces and the sharpened ears, were intent on one man moving through the open space in the middle. He talked in a relaxed and honest way to the surrounding circle as he shambled his way around, casual though intent with meaning.

Then, in an instant, his body would tweak with tension into a new shape, his voice shift a couple of octaves, and he would suddenly be in character. No hats, no props, no costumes, just the inventive mechanics of the body and the voice. The effect on the audience was immediate – gurgles of pleasure, delighting both in his transformation and in their shared recognition. It was theatre at its most fundamental: a single person telling a story on a patch of grass between two trees, under a mountain. I did not understand a syllable, and it was spellbinding.

There were frequent ricochets of laughter, picked up and redoubled by the encircling audience in the light we all shared. Laughing in the dark is one thing, laughing under the influence of both the material and the snorting and raucous faces around you is another. This reminded me of the Globe and its mutuality of pleasure. It was not just laughter: the storyteller could dip a story from farce to satire, from satire to pathos with an arch of an eyebrow or a drop of a shoulder. There was political bite too – anger tore through the storyteller's voice and passed like a pulse through the watching circle. The immediacy of the response implied a newspaper freshness in the material. But as soon as solemnity had settled, it was ruptured, and the performer tore off on a flight of fancy, or into some fastidiously pompous comic creation. Every ten minutes – just to underscore the Elizabethan-ness of the whole experience – the performer was joined by a large woman, under a spreading hat, carrying a tray and drowning out his performance with cries of 'Mango! 7Up! Get your fine 7Ups here!'

It wasn't just the drink-seller who created a connection back to the Elizabethan theatre. The immediacy of contact, the direct relation between performer and audience seen here, was at the heart of what made the first *Hamlet* so compelling, and so radical in its initial performance. Never before had anyone opened up their interior space with such vividness and immediacy. Before Hamlet starts his second great soliloquy, 'O, what a rogue and peasant slave am I!', he turns to the audience and says, 'Now I am alone.' It is a cutely placed metatheatrical joke. There are 3,000 people watching him. But by this stage they are alone together; the 'I' is inclusive and collective. All are travelling as ship *Hamlet* together, sailing uncertain seas.

A see-saw paradox lives at the heart of the play, a delightful inside-outside riddle which can never be resolved. The play is the most intimate exploration of a concealed soul ever undertaken, and that private exploration is achieved by nakedly public declaration. Inwardness and outwardness explode and implode together. The mode of achieving this is the soliloquy, and *Hamlet* demonstrates Shakespeare's mastery of it.

A method of public privacy he perfected throughout his writing, the first signs of the range of this instrument may have occurred to him when he wrote Richard III's thoughts on the night before the Battle of Bosworth. For most of his own play, Richard is the master of buttonholing the audience, taking them into his confidence and charming them with an assured comic entitlement. With a silky wit, a light irony and a boyish earnestness, he makes his appalling crimes appear innocent and natural. 'What else could I do?' is the dominant tone. Then, on the night before the climactic battle, awaking from a dream filled with the ghosts of his enemies, Richard's confidence evaporates. The charm and sociopathic relaxation is replaced by the broken mumblings of the fully fledged paranoid:

> Give me another horse! Bind up my wounds!
> Have mercy, Jesu! – Soft, I did but dream.

O coward conscience, how dost thou afflict me!
The lights burn blue. It is now dead midnight.
Cold fearful drops stand on my trembling flesh.
What do I fear? Myself? There's none else by.
Richard loves Richard; that is, I and I.
Is there a murderer here? No. Yes, I am.
Then fly!

The switchbacks here, the turns, the self-contradictions and the
zigzags are electrifying. It is the sound of a man breaking apart,
and in the process, as he watches himself fragment, discovering
capacities he did not know existed. A self-awareness perceived
with the revelatory force of a man who confronts a mirror for
the first time. It is the man of action discovering what consciousness is – and how doubt and confusion float behind consciousness
like a vapour trail. The excitement of Shakespeare is palpable. He
is discovering how gaps and silences in speech can fill up with
electric charge, and how thinking aloud does not have to be a
steady tread forward of consequent meaning, that it can be acro-
batic and chaotic. The impression he felt in writing it would have
been reinforced when he saw its effect on an audience and
registered the dazzling thrill of its truth.

From Richard on, Shakespeare immersed himself in a variety
of voices: Benedick is light and ludic, young Hal nervily assured,
Falstaff revels in absurdity and paradox, Rosalind furiously tries
to work out truths, Juliet scintillates and tests language against
the turbo-charge of her soul. They all come to the edge of the
stage and talk to us with their own honesty. But it is as if
Shakespeare kept that particular tone, of troubled consciousness,
of the wrestle between authenticity and confusion, in his back
pocket, letting it grow there. He gives it a brief run out with

Brutus in *Julius Caesar*, another mind troubled by the question
of whether to act or not, to kill or not:

> It must be by his death: and for my part,
> I know no personal cause to spurn at him,
> But for the general. He would be crown'd:
> How that might change his nature, there's the question.
> It is the bright day that brings forth the adder;
> And that craves wary walking. Crown him? – that; –
> And then, I grant, we put a sting in him,
> That at his will he may do danger with.
> 　　　　　So Caesar may.
> Then, lest he may, prevent . . .
> Between the acting of a dreadful thing
> And the first motion, all the interim is
> Like a phantasma, or a hideous dream:
> The genius and the mortal instruments
> Are then in council; and the state of man,
> Like to a little kingdom, suffers then
> The nature of an insurrection.

The collapse of the syntax and the eruptive nature of the punctuation – 'Crown him? – that;' – introduces us to a mind disturbed,
and one not in control of its own powers of articulation. This is
speech, not *a* speech. We listen to the reasoning and the self-
persuading, and share in the decision-making. For the audience,
the thrill in being invited into the moment when an act of history
was decided upon, to be not only in the conspirators' tent, but
in the mind of its leader, gives a sense of impertinent privilege.
We are within Brutus's phantasma; we preside in the council of
mortal instruments. The theatre, a community of individuals living

and breathing together on a point of thought, becomes a little kingdom, deciding which way to shift.

No one had attempted anything this daringly intimate before. Greek drama has a piercing interiority and is often directly simple, but it never quite loses the rhythm of recitation and song from which it was born. It rarely slips the grip of its own sculpted form to reveal the isolated human, lost within its stories. The Senecan tragedies from Rome which Shakespeare admired are steady and stately marches towards planned conclusions. Tudor dramatic poetry is not admired for much, but least of all for its sayable freshness. Marlowe opened up a collection of doors for Shakespeare beyond which were dazzling possibilities – epic, lyric and satirical – but his verse always tended gorgeously towards the rich, the marinated and the heavily sauced, rarely to the human and the lost. This speed of thought, this dizzying improvisation *in extremis*, was to a great degree Shakespeare's own invention. He would have been helped towards it more by comedy than tragedy. The fast thinking of a distressed farceur in Aristophanes and Plautus, a quick-witted servant or adulterer speed-thinking his way out of a crisis, were better guides in how to write thought than the stately grandiosity of tragedy. It is doubtful he could have written consciousness so beautifully without his complementary comic voice. Or without a sense of humour. The storyteller spellbinding his audience in the Ecuadorian park knew that humour quickened the mind of his audience and brought them alongside him.

The soliloquy comes to full flower in *Hamlet*, where 3,000 people sitting in a wider circle than the one I witnessed in Quito, in the first Globe, were brought into the seasick mind of a young prince. Richard Burbage stood above the groundlings in the yard, on the same level as the punters in the lower gallery, and below those paying higher prices in the two upper galleries. The audience were on every side of him. A human figure surrounded on all planes, up down left and right, by other humans all sharing the same light. It is not a position from which you dictate; it is a position from which you share.

For several centuries, when everyone chose perversely to present Shakespeare in every form of theatre architecture bar the one he wrote for, actors would agonise over the nature of soliloquy and how to play it. 'Who am I talking to?' actors would ask. 'Am I talking to myself? To another character in the play? To my mother? To ghosts? And why am I talking? Is it a confession? A plea? A justification?' All these questions were necessitated by the fact that the audience were plunged wrongly into darkness, and that the only thing the actors could see were glaring theatre lights rather than receptive human faces. When the Globe was reconstructed and newly opened, the answers to these questions were bluntly supplied. 'You're talking to the audience, stupid. You're telling them what you're thinking.' It unbundled centuries of misdirection.

There is an honesty in this connection which many find problematic. Many want to hide Hamlet from the audience, not only with blinding lights, but also with a shield of tone. He should be anguished, he should be sardonic, he should be bitter, a centuries-high heap of 'shoulds'. What matters most is that he is clear, and that he is fresh and alive in the moment. There is a purity of thought within these speeches, unmediated by a priori decisions. Each thought arrives for the first time, and finds the appropriate words for the first time. Often the words create the thoughts – words and thoughts birthing and new minting each other in that brave and reckless collaboration with the audience. The conversation is live and mutual. The look in the audience's eyes, the intake and the exhale of their collective breath, affects each thought and its progress to the next. It is a young vulnerable man, saying, 'Here I am, this is what I think (or what I think I think), listen to me, please.' The openness in that request, the immediacy of its fragility, is why *Hamlet* has conquered the world. This is a gentle spirit talking modestly in the cold outside, whom we are pleased to ask in.

The only rule of thumb for playing Hamlet's soliloquies, above and beyond clarity, is never to teach, and always to learn. If you arrive with your thoughts pre-packaged before you start speaking, then unfurl them for the benefit of your audience, you are dead before you start. The morally superior Hamlet is as dull as the morally superior person sitting next to you on a park bench or at a table. Academics, actors and directors sometimes want to create a Hamlet who lives at an Olympian height, a character knowing and superior. It is the sort of figure one is as keen to punch on the stage as in life. The person we listen to is the person who is as excited by what he is saying as we are. Sometimes Hamlet's own instruction – 'Let be' – is the best one for directors and commentators. Let the play be what it is.

* * *

Hamlet's soliloquies are events in themselves, but there is also a narrative of intimacy and closeness which grows and shifts with them, the changing nature of Hamlet's relationship with us, the audience. In our first private moment with the young Prince, he hurls his spew of thought at us with the force of projectile vomit. The court, dominated by his usurping uncle, have all just exited. Hamlet has been engaged in a terse, clipped exchange with his mother and uncle. The gnomic taut nature of his responses

communicates the tension bubbling inside. The moment he can,
he turns to us and unleashes:

O, that this too too solid flesh would melt
Thaw and resolve itself into a dew!
Or that the Everlasting had not fix'd
His canon 'gainst self-slaughter! – O God! God!
How weary, stale, flat and unprofitable,
Seem to me all the uses of this world!
Fie on't! ah fie! 'tis an unweeded garden,
That grows to seed; things rank and gross in nature
Possess it merely. That it should come to this!
But two months dead: nay, not so much, not two:
So excellent a king; that was, to this,
Hyperion to a satyr; so loving to my mother
That he might not beteem the winds of heaven
Visit her face too roughly. Heaven and earth!
Must I remember? Why, she would hang on him,
As if increase of appetite had grown
By what it fed on: and yet, within a month –
Let me not think on't – Frailty, thy name is woman!
A little month, or ere those shoes were old
With which she follow'd my poor father's body,
Like Niobe, all tears: – why she, even she –
O, God, a beast, that wants discourse of reason,
Would have mourn'd longer! – married with my uncle,
My father's brother – but no more like my father
Than I to Hercules – within a month –
Ere yet the salt of most unrighteous tears
Had left the flushing in her galled eyes –
She married. O, most wicked speed, to post

With such dexterity to incestuous sheets!
It is not nor it cannot come to good:

We course down tumbling rapids of thought at synaptic speed, repetitions piling on repetitions, sense ripped from thought, exclamations erupting with violence. The iambic beat maintains a forward tread, but the incline is downhill and the ground is gravelly, so every minor eruption loosens the footholds. The actor, the character and we the audience keep slipping and stumbling. The only way not to fall is to give in to the cadence. The headlong rush of this soliloquy is an artful way to dump us, the audience, in at the deep end. Before we have had a chance to get to know this young man, he is pouring out the lava of his soul without mediation or filtering. The directness forces us into, if not agreement, immediate sharing, before we have any chance to consider what is being said. We are plugged directly into this young man's scrambled soul. We become his confidants. Every confession needs a priest, every ancient mariner a wedding guest, every lament a hearer. Hearing a sorrow is not passive. It is as if we are at a large function, and someone has suddenly turned and planted a troublingly passionate kiss on our soul before rushing off. We are affronted, a little shocked. And also keen to see them again.

We track his progress as he is told of his father's ghost, as he meets the Ghost and is informed of his father's murder. We share in his determination to avenge his father's spirit. The next time we meet him, instead of seeing him pursue that ambition, we see him trapped within an antic disposition, processing his emotional turmoil. His friends Rosencrantz and Guildenstern arrive, then the Players with whom he shares memories. With both encounters, he secures a pause from his torment. Delighted as we are to see him, there is a feeling of privacy withheld, of being at an event with someone we now know well, whose secrets we share, but with whom it is difficult to renew our relationship at its full depth. This is frustrating, since we know secrets now, and found the depth of our previous intimacy exciting. We long for the privileged friendship again. After the First Player has moved himself and others to tears with his recitation of the fall of Troy, and the grief of Hecuba, we watch as the stage clears. We know with tantalising expectation that we are about to come face to face again:

HAMLET Now I am alone.
O, what a rogue and peasant slave am I!
Is it not monstrous that this player here,
But in a fiction, in a dream of passion,
Could force his soul so to his own conceit
That from her working all his visage wann'd,
Tears in his eyes, distraction in's aspect,
A broken voice? and his whole function suiting
With forms to his conceit? and all for nothing!
For Hecuba!
What's Hecuba to him, or he to Hecuba,
That he should weep for her? What would he do,
Had he the motive and the cue for passion
That I have? He would drown the stage with tears
And cleave the general ear with horrid speech,
Confound the ignorant, and amaze indeed
The very faculties of eyes and ears. Yet I,
A dull and muddy-mettled rascal, peak,
Like John-a-dreams, unpregnant of my cause,
And can say nothing. Am I a coward?
Who calls me villain? Breaks my pate across?

Plucks off my beard, and blows it in my face,
Tweaks me by the nose – who does me this?
Ha!
'Swounds, I should take it: for it cannot be
But I am pigeon-liver'd or ere this
I should have fatted all the region kites
With this slave's offal: bloody, bawdy villain!
Remorseless, treacherous, lecherous, kindless villain!
O, vengeance!
Why, what an ass am I! This is most brave,
That I, the son of a dear father murder'd,
Prompted to my revenge by heaven and hell,
Must, like a whore, unpack my heart with words,
And fall a-cursing, like a very drab,
A scullion!
Fie upon't! foh! About, my brain! I have heard
That guilty creatures sitting at a play
Have by the very cunning of the scene
Been struck so to the soul that presently
They have proclaim'd their malefactions;
I'll have these players
Play something like the murder of my father
Before mine uncle: I'll observe his looks;
I'll tent him to the quick: if he but blench,
I know my course. The play's the thing
Wherein I'll catch the conscience of the king.

At every moment of this speech, we walk beside Hamlet. From his initial self-disgust, through his disbelief that the Player in his fictional passion can be more authentic than he can within his own real pain. We live on the horns of his dilemma just as he does. All around the world, when our Hamlets asked the question 'Am I a coward?', they asked it directly and simply. They found someone in the audience, looked into their eyes, and pinned them back with the question. Sometimes people looked away, embarrassed, sometimes they offered support, often people replied 'No.' Whatever fourth wall remained by that point dissolved, and we the audience were in an open conversation with our leading man. The moment was electric, a gap of silence when we did not know how the story would proceed. It is disarming to hear an icon asking 'Am I a coward?'

He goes on to beg the treatment that would be meted out to a clown, to 'break my pate across', 'to tweak me by the nose'. This is not an Agamemnon or a Priam. It is the opposite of what we expect from a hero. Burbage, who first played the part, would have been known to the audience as Titus, as Richard III, as Oberon, as Brutus, as Henry V – the ghosts of those sturdy Titans would have shimmered around his frame as he played Hamlet – and here he was dissolving the audience's sense of security in his authority, asking them to tweak his nose. The risk is enormous, as is the courage in presenting weakness. As naked as we know it, and as comically foolish, it is the same eloquent openness as the entertainer on the grass in Quito.

We follow him through his rage at himself. There is something unconvincing in his cursing of his uncle – 'Bloody, bawdy villain' – and effortful in his attempt to embody the spirit of retribution – 'O vengeance'. This is too conventional for the Hamlet we know, this Heroding and roaring. Hamlet knows it; he shares in our embarrassment at his having tried too hard. There is a rueful apology, almost a complicit humour in his 'Why, what an ass am I! This is most brave . . .' This is the Hamlet we know, and we feel a renewed familiarity as he abuses himself for having been such a fool. His resolution to move things forward by producing a play seems more appropriate. The couplet he finishes on is a secure ending, a safe mooring. We share in his purpose and exhilaration as he leaves the stage.

Which makes it all the more surprising that the next time we see him, we hear:

> To be, or not to be: that is the question:
> Whether 'tis nobler in the mind to suffer
> The slings and arrows of outrageous fortune,
> Or to take arms against a sea of troubles,
> And by opposing end them? To die: to sleep;
> No more; and by a sleep to say we end
> The heart-ache and the thousand natural shocks
> That flesh is heir to, 'tis a consummation
> Devoutly to be wish'd. To die, to sleep;
> To sleep: perchance to dream: ay, there's the rub;
> For in that sleep of death what dreams may come
> When we have shuffled off this mortal coil,
> Must give us pause: there's the respect
> That makes calamity of so long life;
> For who would bear the whips and scorns of time,
> The oppressor's wrong, the proud man's contumely,
> The pangs of despised love, the law's delay,
> The insolence of office and the spurns
> That patient merit of the unworthy takes,
> When he himself might his quietus make
> With a bare bodkin? Who would fardels bear,
> To grunt and sweat under a weary life,
> But that the dread of something after death,
> The undiscover'd country from whose bourn

No traveller returns, puzzles the will
And makes us rather bear those ills we have
Than fly to others that we know not of?
Thus conscience does make cowards of us all . . .

Those six grave yet flighted syllables, the bareness and the directness of them, an arrow of expressed thought. A hero, with all that
Shakespeare's audiences had come to expect from heroes, a hero
who has the courage to ask the simplest question of all, and to
ask it in its simplest form. Six syllables, thirteen letters, and
everything packed within them. A question, not a statement. With
no certainty in the right response. Hamlet has carried us thus far,
we are in part him, in part his friend, and now he asks on our
behalf the question that sits at the centre of our lives. The speed
at which it is presented wrong-foots us. I've seen those six words
done a hundred different ways. They've been preceded by post-
modern pantos providing context, they have been repeated musically, they have been screamed out, gurned and churned, and
cued-in by every form of drum roll, literal and metaphorical. In
our production, he simply came out and said it.

The argument then twists and turns, and we shift with its tides.
The opening movement is essentially 'Why not'? Why not release
ourselves from our bondage to the tyranny of the flesh, let ourselves
float free from the shivering beast we are tethered to, and call it
an end? The doubt sets in on the tiny phrase, placed in the middle
of a line to make us stumble over it, 'perchance to dream'. It is
the dreaming, the potential for we-know-not-what which stops
us. Seductive as it may be to disappear into unknowability – 'what
dreams may come' are four words of surpassing invitation – it is
still unknowable. We might want to sink into the pillow of the
three kindly m's in those last three words, but the dark still scares.

He swerves away from the metaphysical to the all too bitterly worldly, and enumerates with political rage the injustices and frustrations of living in the world. But then we stumble again, on an aptly vague 'something'. And on a more picturesquely imagined 'undiscovered Country from whose bourn / No traveller returns'. What stops us is what we don't know, what is in our imagination.

Hamlet stood at a critical juncture in our own development, one of many when those long and uneasy walking companions, mind and body, were set to take a further step away from each other. All the evidence of the body, all that is substantial and can be recorded, is saying one thing, but the mind, its power of argument and imagination and of alternative reasoning, suggests another. How breathtaking to have heard those words for the first time, a lonely figure standing on a wooden stage, held in an embrace of human bodies, lifted by the held breath and fascinated attention of 3,000 spirits, each word defining and illuminating the tightrope we balance on as we try to hold battered flesh and fleeting thought together in one uncertain vessel.

This pure adventure, the radical thrill of new thought, can be done nowhere better than in this sort of arena, a shared light where audience and actor work together to push the possibilities of an evening or an afternoon in the sun. The proscenium arch and the black box are places for control, for teaching, not as much for journeying together. The communion where new thought is birthed in the instant it is said can only be achieved where a whole congregation comes together to make it happen.

Our connection with Hamlet persists throughout the scenes where he does not address us directly. We are complicit in his feelings about other characters; we hear his ironies and his subtexts. He flicks an occasional quick private thought our way. It is all food to maintain the friendship we have forged, though we miss the intensity of the connection we feel when he speaks directly to us. We mourn that absurd sense that we are privileged listeners, when only another thousand or so people are tuning in to the same. Then as the play burrows down its tunnel leading to disaster, we note that we are hearing from him less and less, and that he is drifting away. He stages his play; he shares with us his quandary over whether to kill Claudius or not; he scorches the ground from underneath his mother in a scene of such uncomfortable intensity that we feel we have seen too much; he kills Polonius by accident, then quips brilliantly with the King in a dizzying display of deflection and distraction. These scenes of quasi-hysteria, when Hamlet slips in and out of a madness which is part feigned, part genuine, place him almost too far away, beyond our reach. The boy/man we felt so close to and protective of has now gone to a place we can only observe. It is hard to empathise; it is not even easy to locate him.

He is exiled to England. On his way there, he chances to see Fortinbras, a figure who serves as a distracting mirror image, passing through Denmark on his way to attack Poland with a mighty Norwegian army. He turns to us:

> How all occasions do inform against me,
> And spur my dull revenge! What is a man,
> If his chief good and market of his time
> Be but to sleep and feed? A beast, no more.
> Witness this army of such mass and charge
> Led by a delicate and tender prince,
> Exposing what is mortal and unsure
> To all that fortune, death and danger dare,
> Even for an egg-shell. Rightly to be great

Is not to stir without great argument,
But greatly to find quarrel in a straw
When honour's at the stake. How stand I then,
That have a father kill'd, a mother stain'd,
Excitements of my reason and my blood,
And let all sleep, while, to my shame, I see
The imminent death of twenty thousand men,
That, for a fantasy and trick of fame,
Go to their graves like beds, fight for a plot
Whereon the numbers cannot try the cause,
Which is not tomb enough and continent
To hide the slain? O, from this time forth,
My thoughts be bloody, or be nothing worth!

There are a thousand different ways of reading this speech, each reflecting in some way the reader back at him or herself. It fills me with sadness and a sense of loss at the parting of the ways. The opening thoughts we know and are accustomed to – the worries over authenticity, the disabling effects of consciousness – but Hamlet has by this stage killed someone – Polonius – even if by accident, and we feel a tidal sense that he is approaching the moment when he will be able to act, and have to. The doubts, the thoughts, the confusion are drifting away like low-hanging morning mist burnt away by the sun. The decision and the action which will follow will extract from Hamlet most of what we cherish in him. I love him for his openness, his cowardice, his honesty, his trembling in the face of life. I don't want him to be a man of action, or have bloody thoughts. This is our final moment alone with Hamlet, and something within it feels like a separation.

After his return from his aborted journey to England, there are no more soliloquies. We imagine he is talking to us when he speaks of Yorrick, and of the impermanence of Caesar and Alexander, and of his love for Ophelia. When he embraces a transcendent calm contemplating the fall of a sparrow, we hope that an element of it is a gift for us. When he closes the lid on his own story with 'The rest is silence', we in part imagine it is him finding closure on our behalf. But, in truth, he has drifted away. The man who returns from the sea has a sense of containment around him, and a free-floating independence within. He doesn't have to unburden himself to us any more. Our intimate friend has grown up and grown away. In our production, as the court appeared for the fight with Laertes, Hamlet looked impassively around the audience. It was a farewell in a minor key.

★ ★ ★

The many poets who became Homer carried a mountain of words in their memory banks, locked within musical rhythms and formulaic phrases, and sang their tales of Achilles and Hector and Odysseus to silenced rooms of auditors, happy to sit for hours and hear of an epic past. In the Jemaa el-Fnaa, the great market circus in Marrakesh, hooded figures walk up and down chanting Arabian tales to the rhythm of their own footfall. Crowds of four or five hundred sit and stand enraptured by these stories from long ago, delivered in a chanting monotone which makes them come alive afresh. In Quito, on the bright-green grass, storytellers riff on politics and love, new washing machines and old heartaches, and the faces around them shine. All stories told to people in a circle, all sharing the same light, the lit humanity in their faces magnifying the humanity of each tale exponentially. All told with an open palm, as Alan Garner says is a necessity of storytelling, and never with a pointing finger. Hamlet stood out in front of a group of people in a circle and, with the same presence and the same honesty, told an entirely new story, a story of dread and fear and doubt, and of the birthing of a new consciousness. A story forged in the alchemy that binds together a voice and a listener.

In Quito, the performer finished with a lovely bathetic coda, as if the story he had told in all its vividness was melting back into the world. He bowed with a puppyish exuberance, as the crowd went briefly wild, then the 7Up seller stepped rudely in front of him. He wandered off across the park alone. So every story comes to an end, and the peculiar intimacy between teller and hearer, that momentary bond which trumps almost all others, has to dissolve. We have to leave, teller and hearer, in our different directions. As Armado says in *Love's Labour's Lost*, with the greatest last line in any play, 'You that way: we this way.' The actors to the mysteries of backstage, the audience to the different stories of the world.

10

NEWS FROM ENGLAND

HAMLET *For who would bear the whips and scorns of time,*
The oppressor's wrong, the proud man's contumely,
The pangs of despised love, the law's delay,
The insolence of office and the spurns
That patient merit of the unworthy takes . . .

Act 3, Scene 1

SOMETIMES YOU GET THE FEELING you should adjourn a day halfway through. Too many things are crashing and colliding into each other. Mistake is bundling into mistake in a compressed time period, the compression compounding mistake into potential catastrophe. One of the first things to be at risk at such a moment is your own judgement. Sometimes you feel the wise move would be to go back to bed and hide under the duvet until all the demons of petty disaster have ghosted their way through your immediate environment.

Having rushed from rehearsals to jump into a BBC car to do a radio interview, we realised there was no BBC car there. We booked another non-BBC car, and it was running late. I got into it, but the driver didn't know the way over the river let alone to the BBC. On the way to the BBC, our press department rang to ask me to do another radio broadcast later that night, this one a discussion on *Free Thinking*. Fine, I said, if each knows about the other and are happy with it. The wrong car, the late car and now the misdirected car was stuck in traffic, and arriving late looked odds-on. A text arrived to say the venue had changed, and we now had to go to Broadcasting House. I rang the producer's number I had been given, but it was (of course) wrong, and I found myself talking to someone on *Naturewatch*. Things weren't looking good.

It was the day before Shakespeare's birthday, 23 April 2015, and we were one year into our tour. The next day, we would open our summer season at the Globe, and the day after that we were flying out to Madrid, where the *Hamlet* company was completing a residency of four performances, to celebrate the one-year, halfway milestone. The birthday had woken the BBC up to the continuing relevance of Shakespeare, and it seemed I was the guest du jour – if I could make it to the studio. Eventually, stranded in traffic, I jumped out of the car and rushed through streams of people going the other way (why do more people always seem to be leaving the BBC than arriving?), and presented myself, scruffy, sweaty and breathless, to a nervous-looking producer, who scooted me up to the studio.

The first interview of the evening, for an amiable arts magazine programme on Radio 4 called *Front Row*, was going well enough, until the North Korea question heaved itself elephantinely into the room. It was now becoming habitual. 'So, you're going to North Korea?' people asked, and whatever explanations or contexts you offered, you could not penetrate their caul of moral superiority. This was irritating on two counts. First, it asserted that they alone had spotted what was going on in the most written-about country on earth. The assumption being that we had missed it. The second, it was a classic example of Instant Whip Opinion, providing a brief, sweet-tasting moral superiority for anyone who wanted to find some fault in a corner, and thus felt permitted to ignore the stink in the rest of a large room.

Traffic, missed taxis and wrong numbers were less than great ways of smoothing out an occasionally volatile temper, but I managed to stay temperate. I put our case that the world was bigger than just North Korea, and that it was maybe useful to place North Korea in the context of what we had done in Africa, in Somaliland, in Sudan, in Central America, in Sarajevo, in Kiev, in ninety-seven other countries by that stage. And that, dare it be said, people in North Korea were actually people, and that they might deserve *Hamlet* as much as anyone. My interviewer gave me that look of smug scepticism which journalists specialise in, that shared delusion that their vicarious fascination with disaster gives them a unique wisdom rather than an excessive morbidity. This was usually a red rag to a bull for me, but I kept my alternative smugness in check, and managed to get out of the interview without disgracing myself.

It was doubly irritating because a couple of days before, we had received an ornate and lengthy letter from the People's Republic, telling us with decorously phrased sorrow that we could not visit North Korea. There had been a squabble at the UN, and in a fit of pique they were cancelling our visit. We were in several minds about this. It was impossible to leap to the defence of a regime which didn't merely sack its defence minister, but obliterated him with an anti-aircraft rocket. We were also cautious about going since their quarantine regime for Ebola was three weeks in solitary confinement. But, however wrong-headed to many, inclusivity was inclusivity, and we were still determined. So I said nothing about the decorously phrased letter.

The interview concluded, I now had a couple of hours to kill before the later discussion programme, which would be on Radio 3. The area around the BBC goes fairly quiet after seven, but I spotted across the road a very promising-looking restaurant. The member of our press department who was babysitting me had an equal fondness for top tucker, so we settled down for some good nosh and a little lightening of stress. Fine food demanded fine wine, and days of tension sharpened the thirst as well. A couple of bottles disappeared at some speed, and just when we were considering concluding with a digestif, we realised that I had minus five minutes to make it back to Broadcasting House. I dashed unsteadily back across the road for the second time that day, and was met by a producer hopping up and down with nervousness. We jogged to lifts and sprinted along corridors, and I was bundled into a small round-table studio where my fellow guests were settled. The countdown to transmission had already begun.

This was another moment when I should have called time on the day. The atmosphere was various degrees of Arctic, and I realised in a flash that the three other guests had been sitting in one of the BBC's dead-soul hospitality rooms for an hour or so. They looked like they had been sipping vinegar, with a heavy twist of lemon. They were also all clearly from the tribe of academe, a tribe with whom I had a patchy record. These three looked the antithesis of predisposed towards me. In the thirty-five seconds left before we began, I decided to see how a little bonhomie might go down by charging around the room, shaking hands and introducing myself. They all rocked backwards away from me, no doubt perturbed by my unsteady motion and also by the large red-wine stain empurpling my shirt. It wasn't the ideal start.

The wise man, at that point, would have left the room. But such wisdom was never my strong point, and the programme had begun before I had had time to think. The theme was Global Shakespeare, and it took me a short while to orient myself as to what the argument was supposed to be about. I filled those moments with a brief speech about how marvellous the Globe was and how all-round glorious the tour was. My fellow guests looked at me with a pitying contempt. Global Shakespeare seemed to me such a self-evidently great thing that I was at a loss as to how we were to fill up forty-five minutes of radio with blather about the wonders of the Stratford man. But I learnt quickly from the others' opening statements that I was in the wrong. It seemed that much International Bardery was not a good thing. Since two of the academics ran a course devoted to Global Shakespeare, it seemed rather peculiar that they were arguing against their own livelihood, but there you go. Everyone needs a different reason to get out of bed in the morning.

Having invited many of the world's countries to come to us with our Globe to Globe festival, and now touring our *Hamlet* to many countries that had never seen a Shakespeare production before, I rather foolishly thought I was in a strong position. The reciprocity of this conversation about and through Shakespeare seemed to me a great way for Nation to Talk, in a very BBC way, to Nation. We had only felt entitled to take our tour to the world on three conditions: that the cast was multicultural, that we played to people and not governments, and that it was seen as a response to our previous hosting of Shakespeare from other countries.

I had not realised the depth of our perfidy. It seemed that for two of the others there, anything to do with Shakespeare that involved the United Kingdom, whether it travelled from there or to there, was tainted with all things evil: the East India Company, colonialism, capitalism, soft power, cultural imperialism, you name it. It was impossible to do anything without knowledge of such history, and if the knowledge was there, so too must be the taint. The only people free to do Shakespeare, it seemed, were those who had no contact with the United Kingdom. They could produce these plays, and tour them to other countries, free from all such stains, and with an appropriate virtue and honesty. Their argument may well have been more subtle than that, it probably was, but that's how it appeared to me in my befuddlement.

There are a thousand and one arguments, passionate, cool and profound, to be made against this. After a long day, bad traffic and a bottle of wine, I wasn't the man to make them. There's an old Tommy Cooper sketch where he gives us his detailed and imaginative version of the Jekyll and Hyde dichotomy. This involves him putting a hat on and saying, 'Good, good, good', and then taking it off, turning his head decisively, and saying, 'Evil, evil, evil.' That's it. I found myself invoking his spirit and muttering 'Evil, evil, evil' under my breath whenever I was being told off for doing Shakespeare and being British. That's in the few moments when I wasn't chanting 'Wrong, wrong, wrong' in an infantile manner. I was being boxed into the corner as the wicked white man. Awkwardly for everyone, I was doing most of the boxing myself. But I was a dead man as I entered.

I recovered a little when one of them told me that our tour was compromised since it only played to dignitaries wherever it went. This was so wholly and utterly at odds with the truth, and since I was fresh back from seeing it play to thousands in East

Africa, all of whom were admitted for free, that I regained some traction in the room. But since that lie – the story that Shakespeare is the posh playing to the posh – is such an attractive nonsense, I could sense the synaptic speed with which this untruth flew over the radio waves and into people's minds. When I stated the truth, that we played to huge crowds of everybody, most allowed in for free, that our tour was all about people meeting, people listening and people communicating, I could feel the lumpen slowness with which it struggled to haul its way out of the room. An untruth about how cynically awful the world is will always move at lightning speed, and a truth about the world's clumsy potential for goodness will always struggle to catch up.

Any ground recovered was lost on the question of ownership. I proffered the thought that these plays had been offered up into the world by a disinterested author, an imperfect printing process, and had since then floated through the world free of copyright, and free of claim, for anyone in the world to do what they will with them. This position turned out to be crushingly naïve. The previously forgiving one of the three scolded me that these plays were apparently entangled in and strangled by chains of owner-ship from the moment they were born. First, the company of actors, then the printer, then the shop they were sold in, then everyone who had interacted with them since – they had all covered these plays with their sticky fingerprints of ownership. If I had had the puff, I might have argued the point, but it was late in the programme, and I wasn't good for much more than barking 'wrong' and muttering 'evil, evil, evil'.

I left the studio and turned on my mobile. I knew I had been comprehensively bested, but one still lives in hope. The flat absence of 'well done' messages told its own story. An enthusiastic kicking on social media amplified it. In truth, I had been boorish and had undermined the legitimacy of my arguments with a bullying inarticulacy.

It's hard even when sober and sharp to argue with the aggressive meagreness of this attitude. Producing Shakespeare has always relied more than anything on joy, on innocence and on enthusiasm. But try arguing for those three at a congress of Shakespeare scholars. Without looking like a blithering Pollyanna. For many of the academic community, but not all, these beautiful words left flimsily on paper cannot just be that – beautiful words on flimsy paper. They have got to be about territorialism and control and ownership, fundamentally because those arguing the case want more than anything else to be the owners. They want to be the hieratically ordained priest caste, who can tell others how to enjoy them. The circumstances of the play's productions have to be about power and influence and negotiation, so that they can be the arbiters of how such transactions take place.

Ultimately, a boy in Montevideo, or a girl in Manchester, wake up one morning, and are tickled by the thought of putting on a Shakespeare play. Their primary motors are threefold. First, they love the plays. Second, they think it will be fun. Third, they think that putting on the plays will enable them to kiss whichever combinations of boys and girls they fancy kissing. Those innocent desires sit at the heart of all play production, whether it be a group of kids in a favela, or a Broadway show, or a piece of Polish avant-garde gloom.

It is the same motor which drove us to put on our tour. Without the kissing, of course – we're too old for that. At the heart of the project, as with all at the Globe, was a blithe innocent desire to present Shakespeare. We are aware that such innocence is compromised, that the world is full of different shading, and that there is no shortage of folk waiting to exploit and manipulate such innocence. But what can you do in the face of all the world's squalidness and impurity? Try to absorb and answer all of it, every detail in its immensity, acknowledge every shred, and then what? Adapt your work to answer each and every one of the world's critiques and concerns? I have seen the results of that approach, the despairing attempts to pre-emptively self-exonerate in the face of all possible attacks. It leads to work that is so at pains to be morally upright that it is artistically inert. An aesthetic and moral paralysis, terrified into stasis by the imagined judgement of others. Or do you absorb and understand as much as you can, and then walk forwards, your heart and your laughter pushing you on, and try to show the world something new? You consider and reflect, and then you have two choices, to retreat into self-editing and self-reflection, or you move forwards. We moved forwards.

* * *

As a double irony, in radio disaster No. 1, we were attacked for intending to visit North Korea, just after we were told we couldn't go, and in radio disaster No. 2, we were attacked for cultural imperialism, just as we were in the middle of a row with the British Council. The BC had proved a confounding partner thus far. Many of their officers on the ground around the world had proved supportive and vital partners. They had found us promoters, assisted with advice, drummed up audiences, put us in touch with good local people – even in a very few cases they had given us tiny sums. We always wanted more money – in that sense we were desperate to be a bit more imperialist. Most of the officers were a credit to the UK, young, fired up and deeply connected to the cultures of the countries they were working in. A few were less than great, archaic survivors from a different era, airily saying to us as we arrived, 'God, it's good to have some culture here at last', in the face of countries who had been building temples when Britons had been quizzical about the purpose of toilets. What confused us was the ambivalence of the British Council in the centre, in London.

The British Council is one of those British institutions that often seems strangely at odds with its own purpose. It constructs itself, like many large British institutions, as a fortress, and its first instinct is always to defend the walls of its own fortress. Even if you approach offering it exactly what it wants. The prehistoric simplicity of what we were doing – taking a play to people and countries that had never seen it before, meeting and encountering artists and audiences along the way – was so pornographically simple, and spoke so directly to the original purpose of the BC, as to be obscene in their eyes. We were not the only people confounded by this. The British Council officers on the ground were as confused as to why the BC's centre was so lacking in commitment. After two years of chivvying them for a response, one of their chief timeservers sent us a blood-boilingly dumb email saying our tour lacked an element of dialogue. I hit the roof and got drawn into a tit-for-tat abusive email exchange, which I always find strangely enjoyable but which is also strategically very dumb. It concluded with such naked rudeness on my part that we had burnt our boats for good with the British Council. All this at just the moment earnest academics were telling us off for being pawns of British government policy.

To be honest, the mid-point of the tour was problematic in many ways, not least financially. We were attempting to achieve the tour without any extra money, just as the Globe operates without any subsidy or any unearned income. We were proud of our capacity to wash our own face. The premise of the tour was straightforward. We would charge the wealthy countries over the odds, and the profit we made from them would subsidise the less wealthy countries. Getting in and out of a country cost an average of about £15,000, so the high fees we could charge say Germany would cover our visits to less well-off countries. (Ethiopia offered us, with an affecting pride, a fee of £55, to play two performances in their National Theatre to 4,000 people). It was a simple plan, but with one structural flaw. Sadly, and cruelly, there are a whole lot more poor countries in the world than there are rich ones. Two-thirds of the countries we were visiting couldn't get close to covering our costs, and we would have had to charge astronomical amounts to the wealthier to cross-subsidise. Welcome to the world, many might say, and rightly.

The problem had been brewing for a while, and had now become clear to us, and to our Board of Trustees. This admirable group habitually, during my time at the globe, made everyone else's sang-froid look like screaming hysteria. Tell them that you were launching an international festival, building a new theatre, creating a new Video On Demand platform, or sending out a tour to every country in the world, and they reacted as if nothing had happened, though with a slight stiffening of their collective posture as if someone had done a small fart in the corner of the room but no one had worked out where it came from. However, tell them that a season or a project was in danger of losing money, and they reacted as if a door had been flung open and an Arctic wind had swept in. They became frosty and severe. In many ways, the ideal board.

We had sorted out a solution before the problem grew too large, a problem which involved cost-cutting, shifting of resources and a lot of extra work and performances at the Globe to cover the hole left by the tour. The solution, quite rightly, had to be analysed and then approved in a number of semi-frazzled emergency meetings and across more spreadsheets than were good for man or computer. The degree of concern was justifiable, but at that moment was like a fallen tree across the road, draining energy and commitment away from what mattered.

* * *

So here we were at the halfway point, the tour just finishing a life- and art-affirming leg around Africa, surrounded by the full array of British mechanisms to hinder and slow endeavour – the media, the academics, the apparatchiks, the governance – all out lancing any bubble of adventure or connection which crossed their path. Or so it seemed to our paranoid selves.

We were having a collective *Hamlet* moment. The play was starting to make us see the world through its own perspective. Towards the conclusion of 'To be, or not to be . . .', Hamlet looks out into the world and sees the enemies who have stood four-square in the face of joy and justice since humankind started building communities that couldn't fit in a tent:

> For who would bear the whips and scorns of time,
> The oppressor's wrong, the proud man's contumely,
> The pangs of despised love, the law's delay,
> The insolence of office and the spurns
> That patient merit of the unworthy takes . . .

'Whips and scorns' is easy enough to parse; the rest are a lexicon of the resentments of a grumpy adolescent or of the grumpy adolescent that stays alive in us all – the oppressor is always wrong; 'contumely' is the insulting contempt the powerful have always reserved for the weak (think Simon Cowell); the pangs of despised love is an eruption of broken-heartedness in the middle of political complaint (floating Ophelia back into the room); the delay of the law was a particular complaint of Shakespeare's own litigious age, but has hardly gone out of fashion; and the last complaint – 'the spurns that patient merit of the unworthy takes' – compacts into one telling phrase every instance one has witnessed of humble goodness queuing up to accept its maltreatment from the shits of the world. This is a foundation stone of Hamlet's despair – his moral and social awareness – yet it is often bulldozed out of the way to make room for other sources – his psychological failings, or an excess of aesthetic fineness. Hamlet's sensibility is inseparable from his sense of injustice – he cannot look at the world without seeing its tawdriness and without trying to name it and call time on it.

Claudius is a figure of loathing for Hamlet not only because he killed his father and is sleeping with his mother (though that is a formidable charge sheet). He is also, in Hamlet's imagination, a figure from the old order, given to heavy-headed revelling, and diplomacy at the end of a gun. Polonius is hated for his manipulative exploitation of his daughter's beauty, but also for his antique language, for his obfuscations and for the smokescreens he throws up between himself and the truth. Beyond both of them is a state apparatus which can be interpreted in a number of ways – as an arena of medieval brutality or an unfeeling bureaucracy; as a failing state or a reviving tyranny – but from Hamlet's perspective, it is all shoddy and tired and bad.

'Denmark's a prison' at best, and beyond that the world, too, 'a goodly one, in which there are many confines, wards and dungeons'. It is a place of rampant hypocrisy, where 'those that would make mows at him [Claudius] while my father lived give twenty, forty, fifty, a hundred ducats apiece for his picture in little'. A place where 'one may smile and smile and be a villain'. (Insecure actors playing Claudius, lacking guidance from their directors, have often taken this comment too literally as a character note and spent hours wandering the stage in a permanent state of rictus.) This last insight is such a trite one you feel a brain as sharp as Hamlet's should have got there a little earlier, but anger has a capacity for infantilising the intellect. I expect even the Dalai Lama gets morally diminished in a traffic jam. The behaviour of the Danish court is such that it makes of Hamlet both a tortured genius and an outraged eight year-old.

Hamlet places himself in the long line going back to Orestes, and forward to Jimmy Porter, Bob Dylan and Rooster Byron, blessed with an overflow of sensibility that cannot find a context or a home to live in, and so must hate the world which inflicts such endless bruising. Thus all else becomes the enemy, whether it be the establishment, the man, political correctness, whatever force has taken society beyond coherence into rigid conformity. Hamlet is the prince of such eloquent complainers, the archetype for all who feel oppressed by the clumsy stupidity of the world.

Yet, as with much complaint of this sort, his is excessive. Claudius on the evidence of the play is not just the villain he wants him to be – he has an active insight and conscience of his own. Polonius is not just 'the wretched, rash, intruding fool' that Hamlet labels him. He has children who love him, and a highly active, if wayward, intelligence. Denmark, though it has an act of definitive rottenness at its core, and seems messy and stumbly, is not the bleak antechamber to hell of Macbeth's Scotland, or the blasted loveless dysfunction of Lear's England. When Shakespeare wanted to write a proper dystopia, he did. With Elsinore, he has the brakes on.

Why? It's hard to say, but it appears there was a desire to show that Denmark was not the only problem: Hamlet was part of it as well. A fine-tuned sensibility is a beautiful thing, but it's also tough to fit into the world. Orthodoxies and hegemonies need opposition, but once opposition is let loose, it's impossible to tell it to stop. And should it stop? Isn't such rebellion most useful when most excessive, even when it parts company from the proof of sense? But when it does, doesn't it become wearing? Bob Dylan is a consistent pleasure, touching the spirit in its loneliest and quietest place, but it's always pleasant to break his tone with a burst of Sam Cooke and 'Everybody Loves To Cha-Cha-Cha'. Hamlet is exemplary, and to be so he has to be extreme, but he's not necessarily someone for every hour of the day.

All paranoia, once set running, is hard to contain. Ours had grown excessive, in sympathy with our eponymous hero. The world seemed against us, when it was in fact more often being helpful. Our board, though on the calm side, had sanctioned and approved one of the most high-risk theatrical adventures ever, and had been consistently steadfast in the face of substantial risk. The British Council, though deadened at its centre, included a host of extraordinary people working in thoughtful and enlivening ways to make a contribution to the world's culture. The academic community, though several seemed immured in their own fear and loathing, had proven huge and generous friends to the entire Globe project.

A moment comes within any cycle of perceived injustice, when a good sleep, or a chance occurrence, or a little bit of stray happiness lends perspective, and reminds one that the world is far from all bad, and that the good sits clumsily alongside the bad. For Hamlet, that moment never arrives. The walls close in inexorably, his darkest suspicions are proven true, and thus make his narrative a tragic one. For many of the rest of us, thankfully, the comic tone walks in and throws a little sunshine around.

The corrective for us proved, as it always has, our reconnection with the company. Spending time with them, and experiencing at first hand the work they were doing, had always proved the best panacea. We flew out en masse to Madrid. Matt, who had spent a year playing Laertes, Horatio, Guildenstern et al., had been quietly preparing his own Hamlet, and this was to be his first night. He was astonishing, nerveless as an assassin, not dropping a stitch all evening, and offering up his own, eloquent, sweet-natured Prince. All the other actors rose up to meet him, and gave one of the best performances I had seen. Their characters were so ingrained in their bodies by this time, there was a real sense of not watching actors playing parts, but of meeting people. It felt like Ophelia and Claudius and Gertrude and the rest had walked into the room. We were in a modern theatre, with a lively and engaged audience, all 600 of whom rose to their feet and brought the company back and back at the end. Argument and suspicions and paranoias blew away.

Something of the insouciant, low-shouldered, rolling ease of Madrid seemed to have informed the show. Spanish theatre and Spanish actors have an innate charisma, an ability to stand still and declare 'I am here', which is the envy of other nations. They call it *duende*, and it's hard to quantify. They can be natural and melodramatic at the same moment. You can see it in a Javier Bardem or an Antonio Banderas. They say 'I love you', and you want to cheer, as if they are saying it on behalf of everyone else. They can carry narratives, or hold physical positions, which in anyone else would look ridiculous, but their blend of self-possession and style pull it off. Shakespeare's theatre, one imagines, had a little of this same rooted physical presence, this earthed sexuality, though blended with a strong twist of Nordic angst. Our actors could only borrow such glamour in passing, but they borrowed well.

We adapted socially as well, and came over all Iberian. We commandeered the pavement outside our hotel, and forty or fifty people tapas'd and laughed. I said some words of congratulations to the new Hamlet and to the company on achieving ninety-seven countries in a year, and of our excitement at the tasks and challenges ahead. Then a fleet of taxis arrived and whisked everyone off into the night in search of Madrid's after-hours carnival fun. They spent the night dancing with a transvestite contortionist. I don't know if this was the dialogue which the British Council were looking for in their cultural endeavours, but they were certainly having an effect.

The next day, wandering around Madrid, aimlessly enjoying the stories and histories which pack themselves into every street corner, and relishing the blissful curiosity of unpacking such stories, a flash mob invaded a square and started doing swing dancing. Aware as I am that such demonstrations are about reclaiming space and subverting hierarchies and all that anti-jazz, there was something so gloriously, innocently happy about what they were doing, and the pleasure they were providing, that it blew the remainder of any blues away.

11

WITTENBERG IN THE DESERT

LAERTES *when these are gone,*
The woman will be out.

Act 4, Scene 7

ONE OF THE MANY SOURCE stories for Hamlet includes a Danish legend from the twelfth century which claims that Hamlet was actually a woman, and that his/her mum had hidden his/her identity to secure his/her claim to the throne. Hamlet could not even come into existence without being shrouded in ambiguity.

Though Hamlet was voraciously claimed by Burbage on its first outing – '2,000 lines! Yes, I think I'll have a bit of that' – there was no chance (pace *Shakespeare in Love*) of a woman playing it on the all-male Elizabethan/Jacobean stage. But it did not take long for women to start claiming the role. Theatre people (and especially the men) are whores for ticket sales above all else. Critics are kind enough to ascribe seriousness to our endeavours, but they would be dismayed if they knew how cravenly we chase full houses, and how much that chase dictates choices. Once women started to appear in British theatres by the lascivious good grace of Charles II, and once they proved their astonishing popularity (a process that took about twelve seconds), it was only a matter of time before women started claiming the leading male roles.

Nor should it be surprising that Hamlet, the most complete expression of what it is to be human, should be an attractive role for women. It invites open interpretation. Hamlet lives in a fog, the lines of his drawing are fuzzy and uncertain. Where other leading tragic figures in Shakespeare's canon are more sharply delineated – Othello, the noble Moor; Lear, the mentally vulnerable tyrant; Anthony, the decaying libertine – Hamlet occupies space uncertainly. He is so negatively defined by what he is not, and what he is unable to become – he cannot become the king, he cannot return to Wittenberg to be a student, he cannot fulfil his desire to be Ophelia's lover, he is incapable of becoming the man of action his father's spirit wants him to be – all this inability to achieve clarity as a persona leaves room for interpreters to sketch their own shape. Free space enables the imagination – Hamlet's very own negative capability. His uniqueness is in part his liminality, which makes him available to all.

His supreme intelligence, and the delicate game he plays (and often loses) between feigned madness, real madness and disabling clarity of sight, all leave his identity free. He sees so clearly through the constructions which others encase themselves within – the security blanket of two-dimensionality – and his own fluid identity enables him so accurately to deconstruct others, that he slips free of conventional definitions himself, including male and female. E.M. Forster divided his characters into flat and round, those stuck in a groove and those capable of change. Hamlet is in a separate dimension – a whirling cloud of thoughts, sensations and feelings. He becomes an essence of humanity.

Yet to deal for a moment in old-fashioned gender definitions, he does have something of the feminine about him. He is out of tune with the masculine boorishness of the Danish court, his relationship with Ophelia is a passionate meeting of spirits but far from a conventional love story, and his feelings for Horatio are as much sisterly as brotherly. In his greatest fit of self-loathing, when berating himself for being unable to enact vengeance on Claudius, he bitterly accuses himself of being too feminine:

> Why, what an ass am I! This is most brave,
> That I, the son of a dear father murdered,
> Prompted to my revenge by heaven and hell,
> Must, like a whore, unpack my heart with words,
> And fall a-cursing, like a very drab,
> A scullion!

The expressions here are pejorative, but the anger driving Hamlet is an unease with his own femininity. Edwin Booth, the great nine-teenth-century American actor, wrote of his approach to the role:

> I have always endeavoured to make prominent the femi-ninity of Hamlet's character and therein lies the secret of my success – I think. I doubt if ever a robust and mascu-line treatment of the character will be accepted so gener-ally as the more womanly and refined interpretation. I know that frequently I fall into effeminacy, but we can't always hit the proper keynote.

There are about twelve things within those sentences which make you want to punch Edwin Booth, while still appreciating his point of view.

There is also Hamlet's weight of feeling, a freight of emotion which on several occasions becomes insupportable for himself. That strength of feeling has traditionally been ascribed, for good or bad, to women. And the ability to translate such strong feelings into speech. Women are traditionally understood to be able to 'unpack their hearts', where men are more likely to pack them up and secure them with an undecipherable lock. That volatility, and that openness with the workings of the heart, makes the part available to women, where traditionally the more beefy roles have not been. Also in purely technical terms, actresses are good at summoning tears, where actors more often have to resort to the onion in the hankie.

We are uncertain as to when the first female Hamlet appeared, but by the middle of the eighteenth century it was far from exceptional. By 1775, Sarah Siddons is already being mentioned in dispatches for her brave work in the provinces playing Hamlet. Whether the audience loved her Hamlet or not, she was clearly a fan herself, since she carried on playing it for another twenty-seven years. London's first recorded female Hamlet was Elizabeth Powell at Drury Lane in 1796. Another of the first female Hamlets, Kitty Clive, won effusive praise from Dr Johnson. 'Mrs. Clive was the best player I ever saw,' he opined. 'What Clive did best, she did better than Garrick.' It is hard to imagine what Garrick, Johnson's close friend, would have made of this. Or maybe it's not. Another fan of a female Hamlet was Edmund 'flashes of lightning' Kean. His contemporary Walter Donaldson told of his response to a Hamlet performed by one Julia Glover: 'At the end of the first act [Edmund] Kean came behind the scenes and shook Mrs. Glover, not by one, but by both hands, and exclaimed, "Excellent! Excellent!" The splendid actress, smiling, cried, "Away, you flatterer! You come in mockery to scorn and scoff at our solemnity."'

East-coast American theatre and London theatre were as neigh-
bourly then as they are now, and in 1820 Sarah Bartley became
the first female American Hamlet in the Park Theatre in New
York. Another two American women assayed the role in the
nineteenth century, both deeply unconventional and worthy of
becoming figures as iconic as Hamlet himself. Anna Elizabeth
Dickinson was a Radical Republican firebrand who campaigned
throughout her life for the abolition of slavery and for women's
suffrage. A gifted and powerful orator from an early age, in a time
when standing on a box and scooping a crowd into the swoop
of your rhetoric could still nudge history a little this way or that,
her power over a crowd was used extensively. Both before the
civil war and in the most dangerous zones during it, she was
utilised by the Radical Republicans to help push America towards
a slavery-free future. At a time when being seen and not heard
was still a commonplace for many women, to stand up and ex-
coriate Lincoln for being too soft in front of the House of
Representatives is a testament to her courage. And to America's
unheralded ability to be ahead of the game in forging the future.
When she took on the role of Hamlet, the very act of doing so
was assumed to be a proof of her insanity. With a blurring
Hamletian irony, in later life she was kidnapped and forcibly
committed to an asylum by her own sister. She won her own
freedom and spent much of the rest of her life clearing her own
name from what was then thought the 'slur' of madness.

The face of Charlotte Cushman, another celebrated American
nineteenth-century actress, stares out at us from a series of sepia-
tinted photographs. She is far from a conventional beauty, really
very far, but an iron will and an unabashed strength sail forth
from each image like a Victorian battleship. In the photographs,
she is usually accompanied by a frail female beauty, kneeling in

supplication to her, or garlanding the frame timidly behind. These are several of the lovers who fell by the wayside as she blazed a trail of unconventional living through the Western world. Her soprano voice having failed her at an early age, she turned to acting and took on Lady Macbeth at the age of nineteen. The conventional female repertoire was never going to satisfy her. Her sister became her co-star, the two of them playing to great acclaim the passionate love story of Romeo and Juliet, with Charlotte as Romeo. She later graduated to Hamlet, playing it in Boston and New York from 1851, and, as a mark of high cross-gender-boundaries esteem, Edwin Booth lent her his Hamlet outfit.

She later had a flattering portrait done by Thomas Sully, whose daughter she seduced for good measure. They exchanged rings and performed some form of mock marriage, after which Charlotte went on a European tour that stretched from a planned couple of months to several years. Rosalie Sully, left behind, died of a broken heart. Charlotte's continuing life in Europe proved a hectic merry-go-round of passionate shenanigans as stormy relationship followed stormy relationship. Each punctuated by a moment when the couple of the moment sat and stood for a photograph in grim stillness, dressed with a deliberate male sobriety, for the joy and scandal of their love to be captured in monochrome cheerlessness. For a long period, while she was still performing, she settled in Rome, where she nurtured a community of bohemian and gay writers and artists.

For both of these extraordinary women, and many others like them, playing Hamlet was an act of political reclamation, bound up with their desire for greater rights, social and political, for women. Standing up for rights, and playing the Prince were expressions of a similar desire for equality of respect and expression. Dickinson was the more clearly political of the two, though the communities that Cushman fostered and led were at the forefront of modern thinking on women's rights. In both cases, their acting threw new light on the text and the role. Simply seeing a woman relating to Gertrude and Ophelia within the dynamics of the narrative makes the spectator look anew, and moves judgement away from conventional thinking. Cushman is reported to have gone out of her way to show Hamlet treating the other women in the play with respect. One is tempted to think, given her capacity to engineer romantic havoc, that this might have been less an early expression of Brechtian *Verfremdungseffekt* (alienation effect) and more an actress on the pull, but that would be very cynical.

These two and many others, all across Europe and right across America to the rootin' tootin' Gold Rush west, were using this most iconic role to change ideas of what was and was not permissible. The apotheosis of the journey of a female Hamlet from the edges of culture to centre stage belonged to the French actress Sarah Bernhardt. Her career was a rooftop-scorching comet which flew low over the Western world, and her Hamlet was the climax of it. Bernhardt was adamant about the right way to approach the role: 'I cannot see Hamlet as a man . . . The things he says, his impulses, his actions, entirely indicate to me that he was a woman.' A hyperactive über-passionate characterisation, flaming with exposed sensibility, it inspired cities to draw to a standstill wherever she appeared. Ticketless punters stood in droves outside theatres she was performing in, drawn by the collective hysterical delusion that they could sense what was going on within. As if gravitational waves rippled out from Ms Bernhardt.

Her outsize personality bestrode the late nineteenth- and early twentieth-century world like a colossus, sleeping in a coffin, and according to gossip sharing her coffin with half of Europe.

Certainly when you look at the astonishing footage of her Paris funeral, it looks as if half the men and women in the huge crowds – hats gripped tightly to chests, hankies theatrically crumpled into eyes – felt a personal connection. Henry James wrote of her: 'It would take some ingenuity to give an idea of the intensity, the ecstasy, the insanity as some people would say, of [the] curiosity and enthusiasm provoked by Mlle. Bernhardt.'

Hamlet was a central part of Bernhardt's myth, though sadly all we have left is two brief moments of film which show her to be a fine fencer, with a slim, line-drawn grace and a natural ease. Happily, we have two hours of her great successor Asta Nielsen, who produced her own film of *Hamlet* in 1920. The film is little hindered by its lack of speech, and manages to convey a portrait of Hamlet which is witty, fine, tragic and broad all at the same time. It changes the gender of the character entirely. Nielsen plays Hamlet as a woman who has been brought up as a man by Gertrude and Claudius. This Hamlet is in love with Horatio, who is somewhat confused by his own feelings. The gender transition here spoke eloquently to a moment in Europe when gender was more fluid and relaxed than it had been for a while, and would be for a while longer, a fluidity most eloquently expressed in Weimar Germany.

Then bizarrely, with suffrage for women, the number of female Hamlets decreased. The performance historian Tony Howard has diagnosed two principal reasons for this. First, that playing Hamlet was an act of political defiance, which lost some of its gravity and importance with the gaining of suffrage. Second, that the ascension of the critic, and his (and it was almost exclusively his) fierce adherence to bourgeois values banished women from taking on such roles. What had been a commonplace was deemed by the high critical voice to be improper, and hence unallowable.

One critic, William Winter, ensured himself a long spell in posterity's doghouse by declaring in 1911: 'It is difficult to understand why Hamlet should be considered feminine, seeing that he is supereminently distinguished by a characteristic rarely, if ever, discerned in women: namely that of considering consequences, of thinking too precisely on the event.'

The dead hand of collective consensus drove women away from such parts. It is only recently on our stages that such performances have started to flourish again, although they are still surprisingly rare. The break in this tradition was a weird interruption in a natural continuum where Hamlet was seen more and more as the property of all, a break which hopefully will never re-occur. Hamlet, both the character in the play and the cultural entity in the world, is too comprehensive and all-encompassing to let something as piffling as gender get in the way.

* * *

I boarded the plane for Saudi Arabia and settled into my seat, eagerly looking forward to six or seven hours where mobiles couldn't grab attention, and where pleasant oblivion could reign. It was the last moment you want to see your least favourite schoolteacher walking towards you or sitting across the aisle. I did frantic looking-out-of-window and into-newspaper activity, to make it seem that I hadn't spotted him. I sneaked a look across the aisle and spotted with some disappointment that he was doing the same thing. I was clearly his least favourite pupil.

It was a short trip to join the company for what was being billed as an historic event – the first time that Shakespeare has been performed with men and women on stage in Saudi Arabia. Finding a venue that would do this had proven one of the more challenging tasks of arranging the tour. Several places volunteered to host an all-male version, but we were not prepared to, and after much searching and delicate negotiation, we found a university venue that could accommodate us.

The screen within the seat in front of me carried a fair old freight of religious observance and instruction for the faithful. Being told to pray at the beginning of a flight always makes me uneasy. The list of films available was oddly slanted in a way that seemed to defy logic. I was too stupid to see the connecting thread. I started watching *The Martian*, and spotted the weird way that, within this already sexless film, a strange cloud materialised in front of any woman's chest whenever they appeared, and then followed them daemon-like around the room. It seemed that even the smallest amount of female flesh had to be pixilated into abstraction. Then I realised the thread that connected the films – they all contained minimal amounts of female flesh. Swearing, violence and outrageous comedy all seemed fine; girl's shoulders were unseemly.

We flew in low over Jeddah late on a Friday night. The city was ablaze with skyscraper-sized flashing advertisements. It seemed that the man in the moon was being told to drink Pepsi. We landed and then taxied past column after column of private jets, all sleek and angular and pointing in a uniform direction, looking like an alien army preparing to march. We raced off the aircraft but were then blocked at immigration by a failed computer. This meant we had to stand still for an hour and a half, in a queue. Right in front of me was my least favourite teacher: right behind him his least favourite pupil. For ninety minutes, in paroxysms of stupid Englishness, we explored every bodily angle and every mannerism possible to avoid catching each other's eyes. The sheer fatuousness of it, on both our parts, made me want to faint.

Entering the country was going to be difficult, since I had been told fifteen times by different people that I was not to say that I was here to do a show, or perform *Hamlet*, or do anything theatrical. If I admitted this, I would apparently be sent home, and the authorities would cancel the show. I had been coached like a spy to say, 'I am on a cultural enrichment programme.' 'Cultural enrichment programme . . .' I muttered over and over to myself as I looked for fresh and spontaneous ways not to be simply civil to the person in front of me. I was otherwise surrounded by hundreds of men who were all wearing white towel skirts and wraps and revealing a large amount of very hairy flesh. They were all here for Hajj to Mecca, which was only about seventy miles away. They were far less nervous or intimidated than me, and were moaning loudly about the computer delay. 'For fuck's sake,' they kept saying in broad Birmingham accents. 'What a shithole,' another one opined, in a manner that seemed to lack the requisite religious reverence for a pilgrim.

Eventually, I passed through without anyone questioning why I was there, or indeed showing the faintest interest. On the other side, I found a fellow cultural enricher, a delightful climate-change scientist, here to lecture. A passionate believer in the importance of stopping the use of fossil fuels, coming to lecture in Saudi Arabia seemed rather like putting your head into the lion's mouth, and all the better for that. We both knew little about the university – King Abdullah University of Science and Technology (KAUST) – which we were visiting, and tried to fill out details as we drove through the desert night. The one thing we knew for certain was that the university was co-ed, the first and only one of its kind in Saudi, and for that reason it had invoked the ire of the less progressive. It was on an Al Qaeda hitlist. Some men will go an awfully long and violent way to stop women

Naeem and Tom facing off as Hamlet and Laertes in
Odeon Amphitheatre, Amman, Jordan.
© Sarah Lee

Amanda hides as Ophelia in a merry moment during the first ever
performance of *Hamlet* in Myanmar.
© David Hempenstall

Walking into the sandstorm that stopped our show in
the Zaatari refugee camp, Jordan.
© Sarah Lee

President Poroshenko and boxer Wladimir Klitschko looking a little nonplussed
on the eve of the elections in Ukraine.
© The British Council of Ukraine

Two hundred ambassadors at the UN and, for reasons we never fully ascertained,
Kim Cattrall and Laurie Anderson.
© Russ Roland

Rockstar screens in front of the Pacific in Antofagasta, Chile.
© Magaly Visedo

Our host Jama addresses a press conference in Somaliland.
© Dave McEvoy

Backstage with Phoebe and Keith in a Monsoon in Phnom Penh, Cambodia.
© Piotr Zaporowski

A square of all ages in Prague.
© Karishma Balani

A section of the four thousand who witnessed the show in Khartoum, Sudan.
© British Council in Sudan

Corpses strewn across the stage in Estonia.
© Siim Vahur

Beruce and Naeem do a fight call, the Red Sea rolling in the background.
© Dave McEvoy

Happy holiday snap on the Copán Ruins of Honduras.
© Malú Ansaldo

Publicity in Costa Rica, Guatemala, the Ivory Coast and Japan.
© Malú Ansaldo, Beruce Khan

Amanda points to Norway in a Yemeni refugee camp.
© Jess Watts

Saying goodbye to the Globe.
© Sarah Lee

being educated to understand fully and completely what comprehensive knobs the men are. There were three heavy levels of security to pass through to get onto campus: concrete blocks across the roads, serious artillery at every checkpoint and impressively glaring soldiers. Once through security, we drove on into a pristine paradise weirdly empty of people.

At our hotel, I was met by our host, a brave and sweet American woman who seemed strung out by nerves, like a violin string pulled too tight. In vivid contrast, Amanda rocked up looking far from nervous. In the course of the day, she and a couple of the others from the company had found a professor who had discovered innovative ways of utilising the spartan desert resources and had been brewing his own hooch. Amanda was completely off her face, swinging her laundry bag around merrily. She tried rather comically to act normal for a bit, then leant in and whispered conspiratorially, 'I'm a little bit pissed, you know', which I think they had worked out on Mars. She tried rather clumsily to moonwalk backwards out of the foyer. This didn't lessen the nerves of our host.

Hungry for knowledge, I sat our host down and asked for more info. A violinist herself – why do musicians come to resemble their instruments? – she had come to KAUST accompanying her husband, a leading light in computer technology. He was in part responsible for the building of the eighth biggest super-computer in the world, which was installed here. The university was all tech and engineering, was entirely for graduate students, had astonishing resources for research, and had proved a magnet for top boffins from all over the world, as well as Saudi Arabia itself. The previous Saudi king, whose record of oppression at home and exporting chaos abroad was notable, seems to have been discreetly more liberal than he was allowed to appear. A no-holds-barred modern university was his great dream, and, yes, one with women in it. He went to the government and tentatively suggested it, but was screamed out of town by the ultra-Wahabist Ministry of Education. Undeterred, and probably a little piqued (it was his kingdom after all), the King decided to go it alone and build a university himself. Twenty billion dollars later, the astonishing campus sits proud and clean on land carved out of sea and desert. It was knocked up in less than 1,000 days. It seems to have been built too fast for the world to catch up, and is yet to be filled with students. The most bewildered people are the inhabitants of the small and ancient fishing town which nestles alongside the university. Their rough seaside cafes, having enjoyed two millennia of relaxed evenings muttering about the day's catch, now fill up with refugees from MIT and Stanford talking hyperspace.

Whether built from the King's guilt or from the King's hope was hard to say, but it was a remarkable place. My host's nerves were attenuated, but her determination to make the best of this place, and to change the space she was in, was inspiring. The university campus was the only place in Saudi where women were allowed to drive, and within that context for her to have managed to get us there was some achievement. It was the early stages of chiselling fertility out of rocky soil, from which much can bloom.

★ ★ ★

The campus was an eerie replica of *The Truman Show*. The wall of heat you walked into as you stepped outdoors hazed the brain as well as the sky, everything shifted aqueous, and a smear of Vaseline appeared round the edge of reality like a film from the over-bright Technicolor 1950s. Long, neat rows of identical homes lined pristine roads. They were built from a pale-pink stone that was soft on the eye in the blasting heat and under the searing blue sky. Explosions of flower-dazzle burst out like camp fireworks from the earth. The sense of artificial composition was enhanced by the regularly spaced palm trees (palm trees have a hard time looking real anywhere, don't they?). The only jarring note was the result of natural aesthetics – all the bigger green patches were garlanded with hollowed-out circles of rock, big stony bracelets, oxtail-shaped lumps of the local geology, nature's own Henry Moores.

These eloquent lumps of rock sat in front of some of the most beautiful modern architecture I have seen, gently sleek new buildings floating in the sky. Everywhere I looked I saw echoes of classical painting as huge but human edifices of wood and glass led the eye gently towards newly created piazzas or down towards the sea. Air, sea and building sat together with a natural grace. No matter that the whole was a confection from one of J.G. Ballard's dystopian nightmares, no matter that beyond the segregationist fence there were heaps of rubbish; the effect, while within it, was delightful. Most of the time the eye was led towards a beacon, the beacon of learning standing skyscraper tall on a lump of rock in the Red Sea. The beacon had a powerful light at its apex, together with a sculpted eagle. It was placed there so the King could see it from his nearby island and be reminded of all the good he had done. This Napoleonic grandiosity sat awkwardly beside the modernity elsewhere.

The theatre was absurdly well appointed. It was too big, like almost all modern playhouses, but in terms of kit better equipped than most national theatres. It felt brand new and unused, rather like an over-eager golfer who turns up at a match with all the stuff but no idea how to use it. There was tension about photography. The company were uneasy about photographs being taken when what we were doing was potentially going to enrage many. I was inclined to be more relaxed about it, until the theatre told me that they could not photograph the audience because the Saudi women in the audience could not be seen to have been there. It seemed a bit rum to protect the audience and not the actors, so we barred cameras.

Then the simple miracle of people turning up for a show began. No matter that this was a historic event, or a political one, or a dangerous one, the first show was a matinee, and people simply turned up in their droves excited to be there. What greater force of happy innocence is there in the world than people turning up in high expectation for a show? The security around the building was light, and there was a festival atmosphere. The women seemed exceptionally excited, and thankfully no one was be-labouring them (or us) with speeches or posters or literature. Eyes were shining bright even behind substantial burqas, and smiles were flashing wide underneath dazzle-bright hajibs. There were sufficient American girls to break the atmosphere with noisy whooping, and an astonishingly calm chief of staff, a black woman from Caltech, seemed to be discreetly pulling strings. However achieved, all sailed calmly and happily into a first show to a full house, and a sparky show drew an enthusiastic response.

A small feeling of deflation descended afterwards. This was a significant moment, we had been told, the first professional show on the Saudi stage featuring both men and women. As with many significant moments, it had all ended up a tiny bit flat. Everyone was so determined to downplay historic moments, everyone conspired so successfully to render them as normal, that they ended up, well, a bit normal. We were also disarmed when a charming Saudi woman came backstage to talk to us, and told us that she was an actress regularly appearing on stage in Jeddah and Riyadh. Clearly someone was doing a bit of exaggerating. But there was a sense of a job well done, in that the atmosphere had been relaxed and free, and the show enjoyed. The work of our hosts in attempting something brave and pulling it off had been rewarded.

I wandered off with one of the actors to have a coffee, and listened to a story of a broken relationship, one of the several that had been crushed on the anvil of the tour. It was not easy to maintain a long-distance relationship while whirligigging around the globe. But the conclusion of this relationship had been more than a little brutal, and the actor was smarting.

I needed a little space, as my feet had hardly touched the ground, so I set off for a stroll. There is an uncanny moment in countries on this latitude as the day is ending. For an hour or so before night sets in, with the heat ebbing and the light softening, and with the electrical power of the day still stored in sand and rock and masonry, and with each emitting a reciprocal glow, for a brief moment, all seems still and grave, refulgent and invested. There is a swimming temperature in the air, and in matter, cool and heat shifting and curving around each other. Greene writes about it in *The Heart of the Matter*, how that hour, with its peculiar magic, redeems the stifling nihilism of the day.

The centrepiece of the campus was a mosque, and I headed towards it. It was grand but not overwhelming. Its cool white walls topped with a startling blue minaret, together with interlocking triangles of pillars outside, made it look like a miracle of shade for the soul in a hot world. The light started to dance the same shifting quadrille as the heat, with night and day slipping in and out of each other's hold, the sun collapsing into the Red Sea, the white walls still uttering their lambent murmur, and the dark starting to take over in between. The mosque was surrounded by a network of inlets running off from the Red Sea in a successful imitation of Amsterdam and Venice. The walkways around the inlets were a startling white, the water a sharp aquamarine. Between the heat, the light and the water, a soft dampness conjured itself in the evening air, and right at that moment the muezzin poured out his song. Its clarity and its yearning musicality pierced like a prayer. I was alone on this still dreamily empty campus, and for a moment Islam made a pure and simple sense, and I, who had come to scoff, was wholly disarmed and felt naked before its soft power. The sense of peace was as great as I have known, as well as the sense of a presence softly alive, immanent in the milky light.

The evening show was packed – students, teachers, visitors all crammed in, alive to every moment of a strong performance, which was greeted with a rousing reception at the end. Afterwards, we headed off for a supper with many of our hosts – American, French, African and Saudi. I was surrounded by witty and brilliant mathematicians who talked at a level of abstraction and a machine-gun pace I found it hard to keep up with, but the intellectual fizz was intoxicating. They were eager to tell us about their university and its achievements. About 25 per cent of the university population is Saudi. The rest were attracted by the research possibilities, but also by the chance for the university to effect change. They were there to do original work and to think original thoughts, but also to demonstrate the social use and the importance of such work and such thoughts. As one of them – a veteran of several posts at important Western universities – said, it was invigorating to be at a university where thought itself was radical. So many Western homes of higher education were now mired in an obsession with status, with territorial battles and with egos nervously ring-fencing their own domain, that the whole purpose of a university had been misplaced. As one of them said, 'Every university I've worked at before is so anxious to sit on its own dignity that it forgets to be a university.' Everyone talks up their own meaning, but there did seem something urgently true about this university's claim. Universities are there to change the world, to create new tunes which the rest of the world samples and learns to dance to or to ignore.

Hamlet is, of course, a play about a student. Hamlet is on leave from university at Wittenberg. His friends Rosencrantz and Guildenstern visit from there, and bring with them a bracing tonic of playful student philosophising. Claudius is keen to keep Hamlet in Elsinore to keep an eye on him, but also because he seems suspicious of Wittenberg itself. Gertrude says at one point of her son, as if it is proof of his instability, 'Here he comes, reading!' Polonius questions him on the content of his book as if defusing a bomb. Obviously with Wittenberg there were many Protestant over- and under-tones, but there is also the simple fact of learning, and of new thought. Calling someone a 'student' is often now done satirically or as an insult; it is bracing to recall a day when the name implied something new and radical. To be a student in this Saudi university had that bracing thrill, as it did for Hamlet.

For Hamlet, the problem is the thought he has been infected with. University has created a kaleidoscope of possibilities within him, which the antique heaviness of Elsinore and the personal situation he is trapped within cannot accommodate. 'What a piece of work is a man . . .' is the complaint of someone who has been shown such possibility and finds it hard to reconcile with reality. 'Denmark is a prison', but it is mainly 'thinking that makes it so'. Who hasn't been on that journey to a place of fresh and original thought, then felt a suffocating heaviness on returning home, where no one understands the newness bubbling away inside? Hamlet is the paradigm for every young buck or buckess who escapes a way of thinking and then has to deal with the pain of having lost their previous connections, whether wearing artful black or a burqa.

In the words of Erasmus, the man who dreamt up many of the ideals of the education system which Shakespeare grew up within, '*praecipuam reipublicae spem sitam esse in recta educatione puerorum*' (the first hope of the republic lies in the proper education of its boys). This principle was at the heart of the Tudor grammar-school revolution, as Jonathan Bate has brilliantly uncovered. It is the reason why those of the three generations before Shakespeare endowed such schools so lavishly. They believed that drumming the wise saws of the ancients into young boys for long hours on end would help them grow to be active in society, and wise in those actions. The essence of civility for northern Europeans, the essence for good humanity almost, was a proper education in the arts. Shakespeare himself had a sceptical view of this ideal, since many of his most-educated characters show the least humanity, and many of his least learned the most civility. Hamlet himself is a demonstration of the impossible collection of expectations that such a dream can place on a single individual.

The crucial word in the Latin tag above is, of course, '*puerorum*', of boys. While young men in the Tudor age walked slowly to schools to be force-fed Ovid, young women were not even allowed out. They were expected to stay at home and master their sewing. Many rebelled against this, of course, and the number of educated female prodigies in the Elizabethan age is striking, but the tide was against them. As it continued to be for several centuries. The battles for full educational access were fought over a long time here in the West, just as they are being fought with a fresh ferocity and violence elsewhere in the world now, as Malala Yousafzai's case has shown. What education should be is open to question, but there is little doubt that some is better than none, and to deny the chance to anyone, man or woman, is a crime. Who shall be happy if not everyone?

From the moment of my arrival in Saudi, I had been with strong and independent women who were choosing to be here and make a difference: the climate-change scientist here to speak against the economic basis of this nation; our host who had put the whole enrichment programme together; the chief of staff gently pulling the strings of much of the university; our own actresses and stage managers; and, most impressively, the young women in the audience, with a careless insouciance and a carefree shrug, going against the dictates of much of their own world. Finally, the existence of the play of *Hamlet* is its own ringing bell for the virtues of education. That a boy, Shakespeare, whose father was illiterate, could be brought to a place of such eloquence and wisdom and freedom of thought is its own endorsement. Shakespeare himself never made it to a university, but grammar school served him well.

We walked back through the campus to our hotel, surrounded by an excited gaggle of students. Everyone was bushed, but my mind was still thrumming away, and I needed to walk out my thoughts. So I set off for a couple of circuits of the campus, its emptiness and quiet now complemented by the dark. The same peace reigned. The hotel was surrounded by some eccentric species of flower which blooms and shines most completely at night. I silently paid respect to whichever botanical virtuoso had painted the night in such dazzling colours.

On my meander, I wandered into the piazza where I had sat earlier with the broken-hearted actor. Three students, two boys and a girl, all Saudi, were sitting in the night emptiness on wicker chairs talking animatedly. I asked them for a light, and fell into conversation with them. They had seen *Hamlet*, and were snapped alert with excited thought. They told me it was the politics that thrilled them, a young man going against his own mother, and a king, and the state apparatus. They had no specific idea what Hamlet wanted, but they knew that he wanted something different, something new, and that he wanted freedom from the past. We talked about what we wanted, and they asked me to define my desires. I never know how to answer that, so offered them Chekhov's pithy definition: 'All I ask is freedom from lies, and freedom from violence.' They pretended to like it, but it is a desire from a privileged place, and did not speak to their needs. I asked for their definition, and the girl swiftly replied with a relaxed and automatic clarity, 'We want freedom from want and need, we want freedom to contribute, and we want freedom to love.' The boys nodded calmly, and there was little more to add. I left them to continue their conversation.

I walked down in happy loneliness to the sea, and reflected on the words of the young woman. They turned slowly in my mind like a key in a lock. I thought of the seductive sobriety and calm of Islam, or at least this very cosseted bit of it. Then I saw in sharp relief, as if through an inverting mirror, the context beyond the wire. The virtues of this place, and the palpable relief of those who enjoy them, exposed the nature of the world beyond it. This was a utopia, a manifestly fake one, thrown up in 1,000 days, and like all utopias part of its process was to expose the wrongness of the world it existed in. Thomas More wrote his *Utopia* as a dream of a better world, but also as a critique of his own. This fenced-in modernity, where men and women walk and talk together in something close to parity, was a living critique of the world beyond the fence and the machine guns. A critique thrown up by the dream of a dying king, in a fairy-tale denial of the drift of the rest of his life. Just as Hamlet's fresh and bright new perspective exposes much of his own world, the disjunct between the dream here and the reality beyond – a country which subjugates women, promulgates Wahabi closed-mindedness and coordinates the flow of wealth into the hands of a kleptocratic royal family – that out-of-jointness, together with the simplicity of the young woman's words, gifted me a clarity about much that I had seen. A clarity about problems that run through South America, Africa, China, Europe, North America, everywhere. Problems that recur over and over, wherever humans botch together an attempt at a society.

Freedom from want and need . . . setting the template for all else, the ground zero of our collective inhumanity, the inequity of wealth, the continuing cruelty and insanity of which shames all, and hinders whatever other blundering nonsense we talk about natural justice. There is little point debating small points of good-ness, or the lack of it, when we live in a global society which amounts for many to not much more than a torture chamber of destitution and want. A torture chamber which most of us partici-pate in the maintenance and continuance of. Abu Ghraib wasn't horrifying because it was exceptional; it was horrifying because it was so true.

Freedom to contribute . . . Everyone, no matter on what scale, whether on the street corner or in the parliament building, whether in the *New York Times* or in a local rag, everyone wants to speak and be heard and be allowed to affect their environment. They all want to contribute, to help, to change. They all should be allowed to. Any society has to be created to give sufficient numbers, if not everyone, the outlets for their energies, and the platforms for their ideas. There has to be a fluid and changeable set of opportunities for contributions, and a fair system for recognising such contributions. When that desire to contribute is thwarted and checked, as is the case so miserably here in Saudi, then it is a witches' brew.

And freedom to love . . . If that is singular or prodigious, gay or straight, or any combination – everyone should be able to love in the way they want to love. No one individual, no cleric, no despot, no bureaucrat, no anybody should stand in the way of that. Elena Ferrante says that 'If love is exiled from cities, their good nature becomes an evil nature.'

These three conditions affect each other, result from each other, and interweave with each other. But where all three are negative, where economic inequity cripples freedom of thought and heart, where social restrictions stop people from having a voice or being able to contribute, or when love is policed or proscribed, then you have the recipe for nihilistic violence. That is the negative we live in, or too many live in, or are allowed to live in. That is our ridiculous tragedy and comedy, when its inverse, the positive, can bloom like a night flower so simply.

These thoughts arrived out of the dark-blue air as I ambled my way around the sea views, the artificial lakes and the empty walkways of the night campus. A university of hope, surrounded by despair, living at an extreme between the wished-for and the reality. The light on the top of the King's beacon of learning flashing away in the distance.

The next day, we drove back though tens of miles of flat desert sprawl. The beguiling wilderness was strewn with old rubber tyres, the water bottles of seemingly all the world, and a desert-wide confetti of plastic bags. The astonishing durability of rock and of synthetics.

Shortly before the airport was reached, a beaten-up two-storey shack sat with a shabby dignity by the motorway, the tallest skyscrapers in the world looming in the far distance. It had a sign across its front like an old Wild West bank. 'The National Society for Human Rights' it read.

12

THE WORLD IN REVOLT

HAMLET *Let Hercules himself do what he may,*
The cat will mew and dog will have his day.

Act 5, Scene 1

A HOST OF PHOTOS HUNG from a washing line between two
lamp posts on the main drag of Bogotá, Colombia. It was a bank
holiday, and the streets had been given over to the people, so no
policeman was going to take these photos down, clearly posted
by FARC themselves or a subsidiary. These were the pictures,
washed out through frequent reproduction into grainy black and
white, which you do not get to see on television or in newspapers.
Heads with half their skulls blown off in unforgiving close-up,
lines of slaughtered bodies laid out like sardines as policemen
wander past with a diffident neglect, shattered body parts flung
asunder like jigsaw pieces after an explosion. All these images out
there on the street as kids wandered past licking their ice creams.

Just a couple of blocks down, a modest collection of interlocking eighteenth-century buildings around a courtyard housed
a national museum. At the centre of the complex was the most

delicate icon to inspire a revolution I had encountered. In an upstairs room, lit like a shrine and encased in thick glass, was a chunk of hyper-glazed porcelain, its mottled whiteness crawling with candied green leaves, small outcrops of jewellery and a brightly coloured slithering snake. Maniacally kitsch, it was hard to credit that this fragment of a vase had been the trigger for fifteen years of revolutionary wars. Or that a national identity was organised around a broken bit of china.

Just over 200 years before, on the morning of 20 July 1810, a group of *criollos*, members of the indigenous aristocracy, tired of the bad and disaffected rule of their Spanish masters, stage-managed a theatrical scrap. They carried it out in the centre of Bogotá on a market day, when they knew the right audience would be present, excited and flammable. Organising a dinner to receive a celebrated liberationist, they crossed a teeming square to request from a Spanish merchant, known to be both ultra conservative and a bit of a bell-end, the loan of a vase to adorn their table. The owner of said vase, Llorente, refused in a predictably high-handed manner. The *criollos* took the vase and broke it with a histrionic flourish. Fists flew, and word spread quickly around the square that the Spaniards had yet again revealed their innate racism. Fists gave way to stones, and before the day was out a people's *junta* had been formed, and previously unheard of political demands were being made.

Of course, the vase was the straw that broke a back straining under a complex weave of social, political and economic causes. But there was something about the incongruity of it, the gaudy kitsch against all the blood later spilt, including that documented in the brutalist photos, that compelled the imagination. There was something deliciously comic about the red-bloodedness of the passion set against the feyness of what provoked it. 'What did he do? Refused to lend his vase??? OK, that's it! War!'

Another sequence of photos in another place gave testament to what followed the vase's breaking. On the wall of the gents' toilet of a club in Quito, Ecuador, there was a sombrely presented parade of portraits. It was a sequence of framed photos of the presidents of Ecuador over the last eighty years. Each bristled with self-importance and a visionary gleam, fixing their eye steadfastly towards the future. All presented themselves with the same grave dignity, garlanded with stiff military hats and even stiffer moustaches. Underneath, with no comic comment, there was a small caption outlining the length of their tenure. Some had lasted a creditable decade, some a less creditable couple of years, some no longer than a year, many a couple of months, a disturbing number only a few days, and several ludicrously no longer than a day. It was a fiercely witty joke against their own political turbulence. These countries knew about regime change and revolution in their gut.

Beginning with the wars of liberation, themselves a shifting of alliances between indigenous peoples, imported slave populations, a Spanish aristocrat class who identified themselves as American, and the distant Spanish rulers, the next two centuries proved a merry-go-round of political change. Civil war followed civil war, with many a cycle revolving around a phenomenon called *caudillismo*. This involved a charismatic figure, the *caudillo*, an outsider and a corrective to the current regime, coming in from who knows where and sweeping to power. Each would bring with him a fresh democratic mandate, effective until the next *caudillo* came along. The *caudillos* in the photos on the toilet wall are so indistinguishable, a matter of millimetres in the refashioning of their facial hair, it was hard to know what exactly they were offering by way of difference. Violence and revolution were part of the fabric of life in South America in a way they have (almost) ceased to be in the West. Though economic injustice, the bitter legacy of colonialism and interference from outsiders are clearly the prime motors of instability, it was hard not to gain the impression that power was shifted in part because it was the custom, and revolutions happened because people enjoyed them.

Simón Bolívar, the Liberator of all Liberators (for his fan base, though not for all – Marx took a dim view of his bourgeois aspirations), was something of a Hamlet figure. Borderline bipolar, and brimful of self-loathing, this scion of a grand family brought up in a state of emotional dislocation was capable of astonishing feats of bold action and sustained endurance, and equally capable of collapsing into himself and retreat. He could lead coalitions of soldiers across mountains at one moment, and at another disappear into his own lair for prolonged contemplation. He still presides in effigy over what was Gran Colombia, his statue and face dominating each cityscape. In the centre of Bogotá, his colossal statue stood proud in a colonnaded temple, epically framed between two mountain peaks beyond. However, even revolution-aries need to be turned over around here on a regular basis. Plinth, temple and statue itself were all scribbled over with graf-fiti. Both of Bolívar's knees sported posters for a street-art outfit called Canibal Collectif. Remembering the collective apoplexy which accompanied the adornment of Churchill's statue in Parliament Square with a Mohican made of a bright-green piece of turf, lending the great leader a punkish air, it was hard not to offer up a silent cheer.

Amidst all the technicolour exuberance of the bank-holiday street craziness, there was no escape from a constant impression of political instability. The living statues had a very different tenor from the Disney creations of the West. They loomed like dark figures from a nightmare informed by civil violence. These street performers invoked police spattered in blood, soldiers with melted faces, uniforms with wolfish heads, teeth dripping gobbets of flesh. Bicycles wheeled up and down through the crowds, stopping every ten yards or so for people to observe what sat up six feet tall behind the rider. Tacked on to long poles were essays – not placards but essays – theoretical works about politics. People read them with a grave seriousness before falling into debate.

Politics shouts itself into life here on the streets, and interweaves closely with culture. A Chilean I met in Lima told me of his company's approach to political theatre. They boarded buses at opposite ends, shouted a greeting to each other, then across the length of the bus they started a political argument. As their debate got more heated, they walked towards each other. By the time they got to the middle, they were yelling. They then descended into a scrap, which on a given signal they broke and hugged each other. Public dialectics indeed. This was a politics born from hunger and pain, of course, and it would be a crime to senti-mentalise it. (I once saw Harold Pinter bearing down, arms outstretched, on a Chilean poet after he had given a public reading. The poet turned and fled, but Pinter was too fast for him, caught him, and then hugged him enthusiastically from behind. It wasn't a pretty picture.) Yet for all the dangers of romanticising, it was hard not to fall hook, line and sinker for the energy and the brio of this politics. The revolution starts where there is hunger, yes, but also where there is exuberance.

The Poll Tax Riot of 1989 was one of the most exhilarating afternoons of my life: the palpable sense of power being contested on the streets; the joy of hearing a voice long suppressed being allowed to roar; the reinvention of the physical space of a city by a group giving itself over to a form of judicious frenzy; and the knowledge that many things would change as a result. There was the adrenalin that pumped, indiscriminate and dangerous, but there was also the satisfying noise of a fabric that had been stretched too far and too tight finally tearing, and the release that went with that. When the Gentleman, an otherwise invisible character in Hamlet, bursts in to speak to Gertrude and Claudius with the news that Laertes has returned at the head of a popular revolt, the excitement that he feels pours out of him:

> Save yourself, my Lord.
> The ocean overpeering of his list
> Eats not the flats with more impiteous haste
> Than young Laertes in a riotous head
> O'er bears your officers; the rabble call him Lord
> And, as the world were now but to begin,
> Antiquity forgot, custom not known,
> The ratifiers and props of every word
> They cry 'Choose we, Laertes shall be King!' –
> Caps, Hands, and Tongues, applaud it to the clouds –
> 'Laertes shall be King! Laertes King!'

It's kind of him to say 'Save yourself' to the King, but you can't help feeling that his heart is much more strongly in sharing the excitement than in protecting his leader. It also seems joyously crass to go on shouting 'Laertes shall be King' in the face of the supposed King himself, but the excitement is undeniable. As always, with his deft draftsman's touch, Shakespeare catches the irresistible thrill of what the crowd feels, 'as the world were now about to begin'.

Sometimes when you see *Julius Caesar* staged, the assassination of Caesar is followed by a slow and pained regret. Nothing could be further from what Shakespeare wrote. He portrays a group of men intoxicated by the horrible pleasure of violence, who fall into a demented scream-around of 'Liberty, liberty . . .' They are sugar-rush children driven insensate by their group dynamic. Shakespeare knew, understood and relished the energy of a good riot. His London was full of them – the apprentice population had trouble distinguishing between what constituted a holiday and what a riot. One of his earliest plays, *Henry VI Part 2*, takes flight with the rebellion led by Jack Cade, a popular insurrection which almost destroys a king. Shakespeare captures sympathetically the savage wit of the crowd (its catchphrase: 'The first thing we do, let's kill all the lawyers' – a line which never tires), its giveaway charisma, and its profound and dangerous daftness.

It was hard for the company not to consider this as we passed through countries moulded and remoulded in riots, rebellions and revolutions, still boasting the iconography and bearing the scars of all their turbulence. Russell Brand's book *Revolution* was passed from hand to hand. Commentary on it varied from the offensive to the appreciative, but it was keeping the conversation lively. In many ways, of course, South America is now a beacon of prosperity, and an education to others in how to combine prosperity with a broadly spread social justice. John, ever the contrarian, read to us from a book called *What if Latin America Ruled the World?*, a fat economic and historical volume about how the South is going to lead the North into the twenty-second century. We were all loving it so passionately that we offered up cheers. But the history of violence and change was written into the walls, and it sharpened the cut of the political chat. Is *Hamlet* on the side of the revolutionaries, an emblem for the rage of all those who seek to overturn their present world and give birth to a new future? Or is Shakespeare framing a conservative play to criticise the overturning of the status quo?

The play sits within an uncertain political moment. Denmark is threatened from without – Fortinbras, a young prince of Norway, carrying an inherited resentment about an old land grab, has 'sharked up a list of lawless resolutes'. Not only is that line worthy of a Nobel Prize on its own, it conjures up a world nervously trying to accommodate a population of roaming, disaffiliated men of violence. The armaments factories of Denmark are working overtime to hammer out weapons, which never calms the air. Ghosts are walking the battlements, which doesn't encourage an easy night either. Other nations are starting to think of Denmark as the home of drunkards, and dismissing it 'with swinish phrase'. That comes from Hamlet, who may be biased, though even Claudius admits that other nations think 'our state to be disjoint and out of frame'. This tallies with Hamlet's 'the time is out of joint'. A whole country is being lied to over the succession, and Shakespeare posits that a state that sits on a lie never sits easy. When Laertes returns, enraged by his father Polonius's death, a tidal surge of revolutionary enthusiasm follows him into the palace. That Claudius deals with this problem is a tribute to his political skills, but it doesn't solve the problem.

There are also all the surveillance tropes within the play. Polonius instructs Reynaldo on how to draw out information disingenuously about Laertes' behaviour in Paris, he sets Ophelia to walk up and down within the castle as bait for Hamlet, and he is a great one for nipping behind an arras and doing some overhearing. There is a clear and chiming parallel with Elizabeth's spymaster, Sir Francis Walsingham. It is, however, so beaten to death as an interpretive tool that we shied away from it in our production. If every time you see a production it is packed with video cameras and listening devices and secret doors; if it feels like someone is relentlessly screaming, 'Look, parallels!

Parallels!', it sometimes seems the honourable path is in the opposite direction.

All such topics, including surveillance, were hot to touch for Shakespeare. His parents had seen three radical changes of religious thought within their lifetimes in England; the vulnerability of the state apparatus was revealed by the confusion before the accession of Queen Mary, and Elizabeth herself faced and faced down a number of potential revolutions. These were unquiet times, and sedition, both real and imaginary, bubbled away in every great house and on every street corner. It is hard for us to comprehend this sense of the permanent fragility of the state.

Amongst others, there was one tragi-comic attempt at a rebellion by the Earl of Essex, shortly before Hamlet was written. On the eve of the rebellion, Shakespeare's company had been requested to play *Richard II*, a play about the usurpation of a natural ruler. Forty shillings had secured their service. This commission reveals little more than the incompetence of the rebels. A beautiful, elegant drama garlanded with daisy chains of stunning but otiose poetry, little could be less fitted to prompt people to violence. A little crying, some soft thoughts about flower arranging maybe, but violence? No. Historians have marvelled that Shakespeare and his company were not punished for their two-degrees-of-separation involvement. It surprises me they weren't offered thanks. At an earlier moment of tension between them, Essex burst into Elizabeth's bedchamber when she was only partly dressed, before withdrawing out of a sense of decency. Not the actions of a self-respecting *caudillo*. All sorts of odd energies – gender, class, and history – collide in this moment. It would have been vivid in the minds of the audience when they witnessed Laertes charging into the private space of the King and the Queen.

Any illusions that merry England was a quiet and jolly place were to be shattered within a couple of years when the Gunpowder Plot was discovered. This was a potential terrorist attack on a scale never witnessed before in history, intended to take out the entire apparatus of government in one nihilistic swipe. It was the culmination of a long period of religious schism, and of social unrest. The state violence that was used to suppress dissent was always going to provoke some form of blowback. Elizabeth and James were lucky to dodge it, though James's son Charles and the nation later reaped the whirlwind.

So in its own moment, *Hamlet* would have gained from the heat of contemporary concerns. A young prince in a neighbouring land, bristling with intent, is agitating to gain the throne. James VI of Scotland can't have been far from anyone's mind as the most eligible solution to the problem of succession. The threat of invasion, the watching of the borders and the ceaseless creation of new weaponry would remind everyone of the persistence of the threat from Spain. The apparatus of state surveillance would bring to mind Walsingham and Cecil, and their creation of the manipulative psychologies of snooping. And the dangers of a coup would have brought to mind not only Essex, but the long succession of foiled plots against Elizabeth. Shakespeare, with his genius for knowing how close to hover his fingers over the heat of a contemporary flame, was working with his audience's all-too-real concerns.

★ ★ ★

It was the day before our performance in Kiev, and two days before the first elections in Ukraine held since the revolution begun in Maidan square. A British Council delegation arrived to take us on a tour of the city. We set off at a steady pace and were shown historic this and historic that, but we wanted to catch up on more recent history and smell a little of the residual cordite of revolution. We soon found ourselves by St Michael's Church, a grand Orthodox edifice, which served as a sanctuary during the revolution. The fleeing and the injured took refuge within its walls – the medieval habit of religious asylum persisting in the virtual age. More ahistorical still, the bells of this church served as the most immediate form of communication during the rebellion. Whenever the riot police or the army tried to move in, the bells would toll forth, and crowds would flock in from all corners of the city to put a human buffer between the forces of rebellion and the forces of repression. So alongside the modern tools of rioting – Facebook, texting and YouTube – the heavy clanging resonance of church bells was used to bring a crowd together.

Near the church was the first encampment we came across, this one detached from the main body two streets away. It was as if it had not been allowed to join the gang, or had upset the gang and been told to live elsewhere. Each of these encampments was a large higgledy tent, the size of a couple of rooms, secured straight into the tarmac of the road, surrounded by a small stockade, enclosed by more canvas or an improvised fence. Outside it was a small jar asking for offerings. A small birdcage had some thread-bare doves in it. A young man came out of the tent, opened the cage, and took one out for me to hold. The dove's wings were disabled, which seemed to reduce its resonance as the bird of peace. There was some quick commodification of peace and love going on here, but I put money in the jar.

We walked on and into Maidan square. We entered at about seven, as a hot sun was going down and the day's blanket of heat was starting to admit the night's first breezes. We looked out over a broad square, filled with a little city (or big village) of interlocked and interlaced encampments. Smoke rose from 10,000 tarry cigarettes, from every small stove, and from the mobile kitchen which sat proudly in the yard of each canvas home. Firewood was scrappily stacked here and there. Dismembered cars served for outdoor furniture. Radios blared out cheap music. Hooch permeated the atmosphere everywhere, a miasma of vodka fumes. Every dwelling sported its own outdoors scrapbook of the revolution, photos of dramatic moments laminated into importance — a blaze of fire, a charge of shielded police, a moment of defiance. Beside the photos, other memorabilia — old weapons, improvised mortar devices, unused Molotov cocktails — were laid out as if deserving a museum's respect. The revolution seemed to have been curated as quickly as it was made.

Our guide explained the politics to us quickly — the square was now a state within a state, responsible only to itself. Each unit was made up of around a hundred people, each hundred elected its own representative, and each representative sat on a General Council of Advisers, which together decided policy for the whole of the community. They policed themselves, fended for themselves entirely, and together safeguarded the spirit of the revolution. No single leader, thankfully, seemed to have emerged from this mulch yet. At that moment, as dusk settled, it seemed hopelessly beguiling, a smoky moment of anarcho-syndicalism bursting through the tarmac of an ex-Soviet state, canvas fragility encasing hope.

Beside the politics, the other strong element, although it seems effete to point it out, was the aesthetics. Different shades of olive and khaki-brown canvas overlapped each other, the colours of the forest challenging the grey of the cement. Overhanging the square was a block of offices, burnt out leaving a hollow shell, largely blackened and charred. Against this black, an artist had fired sacks of pink paint, which had hit the walls with a spreading splat, and left behind startled circles of pink. Small, fey and joyous exclamations beside such angry drama. Everywhere people had re-used their once protective gas masks to create sculptures. Mannequin figures topped with masks dangling their hosepipe elephant noses stood to attention and lolled on sofas. Elsewhere the masks hovered on poles above the encampments, like protective deities.

Yet the politics and the aesthetics were all silenced by the unimpeachable lines of photos of the faces of those who had died in the square. Plain faces whose image was captured before they got caught up in history, plain and human, firemen and teachers, students and cooks, all unsuspecting of martyrdom. There was very little to be said about such faces, and their loss.

A stadium stage sat in the middle of the square, where we had intended to perform a few scenes, but our British Council minders were wary of someone taking a potshot at us. This seemed far-fetched, nor did it show great faith in our ability to charm a crowd. We posed for a quick photo in the centre of the square, all dazed and flattened. Then Tom, our producer, and I had to nip off to do some press, and left the actors wandering. Some bought the 'Putin is a Cunt' badges which had quickly become bestsellers on the stalls. As I headed down into the metro, I saw how the barricades were made, the cobbles of the square having been torn up to build walls, and to use as missiles. In rehearsals with *Julius Caesar* back in London, it was clear how little the language and the technology of revolution had changed over the last 2,000 years – fire and cobbles.

The next morning started early at our venue – the Mystetskyi Arsenal. The arsenal was built by Peter the Great in the late eighteenth century, and someone had spent a large amount of money here, to turn it into Kiev's premier modern art gallery. Entrance was through a walled garden, and the outdoor terrace, all sculpted hedgerows and splashing fountains, would be the pride of Paris or Munich. Maidan square felt a long way away. The gallery was presenting an exhibition devoted to *Hamlet* and Shakespeare, to link with our visit. The work, largely conceptual, with much video and film, was fuelled by a palpable anger which made its Western equivalent look very pale. In a witty touch, across the middle of the gallery ran a scaled-down bright-red gas pipe. It ran across at just below head height, so everyone had to duck underneath it, a permanent reminder of the necessity to bow the head to Russia. And the reason why.

It became clear that amongst our hosts, and their mother hen who ran the gallery, there was a growing level of excitement. The *Hamlet* ticket had become a hot one, and there were queues of people outside using any trick possible to squeeze their way in. The audience arrived for the afternoon show, a young and game one, in dazzling couture. There was a relaxed feeling in the air, which felt wholly un-Slavic – the vivid colours seemed to have floated up the Dnieper from the Black Sea, the light style and the big open spaces down from the Baltic. We see the world in a simple West/East polarity, but Kiev seems to have a 360-degree perspective, having inherited its religious tradition from Constantinople below, and having traded and battled over the millennia with Scandinavia above. The matinee began, and though the audience were game and willing, it was an uphill task. The acoustics were in a land beyond the dreadful, and the layout, in a room bedevilled with monster pillars, had of necessity to be a compromise between traverse and front-on. By the end, the company had just about got the audience where they wanted them, attentive and receptive.

By early evening, the over-excitement we had discerned earlier amongst the gallery staff had given way to hysteria. Everyone had a spring in their step, and the British Council staff looked like they'd just won the lottery. We were aware that we were a hot ticket, but seemed to have graduated from that to the show that had to be seen. Rumours were flying around of who might be coming, and the rumours grew a little substance when a small cohort of sharp-suited men, with discreet listening devices in their ears, descended on the venue, closely followed by soldiers with sniffer dogs. We were asked to vacate the stage as it was searched for incendiary devices.

Within all this excitement, the staff of the gallery bubbled over with optimism. They talked of their feeling of freedom and of hope since the revolution. They acknowledged that all was not perfect, but for the first time in a long time they believed they were in control of their own destinies. They sensed natural justice in the air. And it did feel like that. That saturating hopelessness of the wholly corrupt state, the invisible but dense fog which weightens the movements of all within it, on this night, just before an election, with everyone turning out in a beautiful venue on a sunny evening, that hopelessness seemed imperceptibly to be lifting. It may have been destined to last no longer than that night, but that intoxicating expectation, that lift in the heel, that sense that anything can happen, felt a little like freedom.

The British Ambassador arrived, shrewd and charming, and dampened any expectations of who might come. 'They'll never show up. They never do. Not on the night before an election.' The garden outside the venue filled with the chicest crowd I had seen anywhere outside the Paris Opéra. And a lot sexier. I calculated that amongst a crowd of about 700, there must have been about 4,800 inches of heel. And about two miles of leg.

Then, despite the Ambassador's warnings, the big guests did arrive. The Mayor of Kiev, who was on his way out. The Minister of Culture, Yevhen Nyshchuk, a young man who looked like a Eurovision contestant but was one of the heroes of the Maidan. An actor by training and trade, he acted as a spokesperson during the rebellion, and as convener and compere for all the voices of revolt. The flashes popped merrily and then went wild as the purported next mayor of Kiev entered. This was the man mountain that is Vitali Klitschko, former heavyweight boxing champion and human totem pole at the heart of the revolution. He carried the sheen of the extremely well groomed and the very carefully held. Klitschko moved through the crowd trailed by cameras, with the steady confidence of the fighter on the way to the ring. Something in me suspected that he might be more intimidated by *Hamlet* than he was by Lennox Lewis.

Then the big prize arrived – Poroshenko, flanked by a swarming security detail and his family. He walked in with a becoming modesty and deference, but still . . . This was the President-elect, appearing in public on the eve of his election. At *Hamlet*! The Ukrainians found it hard to believe that all these figures were gathered in one place. We couldn't believe it. The Embassy and the British Council were about to spontaneously combust with delight. The brouhaha in the theatre was mental. Our cast came out to greet the audience before each show, and there was an insane scrum of actors, camera crews, politicians and hangers-on at the front of the stage. It looked worryingly as if the show might never begin. Politicians emerged from the scrum to make speeches, very long speeches. Their detail went for little, since it was swamped by the pandemic elation simply about being there. Then finally the show could begin.

Again, it was a trial to wrestle the audience into a state of attention. Secret-service men jumped up and down like jack-in-the-boxes, and the audience was too excited by the audience to focus on the show. To cap it all, they were attempting a live feed of the show to the rest of the Ukraine. To do this, they had picked a Keystone Cops gathering of student broadcasters, who spent most of the first half hour plugging and unplugging leads in the middle of the audience, berating their primary-school-age camera operators, and then descending into noisy conference. Happily, the show was rough theatre, built for the open air, and didn't stand on its dignity too tightly. The actors knew how to blend muscle and tenderness to quieten the audience down. The show, like all Globe shows, was one of connection, so line after line went straight into the eyes of the rows of politicians. Contact was soon made, and connections started to proliferate.

The ousting of one king, and his replacement by another. The poisoning of a king (those who remember Yushchenko's poisoned bright-orange demeanour before the last revolution couldn't miss that one). The chafing of a younger generation against the morality and strictures of an older one. The impatience of Laertes. Line after line pinged into the moment and came brightly alive: 'The time is out of joint' . . . 'Something is rotten in the state' . . . 'Take arms against a sea of troubles' . . . 'No king on earth is safe' . . . Many more lived a brief added life in the resonance of the moment.

Most of all, I was happy that this was a bright *Hamlet*, a renaissance *Hamlet*, a celebration of his energy. On this bright evening for this town, it would have been impertinent to come from western Europe and sulk and moan and pule in their general direction. To joy in this remarkable Prince, and in his desire to find a modern, and a new, in a world that stands stiffly and uncomprehendingly against it, felt right. It felt like a due tribute to the moment we were in. Much didn't land, much did, yet at the end, the audience erupted and cheered. They were cheering as much for who they were, and where they were, as they were for the show, but it was a treat for us to share. The President-elect and his family were beaming and full of compliments, the Ambassador cock-a-hoop, and the Culture Minister couldn't be shaken off, he was so merrily abuzz.

As everyone stood around glad-handing, the stage management and the company descended swiftly on the set, and within twenty minutes it had been dismantled and disappeared. The dignitaries departed, and we all retired to a bar to watch Real Madrid finish off their city rivals in the European Cup final. The matter of the day, of the two days, had been too rich to absorb at speed, so we went to a couple more bars, and washed such matter away with sausages and vodka, and reconciled all the unreconcilables with teasing and laughter.

Up at dawn to catch a taxi and fly away, I drove out as the sun rose over the forested hills and the broad Dnieper. The Ukrainians were waking to go to the polls and choose a future for themselves. They were a people without illusion, they knew that Poroshenko was much of the old and a little of the new, they knew that the tension with Russia would not resolve itself painlessly. But whether in the thickly charged air of Maidan square, or in the lightly scented fragrance of the garden outside Mystetskyi Arsenal, they seemed to know they had tasted a little of their own future, and were hungry for more.

★ ★ ★

Exuberance, exhilaration, grasping the future, street wit and the adrenalin of coordinated protest are all one thing, but revolution has many faces, and many of them are horrifying. In Addis Ababa, we visited the 'Red Terror' Martyr's Memorial Museum, a reminder of the decades of murderous butchery under Mengistu and his Derg regime. A chilling congregation of the detritus of terror – bones and skulls, torture instruments, and the scrips and scraps that the disappeared leave behind them. Mengistu, a figure of towering wrath and vengeance displaced Emperor Haile Selassie in 1974, and a couple of years later, by report, smothered him with a pillow as he slept. In an act of ill grace which confounds imagination, he had Selassie's body buried underneath his own toilet, so that every time he visited his latrine some spirit of vengeance would be appeased. He then announced that he was going to purge the country of the wrong elements, in a speech made outside the theatre we were playing in, and to reinforce his point held up bottles filled with human blood and hurled them to the ground. Long years of mayhem ensued.

Addis Ababa, in sympathy with all the curling a's within its name, has a bewildering street map, with hardly a straight line within it. The streets, roads and avenues are all curves, twists and circles, concentric and interlocking. Few have names. Roads double back on each other and twist into each other. My usual instinct for the logic of a city was confounded. As well as bewildering, the city looks broken, ground down by poverty and by the desperate attempts of Mengistu and others to force a pattern on it. Off its many highways, bashed and beaten street signs announce a dusty driveway to the 'Department of Nutritional Wellness', or the 'Institute of Community Technology', all the dilapidated evidence of the influence of old Russian money and a forlorn attempt at Sovietisation. The collectivisation of farming in Ethiopia had wrecked an ecosystem carefully constructed over millennia, leading to famine after famine. What had destroyed the countryside had also broken the city.

We were performing in the National Theatre of Ethiopia, a monstrosity of fascist architecture. Built by Selassie himself, it showed all the evidence of the baleful Mussolini influence. At the back of the huge auditorium, an enormous pod reared up from floor to high ceiling. In the centre of this rocket-like pod, a wide aperture opened out to the whole house. In it was a single grand chair. This was for the Emperor. Every element of the building, a roof of sudden slopes, violent metal streaks of lightning adorning the walls, the whole architectural shaping – all led the eye away from the stage and towards the central temple built for the Emperor. Selassie may have driven the Italian Fascists out, but he seems to have been unable to drive out their madness.

Outside the stage door, there was a broken-down yard, within it an empty swimming pool, and, as if someone had styled it, in the pool a dead dog. The dressing rooms were lit with harsh flat fluorescents, which exposed the detail in the decay. The toilets in front of house stank so strongly of piss it seemed to thicken the air. Even our company's evergreen resilience came under stress here. The crowd for the show was young, which was great, but the acoustics for the theatre were beyond terrible, and very quickly the company were playing to a tight caucus of people who could hear at the front, and a swelling crowd of people on their mobile phones behind. Cats wandered through the rows of seats. At the end of most rows were small plastic bins, which the cats turned over and then clawed their way through whatever spilled. It was a tyrant's dream transformed into a rubbish bin.

In a tour of bizarre moments, and within a place that was provoking much thought about revolutions, an odd arrival for the show surprised. Before the audience had been shown in, and as we were doing our cue-to-cue rehearsal, an elderly white gentleman dressed in a three-piece suit, together with his elegantly attired extended family, was shown in. They looked like refugees from an Evelyn Waugh novel. The elderly man was Richard Pankhurst, the surviving son of Sylvia Pankhurst, the suffragette of suffragettes. Having opposed the Italian occupation of Abyssinia in the thirties, Pankhurst had continued to campaign for the country through the forties and fifties, and had become a friend to Selassie. In 1956, at his invitation, she moved there with Richard to found a journal. She stayed, and at her death in 1960 received a full state funeral. She is buried alongside the soldiers who fought for liberation from the Italians, the only foreigner in the Holy Trinity Cathedral of Addis Ababa. An exemplary life. The family that remained were courteous, displaying language and manners which seemed to spill out of an Edwardian drawing room.

That night we sat in a hotel and talked about revolution and riot. There was the visit to Maidan, and the sense of a country on the move in the Ukraine. The company had already encountered the residue of civil unrest across the countries of North Africa they had visited, Tunisia, Algeria and Egypt all still locked in the tensions, and showing some of the wounds, of the Arab Spring. There had been rioting during their visit to Caracas, as anti-Chavez factions tried to stir up as much chaos as possible, before blaming it all on pro-Chavez activists. This was still relatively early in the tour, and they had much trouble ahead of them. The Maldives government tottered shortly before they arrived; riots kicked off in Tajikistan as they were flying there; Nauru erupted into violence; and it briefly looked as though we would have to cancel our trip to Bahrain because of disturbances. They came to Hong Kong shortly after the Occupy Movement had finished its peaceful pro-democracy demonstrations, all finding a unity behind the gentle symbol of a yellow umbrella. Jen's family were engaged with the upholding of democracy and the constitution in Hong

Kong, so the company were inundated with stories of how that movement ignited fresh hope.

So many different revolutions: peaceful ones, bloody ones; ruling classes manoeuvring around each other, underclasses unable to hold the lid on rage any longer; different peoples fighting for tribal supremacy, indoctrinated folk fighting for ideas and ideals; nihilists desperate to spread the emptiness in themselves, zealots desperate to reshape the world's variety into uniformity; saints fighting for peace and for others, devils fighting for the love of violence and for themselves; the many fighting for the freedom of all: the few fighting for the bondage of the many; and somehow, somehow, against all logic, the few always seeming to win. So many revolutions.

Hamlet fitted in everywhere, Hamlet the icon of restlessness for a world that never seems able to settle. Hamlet who is restless for truth, unable to bear the lie his present moment is built on; who is restless for civility, trying to forge a new care in human engagement; who is restless for honesty and integrity and cannot bear people faking or borrowing their feelings; who is restless for calm when the moment seems a little too noisy, and restless for noise when it seems too calm. In a world that cannot settle, and never has, and most probably never will, what better hero than a hero of restlessness, what better reflection of the world back to itself?

Two notable delusions probably shaped the beginning of the tour. The first that *Hamlet* is a journey towards peace, that there is a light at the end of the tunnel, and that when he says, 'the readiness is all . . . Let be', that he has achieved some sort of nirvana that he was searching for. But Shakespeare was an artist, and artists don't write journeys; they write truth. Yes, he has found that perspective, but he still has to try to place that perspective in the messy world, and in his own messy humanity. Shortly before saying 'readiness is all', he leaves Ophelia's funeral scene with a curse from the bowels of the underclass, which is just as profound and just as true to his own spirit:

> Let Hercules himself do what he may,
> The cat will mew and dog will have his day.

The second delusion, and an embarrassingly huge one, was that touring *Hamlet* would have some sort of benevolent effect, spread a little world peace, nation talking to nation, etc. Unforgivably grandiose, but true. Shame on us for our stupidity, but you need a small helping of stupidity to launch anything of this size. A few months in, it started to become clear that we were not only failing to spontaneously solve all the problems of the world, but that everywhere we went, social and political problems seemed to get worse and more acute. For a while, on top of the embarrassment at the earlier delusion, this caused a little shame. The curse of *Hamlet*, we started to call it. But perspective shifted, as it tends to with theatre and with life, and all of the unrest and unease started to seem less like a bane, and more like a discreet virtue. *Hamlet* was not put into the world to settle it into a somatic calm. He was given to us by Shakespeare to engineer a little change. To remind us to stay restless, and to keep pushing forward towards the something or other ahead of us. To keep making all sorts of trouble for an all sorts of world.

★ ★ ★

Georgia in the old Soviet Union can seem the most televisually memorialised country on earth. Whether this is a hangover from

Soviet surveillance, or simply a desire to proliferate news channels, is moot. At our performance, which closed one of their several theatre festivals, there were five crews interviewing people at the interval, and ten at the end when the show folded into a party. The venue we had performed in was an old helicopter hangar converted with all sorts of urban driftwood and an anarchist sensibility into a chaotic but energised space. It was very Tbilisi, a madcap conjunction of scraps, wit and art that together made something beautiful.

As the show stopped, a heavy-metal band struck up instantaneously, and as I left, the company were all raving away to a blend of thrash metal and psychedelic jazz flute. Beruce, who had snapped his ankle recently in Hong Kong, was waving crutches wildly in the air; Amanda was dancing tall as usual and attracting a circle of devotees around her shifting totem pole. We were joined at the party by the Schaubühne theatre company from Berlin. They were uneasy. Major European theatre stars, their style, led by their theatre-god director Thomas Ostermeier, is a sort of held-back Californian/Teutonic cool, with complex signifiers of status being stitched into every movement. They were taken aback by the guileless innocence of our company, who wandered around being sweetly open with everyone. And more than a little put out that the Georgians didn't appear to want to play cool-status three-dimensional Connect 4 with them, and had just decided to have fun with our lot. They tried to adjust but awkwardly.

Earlier that evening, I had been drawn in to the most infantile directorial cock-off with Ostermeier. The organiser of the festival, Ekaterina, a local powerhouse and old friend, had brought us together in a cafe, and she and a friend sat and observed the silliness of two directors making fools of themselves. After spending a short time telling me about British politics, Ostermeier started to list the number of Shakespeare shows he had directed. I countered. I talked a little of the Globe, and of the new theatre we had built. He told me he had built a Globe and showed me a picture. My face wrinkled into a 'not great is it?' expression. He told me how long his *Hamlet* had been playing. I conceded, then told him how far and wide mine had gone. He looked a bit puce. He offered up, rather feebly, 'Mine went to Ramallah.' 'Mmm . . . mine is going to Ramallah, and several refugee camps.' This was becoming one of the least edifying encounters of the whole experience. 'Are you going to come and see my *Hamlet* then?' he asked rather desperately. 'Might do, might not,' I said, starting to giggle, because the sheer childishness of this was becoming a pleasure in itself. Eka and her friend started giggling as well. So Ostermeier, who does not seem to see many jokes anywhere, got out his calendar and started listing all the dates it was on in the near future. 'Nope,' I said and then, 'Sorry, busy' and then, 'No can do.' For many, especially those who hang out on theatre comment threads, this man is a living deity, and I a gross vulgarian, so the nature of the encounter gave me a guilty pleasure.

Ekaterina was one of the main reasons I had come to Georgia. She hosted me in 2011, and organised the trip her company, the Marjanishvili, made to our festival in 2012. I have strong feelings for country and city, having spent a month in Tbilisi in 1990, at a time of extreme turbulence. The Georgians had just fought for and attained freedom from the Soviet Union, and were tearing themselves apart in the struggle for post-independence supremacy. Diners were kidnapped from restaurants as we sat there, bombs blew out windows one block behind us and we walked on, murderous single gunshots punctuated the night and we slept on. I befriended a wonderfully blasé CIA man, who sat in one of the few cafes around back then, wearing a cowboy hat and a mammoth belt buckle, and when asked what he was doing said 'Import export' with a heavy wink. He was shot dead a couple of years later at a Caucasian border. All the while the Russian tanks gathered on the edge of town. Revolution is one thing, putting together something stable in its place is a different and harder job. Somehow, through some visionary leadership, and through the steadiness and imagination of its people, the Georgians secured their future. My feelings for the country were great, for Eka stronger, and now that I saw her, her head elegantly swathed in a turban, hiding the hair lost to chemotherapy, and heard how tough it had been to organise her festival, my admiration grew.

Theatre politics in Tbilisi is as riven as all its politics – festivals and companies vie with each other, and several of them were still in the rigor mortis grip of those who thrived in the old regime. Eka was of the new generation, and in some ways it seemed like old Cold War battles were still raging here. We talked of my 1990 memories, and she told me of the recent war with Russia, reminding me of the difficulty of imagining alien tanks bearing down on your own city. She railed against the theatre veterans who hated anything new and still craved the old days: 'They eat us. They eat us alive with their disappointment. All of their, "we used to do this thirty years ago and it was a big success", and their, "oh how they cried twenty years ago" . . . They eat us alive with their memories and with the past. They want to suck us back into history. They are a tumour which grows within us taking away the future.' All this from a young woman whose turban had been swept off to reveal stubbly white hair. 'I cannot remember a single one of my shows. I move on. The future is everything.'

'But look around you,' I said to try to cheer her, waving rather hopelessly at a swish hotel foyer, filled with swanky new Western shops. 'All the money that has come in, all the investment, how different everything is from twenty-five years ago . . .'

'Maybe the future is more worrying,' she smiled. 'Change and revolution takes time and care.'

I rebuked her gently for not having told us earlier about her illness, and told her how much we thought of her. I asked her how the illness had affected her, and her earlier gloom lifted off and away: 'I feel more clean, more clear, and a thousand useless worries have flown off the top of my head. I have cleared out love. Everything. Now I want to live in a country house with a garden and with many children. It doesn't matter who the father is. It is stupid and optimistic, but that is all I want now. Children running around in roses.'

There are many different kinds of revolution. As many as there are people.

13

FIGHTING FOR EGGSHELLS
AND REVENGE

Enter FORTINBRAS, a Captain, and Soldiers, marching.

PRINCE FORTINBRAS Go, captain, from me greet the
  Danish king.
Tell him that Fortinbras nephew to old Norway,
Craves a free pass and conduct over his land,
According to the Articles agreed on.
If that his majesty would aught with us,
We shall express our duty in his eye;
And let him know so.
CAPTAIN I will do't, my lord.
PRINCE FORTINBRAS Go softly on.

Act 4, Scene 4

THE APPEARANCE OF FORTINBRAS COMES almost as a complete
surprise. The story is set up at the beginning of the play, there
is a brief continuation of it with Voltimand's embassy to the
young prince's uncle, but amidst the other dramas, it falls out

of sight. As with many of Shakespeare's tragedies, as the play progresses the focus gets tighter: the wide open landscape of the early acts pulls in to the castle, then from its large state rooms to its bedrooms, and then tighter still to its corridors, staircases and cellars. The initial sea-blasted expanse gives way to something close, sticky and claustrophobic. We have burrowed into the dark heart of Elsinore's power, and the family's dysfunction.

Then the sky clears, and a host of marching soldiers appear on the stage, led by a new character. It is a major switch of focus, a blast of Nordic air blown into a fetid stable. This is Fortinbras leading his army on an expedition against the Polack. We remember hearing something about this earlier, and parking it somewhere, but are still playing catch-up as the scene moves swiftly along. Our immediate impression of Fortinbras is favourable: he plays according to the rules and is respectful to the Danish King. There is something about 'Go softly on' that, though it can be played sinister (and Lord knows people have tried), smacks of a gentle authority. Our impression of Fortinbras remains immediate because he is off almost before he has started talking. Unlike his distorted doppelgänger Hamlet, he is clearly not given to hanging around and pondering. Hamlet, having glimpsed him, calls him a 'delicate and tender prince', and though directors are always looking for ways to distort Hamlet's tone, by and large he is a trustworthy witness.

The scene that follows between Hamlet and the Captain is a miracle of compression, and another example of Shakespeare's draftsmanship. With a few brief overheard lines, he gives us a character we can believe in, and creates a situation that is both familiar and surprising.

Enter HAMLET, ROSENCRANTZ, GUILDENSTERN,
and others.

HAMLET Good sir, whose powers are these?
CAPTAIN They are of Norway, sir.
HAMLET How purposed, sir, I pray you?
CAPTAIN Against some part of Poland.
HAMLET Who commands them, sir?
CAPTAIN The nephew to old Norway, Fortinbras.
HAMLET Goes it against the main of Poland, sir,
Or for some frontier?
CAPTAIN Truly to speak, and with no addition,
We go to gain a little patch of ground
That hath in it no profit but the name.
To pay five ducats, five, I would not farm it.
HAMLET Why, then the Polack never will defend it.
CAPTAIN Yes, it is already garrisoned.
HAMLET I humbly thank you, sir.
CAPTAIN God be wi' you, sir.

It is fine craft, hearing both the right words and the right
silences, leaving the appropriate space for characters to work
each other out, and leaving whatever needs to be silent unsaid.
Each 'sir' is placed and distinct, showing deference from above
or below. The comma after 'Yes', before 'it is already garrisoned'
is delicious, leaving the briefest amount of air for irony.
Somehow, and the art within it is unfathomable, he summons
up the army beyond, and the landscape around. We struggled
a little in our tight production to achieve a host of soldiers
marching – the resources were beyond us – and our compensation with singing an old military song and wandering around

didn't always pass muster. The scene with the Captain was, however, a joy to play.

A strong solid man, who knows and is at ease with himself, terse almost to the point of impertinence, he shows little deference. It is the soldier's withheld and subversive economy of language. In answer to Hamlet's callow question about military purpose, the response is brutally plain:

> CAPTAIN Truly to speak, and with no addition,
> We go to gain a little patch of ground
> That hath in it no profit but the name.

This elliptical encounter sums up the enduring daftness of war: young men dressing up in meaningless uniforms in their thousands and crossing continents to kill each other, all for nondescript parcels of land.

At this moment when you would expect Hamlet to pivot one way, he flips the other. Having seen his insight and his thoughtfulness, we expect him to see through the absurdity of this endeavour and to lacerate it, which he does:

> I see
> The imminent death of twenty thousand men,
> That, for a fantasy and trick of fame,
> Go to their graves like beds, fight for a plot
> Whereon the numbers cannot try the cause,
> Which is not tomb enough and continent
> To hide the slain?

But instead of thus condemning it, he surprises and confounds us, by drawing the opposite conclusion. This he sees in his present state of mind as proof of the highest nature of human endeavour, where men fight, not for a worthy cause, but for nothing, 'for an egg-shell'. 'Rightly to be great,' he says 'is greatly to find quarrel in a straw.' Nooooooo, we cry out in our hearts and heads, but Hamlet is not there to be the person we want him to be or to mollify our contemporary concerns; he is there to be Hamlet. There is a rush of blood that rushes through him rather like that which Tolstoy describes coursing through the young Nikolai Rostov at the sight of the Prince of Russia inspecting his troops.

Soldiers criss-crossing northern Europe felt poignant and perti-nent as we made our way around the globe. Just before our tour began, Russia annexed the Crimea. They began with biker-gang diplomacy, sending in Putin's thugs to stake a claim, then shipped in military without insignia to seize the nodal points of power, then finished with smoothy-chops lawyers organising a referendum and strenuously arguing the legality of the whole thing. Simultaneously, in concert with separatists from eastern Ukraine, they began a low-level civil war in an area around Donetsk, and fed the fire with armaments and soldiers. A couple of months after the tour had begun, a civilian plane was downed by a rocket, fired from the area of fighting, which practically had a sign on it saying 'Made In Russia'. The Russians denied this had anything to do with them. Tensions ran nerve-shreddingly high between Russia and the Ukraine, and beyond that Russia and the rest of the world. All this as we steered our way through Russia, the Baltic countries who were now feeling freshly threatened, and Ukraine itself. These eggshells may have been fragile, but they were still endlessly attractive to men who wanted to stomp on them.

We had dealt extensively with Russia over the last few years with a variety of shows. They were charming and have a theatre culture which is the envy of the world. They also have their own way of doing things. In setting up our tour, we had originally planned to play *Hamlet* in St Petersburg. However, our regular promoter wanted us to come to Moscow. He was adamant when I was there on some other business. 'Come to Moscow with *Hamlet*,' he said. 'No thank you, we're going to Petersburg,' I replied. 'Come to Moscow,' he said. 'Erm, no thank you, we've already arranged to go to . . .' 'Come to Moscow,' he said. 'Well, very sorry, but we can't.' Two days after I returned to London, the St Petersburg theatre rang and said nervously, 'We're so sorry, but you can't come any longer.' Twenty minutes later, our regular promoter rang: 'Come to Moscow.' We had a problem getting in to Belarus. We had a long-standing relationship with the Belarus Free Theatre, a company working in exile from one of eastern Europe's last old-fashioned dictatorships, and had supported their frequent attempts to throw a light on the tyranny and repression within the country they could not return to. Because of this, the Belarus government were refusing us entry to their country. We rang our friends in Russia and explained our problem. A day later, the National Theatre of Belarus was on offer to us. We felt compromised by all this, but we had to get our tour done, and every country is every country.

In the middle of all the mayhem with Ukraine, and shortly after the downing of Malaysian Flight 17, I flew in to Moscow. Dropping in to Domodedovo airport, you are surrounded by forests of silver birches. They look like long thin arms stretching up, branch and twig hands splayed out at the top as if pleading to be let free from the prison of the earth. It did not take long for the conversation to turn to the Ukraine, our old friend Irina being pre-emptive with the justifications. 'The USA can do what it wants, they can conquer Iraq and Afghanistan and Libya and now Syria, but Russia, no, Russia can do nothing . . .' I tried a little of the two-wrongs-don't-make-a-right line, but it felt exceptionally feeble. A lot of the people we know and whose judgement we trust were swept up in a semi-judicious, semi-hysterical nationalism. People who would have cared nothing for Donetsk, who would not have farmed it for five ducats, were now staking their dignity on the fate of this small patch of land.

At the interval of the show, I was summoned into a little room. There were layers of men with bulging jackets and self-important earpieces to get through before I got to the inner sanctum. There was a palpable sense of threat. The man who is No. 3 in the Russian hierarchy was there, and I was being granted an audience. It was a lively little group, but the man of power was instantly recognisable – thin, seated and leaning back out of the circle. He was silent and playing a deliberate lack of engagement. Putin-Lite basically. It was a hackneyed status play – I'm too powerful and cool to contribute. The whole non-engagement culture started in California (the central dumbness of it brilliantly eviscerated by Nik Cohn in *Awopbopaloobop Alopbamboom*) and has now spread across the world like an infection. Cool plague. Most of the world has grown out if it, but like a country that is still playing records which went out of fashion years ago, it was still au fait in Russia. They clearly run workshops in how to be Steve McQueen in the FSB.

He was surrounded by sweet women who wanted to talk, and charming men, but he clearly felt that contributing would lessen his authority. I was having none of it. 'You don't say much, do you?' I asked him directly. No one translated. 'What do you think of Shakespeare then?' Someone did translate. Once he had got over his affront at being asked a direct question, he offered a few words of rather hackneyed wisdom about the

Bard, as if they were crystal drops from the Lake of Clever. 'OK, now I see why you don't say much,' I returned. The atmosphere started to get a bit sticky. I burnt some brandies quickly down my throat, then burbled some stuff to the charming others, before they returned to the theatre. During the second half, I went for a swim at our hotel, where I was surrounded by huge sullen lumps of Slavic muscle, several garlanded with gangster tattoos, all deliberately radiating a contained violence as a badge of honour. The No. 3 man thought he was doing it with style, the thugs in the pool couldn't care, but they all looked as stupid as each other. All followed a redundant and out-of-time masculinity, hopelessly clinging to a defunct old archetype in a world that fundamentally found them funny. Yet they were prepared to kill people in their effort not to see the joke.

The covert and not-so-covert war raged on within eastern Ukraine as we worked our way out of Russia, through Belarus and towards Kiev. We were walking through diplomatic minefields here; they were still picking up bodies and bits of aircraft from the fields around Donetsk; young men were still being sent in in convoys from Russia while they disclaimed any involvement. The Crimea, the scene of so many young men fighting for eggshells over the centuries – brilliant and brave and plumed young Englishmen hurtling into certain disaster in the Charge of the Light Brigade amongst many other flourishes of gallant stupidity – had now been taken over. But the Ukrainians were determined to stop any further loss of territory. Face was lost in the Crimea, and, for young men who treasured their honour above all else, face had to be regained.

In Kiev, on the morning of our performance, smart media girls clickety-clacked in high heels and marshalled us into a press conference, where we spouted platitudes about Shakespeare and fielded tough questions about politics. Russia, Belarus and now Ukraine, all distinct, all troubled, all eager for *Hamlet* in different ways, all had wanted something different from it, and all had wanted us to state a different allegiance. But our allegiance was to the play, and to the infinitely obscure and obscurely infinite good within it. The election the next day was focusing minds sharply, and they wanted to talk of little else. They asked a series of questions begging the single answer, 'Putin is a shit', but we steadfastly refused to fall into their not-very-discreet trap.

After the press conference, and once the matinee show was settled, I decided to dip back to Maidan square, which had enchanted us the previous day. The descending twilight the night before had bestowed a magic on the tented city, but the harsh mid-afternoon sun was less kind. I wandered round the square and the satellite streets, all enclosed by battered barricades. The population of the square started to look monolithically similar – angry, bored, disaffected young men. They sat withering in the sun, or hid angrily inside their tents, the road heat melting their joy and their will. This was not the Occupy Movement, with its rainbow diversity and its fundamental niceness; this was much closer to a bunch of sullen skinheads in paramilitary gear, who looked like they'd been drinking homemade vodka 24/7 for four months. Their eyes were bleary, their skin shot, their will sagging as they flopped carelessly on deckchairs and rugs.

This was not true of all – one family in traditional costume bashed out folk songs to try to entice people into their trestle-table improvised restaurant; another enclosure seemed to be offering advice and counselling – but it did seem to be the majority. Other details jarred and disturbed – a boy who looked fifteen wandered around glowering with a Kalashnikov, beside a group of older paramilitaries quaffing lagers. The violence in the air which had a sort of hope in it the night before now looked just threatening, a group of people who were trying, as has happened through history, to use violence to elect themselves as king-makers, to be the Praetorian Guard.

But more than anything the impression was of weariness, of a midsummer heat-soaked lassitude. This didn't look like a revolution waiting to happen; it looked like one waiting to stop. It didn't look like a fire waiting to blaze, but one which had blazed gloriously and now didn't know how to put itself out. An energy that was pure in late winter had now given way, sozzled in booze, to a late-summer heat-haze confusion. I suppose the hardest thing with any revolution is to know how to end it.

The Russians called these Ukrainians 'fascists' and 'nationalists', but more than anything they just looked angry and left behind. Soon after our visit to the country, once Poroshenko was duly elected and the new political class established, they had to work out what to do with the energy of this revolution, and with this body of people, newly enfranchised and still smouldering with purpose. What did they do? What they always do with young men: they sent them off after a small patch of ground. To free up the square, to sort a social problem, and to export a potential danger to the city, most of the remaining members of the Maidan square were fired up about all the evils being perpetrated by the wicked Russians in the east, and formed the vanguard of the forces tasked to reclaim Donetsk. They were sent off to make mayhem out there, and they:

> . . . for a fantasy and trick of fame,
> Go to their graves like beds, fight for a plot
> Whereon the numbers cannot try the cause,

Which is not tomb enough and continent
To hide the slain . . .

It would be an over-simplification to say that all the mayhem we encountered was purely old men exploiting the appetite of young men for the 'bubble reputation'. Many were fighting from a passionate religious conviction, from a desire to see land freed, for a powerful idea, to avenge a wrong done to their own family or people, many; but yet more *were* being steered into it by cynical old men who could see a way of profiting from the resultant mayhem. Generation after generation give themselves over to the hopeless vanity of it. The styling may have changed from medieval plumes and extravagant nineteenth-century uniforms – it may be more beach-boy psycho now – but it is still vanity. All over the globe, as we were attempting to arrange our schedule, we had to keep a weather eye on the world map of confusion, and keep our ear to the ground to guess when and where the next eruption of chaos was coming from.

Russia and Ukraine were discreetly carrying on their running war; Tunisia was nearly overrun by jihadism after we'd left; before we arrived in Pakistan, a suicide bomber from their Taliban killed sixty-five in a park, including many children; Paris and Belgium were both scarred by the sort of violence which remaps a city for ever in the heads of its inhabitants; there were attacks in Burkina Faso and Mali to precede our coming, in Mali in the hotel we were due to stay in; there was an escalation of terror in Bangladesh around our dates; the Peshmerga's counter-offensive against IS began just four days before we got to Erbil; when we started we were hoping to visit Libya with the British Council, then it got progressively worse and became impossible to enter; Saudi went to war against the Houthis as we confirmed; and just for good measure, in Afghanistan the Taliban bunged a couple of mortars at the US Embassy the evening of our arrival. In Africa, we drove past pick-up tricks filled with young soldiers buoyantly bouncing across crumbling roads, guns lazing on their laps, heading off for 'small patches of ground', soldiers who will leave you with a cheerful 'God be wi'you, sir' as they head off into the depths of chaos. In Jordan, we stopped and a personnel carrier filled with young soldiers on the way to its border with Syria pulled up alongside. They were silent, and stared quietly into the distance.

The Earl of Essex was the star military adventurer of Shakespeare's time, the Flashheart of his day. He seems to have been a wilfully anachronistic throwback, strange even in his own time. He seems, though how much credit he is due is moot, to have launched a successful invasion of an undefended Cadiz, to have chased a few Spanish galleons around the Atlantic in a suitably piratical manner, to have invaded one of the Canary Islands, again undefended, and to have hung around some of the larger actions, led by the rather more authentic warrior Walter Raleigh. No matter, his PR machine was effective, his costumes from the many, many portraits of him extant look terrific (it's amazing he had time for anything beyond modelling), and he knew how to carry himself well. Not only did he get the job to lead a major expedition to quash the nascent Irish rebellion in 1599, he got the most lavish encomia of praise ever ladled over an outgoing hero since Roman times, Shakespeare not least amongst them, who predicts his return as a 'conquering Caesar' in one of the choruses of *Henry V*.

On departure, he looked the exemplar of a delicate and tender prince, off to find honour greatly in a quarrel over a straw. But the Irish expedition ended up as a comical and squalid disappointment. Sent to destroy the rebel Tyrone, the English marched hither and thither, but the Irishman was far too canny to meet them in open battle. A whole class of overpreened aristocrats, tricked out like a pageant from a medieval tapestry, lost their way charging dumb and vainglorious English energy into Irish guile and mud. Essex tried manically to maintain an atmosphere of glamour by knighting everyone in sight, but it was not enough to instil purpose. Finally, they concluded a clumsy peace, favourable to the Irish, and with tails between legs, and plumes rather droopy, made their way home.

In some ways this was the last hurrah for a whole way of being; it was, as James Shapiro has beautifully described in *1599*, the death of chivalry. Shakespeare, his antennae as ever attuned to surfaces and subtexts, was registering the movement of tectonic plates grinding inexorably against each other below the surface. *Hamlet* is born at the moment that one world was giving way to another. As the play was forming in Shakespeare's mind, in the Founder's Hall in London a group of merchants were coming together to form the East India Company. They refused to engage any knight adventurers in their first expeditions. This was a new class, the merchant, with new ambitions, and a different way of going about them. *Hamlet* was born as chivalry was flailing its last histrionic limbs (the Ghost is in many ways the emblem and the echo of that chivalry) before giving way to a new world of trade and globalisation. The next time the English went back to Ireland, they did not go to put on a glorious show; they went to kill. *Hamlet* sits in the intersection of these two moments, as a deep and quiet revolution churned beneath the earth.

It often seems that some illusory glamour and chivalry has returned to murderous warfare in the age of the fractured nation state, or the even smaller polity. This may be one of the reasons why Shakespeare has seemed so *newly* fresh over the last twenty years. The separatists in eastern Ukraine, with the assistance of a churning media machine, love a bit of the self-mythification these small dirty wars allow. With the return of warlords in the factional fighting in Central Africa, in the Balkans where football hooligans like Arkan restyled themselves as Chief Psychopaths, in Afghanistan, or now in the swirls of influence within Syria, you can see in the way that armies dress, and memorialise themselves in selfies and social-media profiles, the return of the desperate styling in death that was part of the chivalric code. It was flattened out of existence in the age of the Cold War and the faceless modern mega-army, but now it has returned with a flourish. IS are the masters of self-styling as glamorous warriors, lolling in their jeeps, kaffiyehs draped across them, and great sweeping horizons behind. All memory of their previous life sniffing glue in Cardiff bus stops, or stealing from grannies in Le Havre, is left behind them. It is a horrible con of both the world and themselves. They are trying to paint a picture of freely impelled individuals following the passion of their hearts. When in fact they are as closely controlled as any army, Saddam's old Republican Guard thugs transferring the expertise they gathered running a terror state in Iraq into a different arena.

Essex's foolhardy romance of warfare, and the murderousness of the realpolitik which took the tide against him, both hover in the background of the play. Fortinbras is an enclosed, mysterious figure, praised by Hamlet. We see his short walk-through in the section above, then he appears briefly at the end and does a capable job of tidying up a horrible mess. In that brief scene they share, we see a shift in Hamlet and a new understanding of how romance and realpolitik walk together. We see a man who realises that all forms of human achievement are chasing feathers in the wind, but accepts that that is what humanity does and is – an animal chasing feathers in the wind. Hamlet now knows that the world is a vain fiction, and that action is a sort of tricked-out nothing, and since it is so, his failure to do anything thus far bothers him no longer. Now, to our disappointment, since he has seen through the trick of it, he can do it. Now, to our sadness, he is ready to join in the game. And ready to complete his mission of revenge.

★ ★ ★

Revenge has sat alongside the play like an unwelcome and heavy guest for 400 years. There is no argument that the revenge play was a form, and that Shakespeare was writing within that form and in response to that form. Revenge plays were great box office. The clearly identified superobjective for the leading character and many of the subsidiary ones served as a strong thread to pull a play together. The promised bloodbath at the end kept the audience standing, or sitting on rough benches, eagerly looking forward to the inevitable pile-up of corpses.

The previous *Hamlet* play, which played with some success to Elizabethan audiences before Shakespeare set to improving it, seems to have leant heavily on its revenge theme. From the little we can guess at of this play, whose text has been buried by posterity, and from our knowledge of other contemporary revenge dramas, they seem to have leant heavily on extreme emotional states, highly burnished charnel-house language, plenty of plotting, and no shortage of hysterical cackling as characters left the stage.

This is the form that Shakespeare was simultaneously working within and running away from. I had always been inclined, when approaching the play, to join him in running away from it. Shakespeare exploded the form, not because he sat at home studying a whole collection of them, carefully working out how to deconstruct and reconstruct the genre's genetic code, but simply because he took one look at the story and fancied a bit of that. He saw in the format a good portmanteau to carry his own baggage – stuff about fathers and sons, about clashing sensibilities, about identity and madness, about life's purpose or lack of it, about the theatre and its uses and abuses, about love and its disappointments. He spotted a loose format which he knew could provoke in himself the swirl of the best creation. The place where life and art can meet and dance in patterns which seem natural and true.

Some structures can spark great writing and deliver lethal stories, but the architecture of their narratives are too linear and too strict to allow the ultimate freedoms. *Romeo and Juliet, Julius Caesar, The Comedy of Errors* are all in different ways great, but you always know where you are within the story. You land in a town and you know the layout and the grid. That can be and is reassuring. But there are other structures, where a seemingly lucid and clear beginning carries on to a certain point and then gives way to something stranger and more dreamlike. You lose your way, and happily; *A Midsummer Night's Dream, King Lear, Love's Labour's Lost, The Tempest* and *Hamlet* all share this quality. With *A Midsummer Night's Dream*, it is often hard to remember even in the middle of deep acquaintance which scene follows which; something of the forest's bewitching miasma becomes general. In *Lear*, the scenes on the heath and within the King's slipped wits are meant to bamboozle, and they succeed. *Love's Labour's Lost* is just delightfully silly. A similar deliberate swirling aimlessness takes over in the middle of *Hamlet*, the long section where we circle round the endless corridors of the castle. A play which begins so full of purpose – 'Revenge!', 'Yes, I will!' – slips out of its own straight lines and gets excitingly loopy. Language and character, feeling and thought, trump plot or structure, and we all float together on strange seas.

Some have seen this as the deliberate pouring of fresh stuff into the revenge mould; I think Shakespeare just saw a well-sprung diving board, which he could bounce on a few times and then float somewhere dynamically other. Within that freedom, the moral issues around revenge or no revenge diminish in importance, and the play becomes about something more mysterious and more important than a Brechtian parable on ethical choice. Up to a point, probably up to the beginning of Act 2, there is an infrastructure, but then it melts away. To see what follows as a collection of deliberate intentions and formal games is to diminish what Shakespeare is doing.

We are not watching an intellectual construct, we are watching a light, the light of a young life, and a very bright one. We watch that bright light flicker, and then fade, and then die. Having now witnessed it with captivated audiences all over the world, many of whom did not understand a single one of the words, that is what keeps people drawn in. Not the choices about revenge. It is great when we get to the last act, and we know there is going to be some tying up of loose ends and a little meting out of justice. It's a reliable moment to observe the quickening of interest in the room as the audience smells first danger, then fighting, then death. But after the strange beauty of what has gone before, it feels like a lessening. If you don't know the words, don't you just watch a boy burn and all the more brightly with the fore-knowledge that he will die? And that burning, taper-light against a dark world, isn't that the spectacle?

★ ★ ★

We had spoken much of revenge and its meaning through the course of putting the show together, and through our movement around the world. There were always moments on our travels which brought the company up short, moments when the reality of a line would suddenly become apparent. The company talked of a sudden silence which fell in Bosnia after Horatio said, 'Put the bodies in the market place', in a country that remembered all too vividly the sight of bodies in the market place. In Rwanda, the completeness of their understanding of mortality, and of bodies buried badly, came home all the more forcefully. The knowledge filled the air and changed the gravity of the thought. It was late in the tour before we came face to face with revenge.

We were in Erbil in northern Iraq, in the Kurdish region. It was one of the toughest gigs of the whole tour and madly security conscious. When I arrived at the hotel at four in the morning, each door of the car was opened simultaneously by a masked man with a machine gun, and a dog gave me a good thorough sniffing to check for explosives. Only thirty kilometres away was Mosul, a city entirely run by IS. As in Somaliland, and as in so many other places, we were the first cultural visitors in aeons, and the world and his wife gathered the next day to watch the show. But the day before, the company had been taken to a refugee camp to meet those displaced by the invasion of IS. One man was eager to tell his story, he had been shot in the hip, and he told us of the fighting. He was steady and measured, his translator was imperfect and excitable, but I give the translator's words here verbatim:

After Mosul collapse, ISIS, after they control Mosul, he kill and he hang eleven member of my family . . . my brother, my brother and all his sons be killed, be hanged by ISIS . . . my brother he was handicapped, he was on wheelchair, when they hang him . . . even the friend of my son's they kill him, they hang him, my son's friends . . .

All the houses that belong to me they destroy, demolish . . . and even, they cut even the wood, the trees, and after they say allahu akbar . . .

When we say human rights, they telling you be better than ISIS, an animal could be better than ISIS, there is no description for ISIS . . . and after I am taking my revenge, the human rights come to me and they say . . . oh you should stop, not revenge . . . what kind of human rights if they say do not revenge against the beast, against the criminals . . . I am telling you they are not human beings.

Dead hole, the hole of death, he was in wheelchair, and they push him in and he die . . .

(*pointing to someone*)

They kill his father and his mother front of his eye, now he is stammering and stuttering, front of his eye, naked . . .

(*pointing to another*)

Everything start from the zero point . . . They exploit sick people and vulnerable people . . . Islam is the religion of justice and peace . . . to deface or stigmatise the religion of Islam to make it ugly and nasty . . . my neighbour was a Sunni, I did not know, my manager was a Christian, it was not a problem, never a problem . . . there is something behind the scene, there is some hand behind the scene did that, I don't know what happened . . . Is there any religion on earth asking people to rape, to take money from people . . .?

They have new techniques of killing, new ways of degrading people, new ways to killing human . . . I curse that religion, if any religion do that I curse them, I damn them if it is a way of destroying the human.

Someone asked, 'How do you look forward from here?'

> I am very optimistic because they will be banished, they will
> be killed, now all the people who is ISIS we can determine
> who they are, so there will be no place for them . . .

There was something raw and naked and unmediated about the
wound here, and about the desire to avenge it, which lived in a
world – reality – entirely separate from the fiction of our play.
Naked hurt, naked rage. A trace of it pulses through Hamlet's
raw scream 'O vengeance', and through Fortinbras's desire to gain
retribution for the loss suffered by his father. There was much of
it that we discovered still alive in the world, the people of Russia
and of Ukraine still feeling the pain of wounds that were fresh,
and wanting to lash out to alleviate that pain; the chaos that was
left behind in the world after the USA felt the need to gain
atonement in blood for the wound they suffered on 9/11; conflicts,
local, regional and international, where the pain of loss could
only be solved and dissolved by inflicting more pain and more
loss on others. It often felt, as we travelled from country to
country, that we were in a world filled with hatred, a world
without forgiveness, and with an unslakable thirst to honour
historic promises of vengeance.

Hamlet speaks directly and simply to that world, and that is
little but saddening. The world of forgiveness and healing and
reconciliation which Shakespeare mapped out in his late plays is
infinitely generous and touching. I'm not sure we have made the
world to suit those plays yet.

★ ★ ★

Like Fortinbras and his army passing through a country and moving on, chasing a bit of honour, we went from country to country asking for permission to play, then passing on. There was an element of 'fantasy and trick of fame' about what we were doing, but we were not aiming to win any small patches of ground or to gain anything for keeps. We merely wanted to leave a story floating in the air of a country, lingering in some memories, and maybe staining the earth a little. We hoped *Hamlet*, with its doubt, its confusions and its questions, would persuade a few to let the eggshells be.

14

MISSION CONTROL

HORATIO *Let there a scaffold be reared up in the market place,*
And let the State of the world be there.

Act 5, Scene 2

FOR OUR GLOBE TO GLOBE festival in 2012, our carpenters built
a daft but fun wooden structure, a signpost pointing crazily in
thirty-seven different directions to each of the capital cities of
the countries visiting us. Knocked up as a gift, we placed it on the
piazza outside the Globe. It became iconic in the course of the six
weeks of the festival, companies and audiences standing around
it, laughing and contemplating. Stuck in Istanbul for the day, I
was standing in front of the Milion stone, the last remaining
fragment of a once domed edifice erected in the fourth century
AD in what was then Constantinople. This was the Byzantine
zero-point, the place from which all distances to far-flung corners
of its empire were measured, and were pointed to. It was a
reminder of the internationalist tradition we stood within,
though happily we were less concerned with trade and conquest
by the sword.

Having missed a connection to join the company in the Far East, I was gorging on a fast feast of iconic sights before catching the next plane out. The Blue Mosque, started a few years after the first performance of *Hamlet* and topped off in the year Shakespeare died, squatted like a fat Buddha, happy in its own bulk, spreading out ripples of meditative fat. It was under reconstruction, so flights of scaffolding climbed up inside. The colouring within was a cooling breeze, a patchwork of duck-egg blues and greying reds, with a dance of old script running through it. Traces of ferny leaves snaked through the other colours, looking very like Elizabethan fabrics. A busy cluster of visitors was corralled in a crowded section to lift their phones and take hasty pictures of the devout at prayer, who had all the room in the world.

I charged across to the monumental Hagia Sophia, built in AD 537, which had a clean 1,000-year run as the largest religious edifice in the world and is still far, far too big for common sense. The baffling conundrum of how they got to the top to squeeze in the last brick was partly answered by half of it being occluded by a forest of scaffolding, since it, too, was undergoing refurbishment. After the watery colours of the Blue Mosque, here was a vivid colour contrast, with a rusty brick and the yellow and orange echo of Roman sensibility in the traces of paint that remained. It left an impression of peace and of a mango sweetness. Scratchy graceless birds flitted across the upper reaches of the topmost dome.

Amongst the graffiti, there was a line of Viking script scraped into the stone in the ninth century by a guard called Halvdan, who thus ensured his grip on posterity. This reminded me of the journey we had come, including Scandinavia and Kiev, and the chains of rivers which connect north to south. Although we like to segment our history into tribes and factions, borders and boundaries have been porous since people's first curiosity sent them off in search of different-tasting cheese. To be honest, the Hagia Sophia was something of a mess – low-hanging chandeliers, and anachronistic galleries, and the warring aesthetics of clashing cultures all contrived to detract from its monumental simplicity – but the breath of Byzantium had been somehow frozen within it, with all the promise of imaginative richness that word offers.

Only a couple of weeks later, I was similarly stranded in Istanbul's old wrestling opponent, Athens, again on *Hamlet* business, and again frustrated by the vicissitudes of airplane travel. I had been in and out of Greece many times but had never spent time in the centre of Athens doing the classical dance, so I grasped the opportunity. Having been a classical student of almost unique poorness, my reactions to the evidence of the civilisation I should have studied were complex. My aesthetic sense was awakened by the grace of all on display – 'Great pot', etc. – but I couldn't help feeling my response should have been better informed. I spent a lot of time admiring the quality of the pleats on much of the statuary, and how they fell across the body in a way to make even the most broken fragments still strangely erotic, but I was ashamed of my ignorance as to which goddess was which. This awkwardness was only compounded when I got to the top of the Acropolis and a Greek guide was winning multiple brownie points with a group of Americans by telling them how evil the British were for stealing their Elgin Marbles. I skulked back a little. But the experience of the Acropolis was again compromised by the same factor which affected the Blue Mosque and the Hagia Sophia: a huge quantity of obscuring scaffolding. Having had my third experience of antiquity obscured in a short while, I started to think about scaffolding.

There is hardly a building of stature anywhere in the world

that we stand and gawp at now, that was not previously encased in a prior edifice of equally awesome scaffolding. Whether the Parthenon or the Blue Mosque or the Taj Mahal, before the building was there it had to have a shadow state, or an outer mask – its scaffolding – upon which thousands and tens of thousands of artists and artisans, great armies of muscle and finesse, laboured to create that building. Only for the scaffolding to be torn away so that the building could stand clean and new born, pretending like an ingrate that the scaffolding, which allowed its creation, was never there. Those thoughts passing through me, I felt a ludicrous flush of sympathy for scaffolding, poor neglected, forgotten scaffolding. The Parthenon stands there all perfectly proportioned, the Hagia Sophia all outlandishly monumental, the Taj Mahal all gleamingly pink at dawn, as if they had just appeared out of nowhere, incapable of paying respect to what first made them. Until repairs are needed, and they all scream 'Scaffolding!', like spoilt children, and await the return of their supportive parent. Scaffolding is the midwife of every building great and small, and brings it into the world. It has to hug the building close, clinging to it to keep it steady, before tearing itself away to leave the building to stand on its own feet. It is the mother of all edifices.

Plays appear on stages attempting (not always succeeding) to look like life new born, existence occurring in front of you. Whether kitchen-sink realism, drawing-room mystery, Greek tragedy or Hamlet wandering around Elsinore, the actors have to walk onto the stage as if they have arrived in that moment. They cannot show the long months, then intense weeks, then hyper-intense hours of care and construction which go into their attempt to look effortless. That is true for all theatre. For a tour, you add in multiple variables: transport of people, of set and props, accommodation and dealing with all the technical particularities of each venue. When you're touring abroad, you have to factor in further extras, from visas and licenses, to translation, security and the vagaries of air travel.

Yet you must ensure that the actors can wander onto the stage as well-equipped as possible and look as if they have not a care in the world. You have to set in place a complex system of scaffolding which can be detached with ease and leave the show gleaming. Or, if not gleaming, at least upright. Somehow, somehow, and it remains a mystery to us how it was managed, over the course of two years, and through almost 200 countries, and doing 280 odd performances, we never missed a single show. We turned up on stage at the given moment and started with a song in almost every country in the world. At the Vatican, after a delayed flight and then a broken bus, the actors had to walk straight off the bus and onto the stage. Cancelled flights between Guinea–Bissau and the Gambia meant not all the actors could fly, so two of them and two stage managers had to cross the country in a commandeered hearse. In Pacific islands, where the attitude to air travel and time-keeping is relaxed to put it mildly, feet had to be stamped to ensure that planes left at the right time and headed for the right destination.

At the sharp end of most of the construction and the care were the four stage managers who travelled every leg of the journey: Dave McEvoy, Becky Austin, Adam Moore and Carrie Burnham. Their resilience, consistency and steadiness were sufficient for them to have constructed several Taj Mahals, and a Machu Picchu to boot. Every airport, and there were several hundred, was an event in itself. As a precaution, the start of every journey was timed to give several hours' leeway. This was sensible, though it proved a form of slow water-torture in practice. As well as the disorientation of swapping time zones, almost every other day started between three and five in the morning. The company would arrive, usually zombie-like with exhaustion, a vivid shamble of tired bones dressed in bright chilled-out fabrics, loose trousers and shabby T-shirts in razzle-dazzle colours. As they were a handsome bunch, this proved something of a technicolour spectacle in itself.

After disembarking their bus, all – silent, still half-asleep and running on autopilot – would head straight to the accompanying truck. From this everyone would lift the sixteen hefty flight cases. These formed our set wherever we went, and carried everything needed for the show, including costumes, props, canvas flats, steel uprights, swords and a couple of skulls. Then a caravan of trolleys, bearing the flight cases and personal bags, would move through the sleek architecture, or across the crumbled yard, or through the wooden sheds, of all the airports of the world. A colourful caravan, it would attract no small amount of attention. Once at check-in, Becky or Dave would go to the front, and with courtesy and firmness, and with little or no knowledge of the appropriate language, explain that they were checking in enough cases for a small army. They developed a confidence and a calm at handling this that never ceased to astonish, and behind them the patience of the actors – chatting, listening to music, reading, watching the world bustle in transit – was Zen-like. Somehow bags and bones would all get on to the plane together.

Once delivered to the new country, the bags would be lifted from luggage carousels and trolleyed up again. There would be a brief excursion to sort out local currency, or shbibli. This is what the company renamed the currencies of all the world. Since they were moving at such speed and couldn't learn the name of each individual currency, they would simply go to the bureau de change at each new outpost, pass over the currency they had, and say,

'Can I have some shbibli, please?' Amazingly, it never failed. Passing through immigration and customs was again a matter of confidence and bluff. Cases often had to be opened, and swords explained, but what surprised on the journeys I took with them was how accommodating officialdom was. Once it was explained who we were and what we were doing, doors usually opened. 'Ah, theatre!', 'Ah, *Hamlet!*', 'Ah, Globe!', usually accompanied by some baffled smiling then enjoyment at joining in. Theatre can prove the ultimate passport – there is something perennially innocent about it. Bergman's medieval films feature touring companies, scruffy bundles of life fizzing out vitality around horse-drawn carts as they move through the Nordic landscape, small Tazzes of energy in the enveloping gloom. I thought of them as I saw our company moving through airports, the same anarchic buzz of humour and life. Our tour, by nature of its patent insanity, promoted yet more goodwill.

Out of the airport, and our local fixer/promoter/friend met, the cases were loaded onto new trucks and taken straight to the theatre, or the place we were turning into a theatre. That day or the next, the stage managers would go in ahead of the actors, build the set from what was in the cases, create whatever rudimentary lighting was possible, unpack costumes and set them on racks, and set out the props on whatever tables could be managed. All this while dealing with backstage crews and theatre managements of all nationalities. The show was no rest for them, since they had to manage it, to play musical instruments (some of them), act a little (some of them), and do what minimal shifting of minimal scenery there was. And then the instant that the show came down, almost before the applause had finished, they began dismantling the set and packing it away. This was all hands on deck – actors (some of them), stage management and anyone around helping out. I prided myself on my limited ability with a power tool and was always first in with the Nikita to unscrew what bolts there were. The sight of me bending over with a tool in hand being generally useless made it hard for our hosts to believe that I was the artistic director. There was something determinedly and pleasingly collective about this dismantling and packing together. I once showed the egregious Boris Johnson, then Mayor of London, around the Globe after a performance, and he was astonished to see the actors packing up the set. 'But, you've just been on stage doing all that acting! You can't be doing this as well!' he blustered. His inability to comprehend such collectivism was its own reward. Once packed, the cases were carried out by everyone to whatever truck or coach was waiting, ready for the trip to the airport and for the whole cycle to begin again.

That routine of swirling through a city and pausing briefly to drop off a *Hamlet* performance was repeated more than 200 times in a bewildering variety of settings. The stage managers would whip the scaffolding instantly into place to hold the show, and then make it disappear again with a conjuror's speed, so that the set, or in many cases the newly built theatre, were ready for the actors to go out and tell their story for the hundredth time, as if for the first time. On top of that was no shortage of pastoral care, and occasionally health care, and some tour guide activity to boot. It sounds an unromantic compliment to compare the stage managers to scaffolding, but without it there would have been no Taj Mahal, no Blue Mosque, no Parthenon. And no *Hamlet*.

★ ★ ★

In any good space movie, the tropes of climax and danger are familiar: docking procedures going wrong, the oxygen tanks running low, the astronaut preparing to sacrifice himself for the good of the others. But what always sneaks under the wire, and engages us without us being fully aware, is the drama on the ground: mission control and its inhabitants, where men (and it is usually men) with buzz haircuts and short-sleeved shirts and underarm sweat patches stay up night after night listening to and observing the endangered rocket, trying to come up with any solution that might save it, asserting grimly that 'Failure is not an option' and that nothing will go down on their watch. There is a romance to their teamwork, their ethic and their determination, that I have always loved. The fragility of the real moon expeditions, an easily buckled tin can hurled out into the infinite loneliness of space, served as a metaphor for ourselves and all our fragile journeys, and for much of what is best in us. Mad dreaming, daft courage, insatiable curiosity and a foolish hope that good may come from it. And behind it the hard work, the optimism and the unshakable loyalty of teams of people. What have we achieved that is better than that?

Mission control for our expedition was based in our office on Bankside. Everyone contributed to it, but as a department we had much else to do – opening a new theatre, doing other tours, making a series of films and mounting a string of productions in our (now) two theatres – so most of the work devolved to a team of five people: our executive producer, Tom Bird; three producers, Tamsin Mehta, Malú Ansaldo and Claire Godden; and one marketing associate, Helena Miscioscia, whose task was to raise audiences everywhere from Auckland to Santiago. Buzz cuts, short sleeves and sweat patches were in short supply, but there was no dearth of hard work, optimism and loyalty.

Visas were probably the biggest task and the biggest expense. The company each worked their way through eight passports, stuffed with stamps and forms. They would always have one passport with them on the road and another in London being carted round from embassy to embassy. Often we had to travel to other cities – Dublin or Paris – because the embassies in those countries were better equipped to deal with our requests. The weight of form-filling would have defeated the bureaucracies of many a small corporation, but it was achieved by three or four people. Individuals were often stuck at desks from dawn to dusk, checking and rechecking visa applications for fear that a minor detail might be wrong; none ever was. Brinkmanship was often required. Nigeria held out for an absurdly large amount of money for entry, quite justifiably aggravated by what the British Home Office charged Nigerians who wanted to visit the UK. Bhutan was similarly expensive, until we went to perform there, and the King announced himself so pleased that he was going to pay for all the visas himself.

Contact had to be made with host venues and promoters, and dates secured. This could stretch nerves to an attenuated point. In the majority of countries, dates were made long in advance with national theatres and established local promoters, and all proceeded in a grown-up manner. In many, there was no such infrastructure in place. In several cases, I would ask where we were going to play in a country a week before we arrived, and my question would be met with nervous smiles and hopeful assurances. No matter, I thought blithely, things would sort themselves out. How? No idea. 'It's a mystery', as the character Henslowe says in Stoppard's *Shakespeare in Love*. With their usual mysterious propitiousness, things did sort themselves out. We ran closest to the wire when we flew into an island in the morning while still not entirely sure where we would be playing in the evening, but a hut was secured and the show went on.

Even more surprising was how everywhere the ticket became hot. No matter how late the show was announced, it was almost always full to bursting. Shakespeare obviously sells, *Hamlet* too, and the Globe has a cachet, but it was the madness of the endeavour that people bought into. One example of a general enthusiasm was Algeria. This was another late announcement, with the show in their national theatre only going on sale three or four days before we were to play. Tickets went within hours, and on the night an extra thousand people showed up. More chairs were put out, and audiences packed into the aisles, but six or seven hundred were left outside. They got angry and started banging on the outside doors demanding admittance. The noise was too great for the show to start. Tamsin stood watching it from the theatre's balcony with the theatre's managers. They turned to her.

'What are you going to do?' they asked.

'Well, it's your theatre, you should do something,' said Tamsin, who is from Birmingham and is a long way beyond 'no' in the lacking of nonsense department.

'You must go out and speak to them and tell them to go home,' they persisted.

'I don't know the language; you talk to them.'

'But you are blondes, and they will believe you!'

There was no effective rejoinder to that, so Tamsin went out on her own and spoke to the crowd, and they melted off into the night. It was an excitement repeated elsewhere. I saw riot police out in Quito and Lima to control the crowds. The flipside was a handful of dates where only thirty or forty people showed up. Wittenberg in Germany, which we had felt compelled to do because of its resonance, was a rather disappointing crowd in the town's old disco (what would Luther have thought?); a couple of the Pacific Islands showed a valiant lack of interest; and the Francophone countries of West Africa showed a touching loyalty to their old colonial masters by miming 'Ooo, Shaksperrr? Bof!' with a Gallic shrug of the shoulders. When this happened, it was the company's responsibility to keep their energy high, and mission control's job to keep morale up.

From the centre, we had to book all travel (trying to juggle cost with reliability); to book accommodation (trying to juggle cost with comfort, which in some places could have been demarcated with 1 to 5 cockroaches rather than stars); to make sure that each trip was tightly scheduled; to monitor insurance; to monitor health, which meant that in many of the weeks of rest back at home, the company had to troop to rare-disease clinics to get immunised; to liaise with the local government bodies to see how they might help; to try to cut deals wherever we could which might reduce costs; and to see if anybody, but anybody would put their hands in their pockets and defray the expenses. All that and a thousand other things at a rate of roughly three countries a week for two years.

Publicity was a mixture of a pleasure and a trial. The pleasure was the enthusiasm with which much of the world's media caught on to the idea and played merrily with it, using it as a platform to discuss Shakespeare and *Hamlet*, and the cultural history of their own country's interaction with both. The dullness was the manner in which the British media either didn't get it, or tried to take snarky potshots at it, shooting arrows of the 'why-aren't-there-more-balloons-in-it?' kind from the culturally complacent left, and 'where-oh-where-is-the-money-for-all-this-culture-malarkey-coming-from?' kind from the right. *The Sun* did a rather underwhelming front-page exposé of how we were wasting government money, when, unbeknownst to us, about £4,000 had been given to an educational programme in Haiti, and towards the end of the tour the usual pressure groups tried to orchestrate a shaming of us for going to Israel. We soldiered on. Sometimes you wonder how anything gets made in or gets out of England, though if you can squeeze anything past our old media, and our new trial-by-social-networking culture, it is a triumph of sufficient robustness that you are proofed against further challenges.

Raising money remained a problem throughout, but happily we enjoyed the subsidy which came, as it always does, in the form of the endless hours given by those working on it – our mission control. Each got to go out and join the tour here and there, and each would return energised, yet also heartbroken that they had to return and could not run away with the circus. The rewards in London were disconnected ones, since we were so far from the endeavour, but they were still substantial. We would gather around photographs of crowds massing to see the show in extraordinary settings – Pacific and Indian and Mediterranean seas behind them as the sun went down; we would watch phone-films of crowds on the sand in deserts clapping along to the jig, or of Tommy teaching a school full of children in Nigeria how to dance it; we would all share long press stories plastered with photos about the effect of the show, pass emails of gratitude from our co-promoters to each other, and take pleasure collectively in the tweets and Facebook posts of those who had seen it. The company would send a postcard from each country back to the office, which would sit on our communal table, a pleasingly antique method of staying in touch. It was not the same as being there, but it was enough.

And somehow knowing the show was out there, out in its

lonely and far-flung places, doing its *Hamlet* thing, was its own reward. To have asked for or wanted more would have been to miss the point. It was not a show or an experience built around what people could take back from it; it was about what they gave. We never defined why we were doing it. Such definitions almost always disappoint, and they have much less authority than silence. And being able to look at each other and know why.

15

FRIENDSHIP ON THE ROAD

HAMLET *Give me that man*
That is not passion's slave, and I will wear him
In my heart's core, ay, in my heart of heart,
As I do thee . . .

Act 3, Scene 2

THE WORDS FLEA MARKET DIDN'T encompass what was opposite
our hotel in Bogotá. Thirty stalls packed into an open yard, it
was a riot of stuff, a jamboree of junk, a visual poem of the
discarded. On one rather sparse table, there was a small wooden
chest, a Bakelite telephone, three pairs of spectacles, a tiara, two
old Aztec masks (one gold, one green), and in pride of place, a
television remote control. Another table had nothing but inch-
thin tall wooden Giacometti figures of either an angry beardy
Jesus, or Mary with an infant Jesus bursting *Alien*-style from her
midriff. Another had a swarm of coloured beads swirling across
it, bands of colour clashing and colliding like a Rothko. Another
had refined crockery beside samurai swords. Another sported old
Mayan ceramics against Walt Disney plastic figurines. One table

was peopled by 400 tiny dolls all doing unspeakable sexual things to each other in a great miniature plastic orgy. My favourite table had at the back a line of sentimental porcelain madonnas, and laid in front of each, as if in supplication, an old clay dildo.

All these odds and ends of recent history were arranged with precise care, however lowly the content. I watched one stall holder turning and re-turning an old hammer for five minutes, shifting it millimetres this way and that to make sure it sat within the chaos in the right manner. These poems of cluttered jumble were stacked with the artisan care of a Normandy log pile. The result was a dazzle of contrast and colour, all the baroque excess of Catholic decor jostling with a more ancient exuberance. Like a García Márquez novel stacked into each small space, you read a teeming profusion of narratives. You needed to take cocaine to calm yourself down. On another stall, a crude puppet theatre sat beside an old sewing machine and a smart new printer. The words above the theatre ran 'Nuestro teatro tiene vida' – our theatre holds life. You could have said the same for the whole market.

García Márquez was beyond ubiquitous in Colombia. His photo greeted you at the airport, our hotel was wallpapered with pictures of him meeting famous men, and quotes from him were plastered everywhere, lending validation to everything, whether a political movement or a cup of coffee. I even spotted a cupcake with his teddy-bear face on it. There was a cultural centre dedicated to him, but in many ways the whole of Bogotá seemed his cultural centre. Just as with the market, the life of the city resembled an outcrop of his teeming imagination, narratives spilling from every corner, each über-narrative birthing four minor narratives within itself. The spirit life, the political life and the life of the heart fight for space with a hectoring clamour on the streets, as in his novels.

Beyond the market, Bogotá was in festival mood, the main drag taken over for a holiday. The vivacity and variety of the market found its complement in the human behaviour out on the streets. Every fifty yards, a section of the road was claimed by a street-dancing group, the best of them defying logic and biology, swiftly creating new shapes of body art to a hip-hop beat and then whisking them away with a conjuror's lightness of gesture. Glass-blowers torched new shapes on the pavements. Avuncular old men leered their way up to me with a dirty chuckle and opened out folds of paper to reveal bright-blue rhomboid 'viagra' pills. Music pumped out of everywhere – tannoys, bands, lonely accordions, impromptu choirs. Keith and I met and spent a brief five minutes betting on a guinea-pig race in the centre of the road. Respectfully hushed crowds surrounded street chess, bright-eyed boys taking on grizzled masters – intellectuals, hustlers and tramps all sharing their fascination with the game. An anarchist collective folk band played some mean jazz up a side street. Small-time gangsters wandered around with Cerberus-like clusters of pit bulls. A thin man sat on a pile of broken glass, then stood up and did a little dance on it as he took a long knife and stuck it up his nose. Everyone was contributing: it was a fully shared theatre. One girl I saw, who had nothing better to contribute, sat rather forlornly by the side of the road, running a knife up and down a cheese grater just so she could join in. To cap it all, in the large square outside the presidential palace, with toy soldiers doing half-hearted synchronised marching in the background, an ancient transvestite importuned me to have a ride on a midget llama. And it felt normal. I was a long way from home.

As with the market, it felt like a holiday from hierarchy. No one was worrying about value, no one was saying this is more important than that. Madonna and dildo sat happily side by side, professor and punk played chess together, ghetto blaster shared the soundscape with sorrowing violin. Everything was out on the street together, and everything coexisted at the same time. This reminded me of the essence of García Márquez's magic realism: it is not just that there are so many different jostling dimensions and realities in the world of *One Hundred Years of Solitude*, it is that they are all equally important, they are all on the level.

'There are more things in heaven and earth, Horatio, than are dreamt of in your philosophy' sounds a ponderous line in isolation. A patronising lecture by clever-clogs Hamlet to his dull friend. It has a whiff of superiority when frequently quoted, the mystic man who has seen stuff, talking down to his less visionary companion. This is all wrong. It is an urgent and excited plea from the heart. Hamlet has just seen a ghost, the ghost of his father. Reality has just opened a new portal. Possibilities have multiplied. Horatio is shrinking from it: 'O day and night, but this is wondrous strange!' he says, filled with foreboding. Hamlet snaps back at him in an instant one of the central lines to the whole play: 'And therefore as a stranger give it welcome.' My instinct for this line was always the same: flush a rage into the first two words, then take a beat, breathe the anger out of yourself, and walk gently through the rest of the line. 'As a stranger give it welcome' is central to the new civility, the new openness that Hamlet (and for my money Shakespeare) was trying to live. If something is new or strange or foreign or different, don't walk away from it, or fear it, or shun it; give it welcome. The 'more things in heaven and earth' (and isn't that 'thing' another of Shakespeare's delicious vaguenesses?) are there to be delighted and excited by. He is not saying I know more than you; he is saying take it in, take it all in. It thrills.

The company became adept at diving into a city and accepting the 'more things' they found. They moved at speed, often with only three or four hours to scope out a town, and their skill at covering monuments, street food, dangerous corners and public squares was impressive. Their searches were rather like the experience of shows by the Punchdrunk theatre company, unmapped and unplanned immersive events staged within a space, where your instinct tells you which stories to follow and which to leave. As with a Punchdrunk show, a willing passivity is often better than a planned attack. The amount of information and joy our company could glean from a new city was huge. The freedom to slip down this alleyway, to follow that crowd, to settle in this meaningless space was limitless and as close to pure joy as I have known.

Before travelling to South America, I had a long chat with one of my daughters, who had just finished Jack Kerouac's *On the Road*. Her fresh-as-a-daisy enchantment with that book, with its sugar-rush thrill at the excitement of being alive, in the moment and on the move, reminded me of my own infatuation at the same age. And of my desire to live like Sal Paradise and Dean Moriarty, to keep searching for the new, and 'digging' as much as I was able. The sharpness of the Kerouac connection was brought home one evening in Quito. We had just done a good show to a vociferously happy crowd, and sped off to a jazz club. Many of the customers there had seen the show and happily brought us into their midst. An outfit of experimental jazzers came out and started noodling and nurdling. A modest outfit – trumpeter, clarinettist, bongo drums and keyboards – but no modest talent. There is something about the best jazz, the easy aimlessness to begin with, the lack of destination, the trace of a melody elsewhere, the swaying earthed sashay of it, then the bursts of virtuosity, the slides and slips of the harmonics, and then at a certain moment the sense that the whole crowd have been scooped up en masse into the adventure of an improvisation, that all are trying to go collectively to strange and exotic new places of noise and sex and humour and spirit and warmth, and then as the music stretches higher that we're all somehow getting there, to the pith and prune juice of it, all together and at the same time, and yet not staying too long there, because the itch to move on and to keep moving on is always there, and so we shift and shunt on through . . . there is something about that which only jazz can do.

That night in Quito it happened, the whole room was taken on a flight, and I thought of Dean Moriarty and Sal Paradise sitting listening to George Shearing on the piano, and felt happy and relieved that my life had landed me in a similar place. I realised that the *On the Road* spirit is not about the awful deadening cool – the cool exemplified to me earlier in Moscow. It's not about dark glasses and Marlboros drooping from lower lips, or who can look least affiliate and least engaged; it is the opposite. Being that sort of cool is really for the dullest pricks. It is about sweetness of spirit and boldness and appetite; it is about daring to look further and to discover more. Moriarty and Paradise, Kerouac and Cassidy, Hamlet himself – all explorers in the spirit, out looking in the world.

As John said as he wandered around Lima with eyes wide open; 'You can't take a wrong turn,' he said, 'You just can't take a wrong turn.'

It's not only what's there, but also how you enjoy what's there. The company were great at mapping and investigating, but they also engaged. Compliments for a plate of food, debate with a protestor, a haggle with a vendor, lazy chat with a barman, quizzing of local historians. Keith was always charging off on nature trips; Miranda recorded a native song in every country; the boys went out drabbing to clubs; Amanda sought out and bought a musical instrument particular to each country; all looked for nuggets of detail and anecdote and information that opened up the world to them a little more. They knew you have to be alive to the world for it to come to you. Just as Dean and Sal do through fifties America, and just as we imagine Hamlet doing before the roof falls in.

The level of surprise was still strong. In Lima I was standing at a crossroads, and someone suddenly appeared and did a handspring nearly over my head. His partner appeared, and they did acrobatics together, hurling each other this way and that. Music abruptly started, and the acrobatics morphed into break-dancing. An audience gathered, but no one seemed to have asked them to; they were just happy to do their thing. That commitment to unembarrassed joy, to expressing an alive public contentment felt a long way from home. There was something free here. It felt like a veil of fear and loathing and guilt had been lifted.

To take a moment of peace from this riot of sensual excess, the sanctuary was the same now as it had been for centuries. The heat, the noise, the bustle and the motion – all came to a halt just by passing through a heavy wooden door and sitting for a moment in a church. Whether it was through the high arched door of a basilica, or down a corridor into a cloister, or slipping under a low lintel into a discreet chapel, the temperature drop was a cooling necessity. The sun was blocked out, the heat disappeared, and stillness reigned. It was the church as a spiritual fridge, where we park ourselves on a shelf, shut down our antennae and try our best to keep ourselves fresh. Realignment in stillness, letting the quiet of centuries lower your shoulders a little. I'm not sure it opens up 'more things in heaven', far from sure about heaven in fact, but there are surely 'more things' than what is just in the markets and on the streets. A confirmed agnostic, I can't see the point in not leaving oneself open to everything. Why miss a party?

In the magnificent Basilica San Francisco in Quito, an imposing white without, a palace of shining gold within, I sat still for a moment. A flush of guilt passed through me about the spoiling of happiness I was receiving. Kerouac's 'digging' was all very well, the sampling and the relishing of the world, but what was the quid pro quo? The question popped up, and the answer sailed in with a modest grace, blown in by the still and the quiet of the room. All that matters is the sum of happiness, and that you increase it, however you are able. You can go to the sad part of a town and give a little happiness, or you can go to the happier place, sit and drink in what they offer, and then give some back. What matters is the sum of happiness, and that you grow it and don't diminish it, now and beyond.

What we were doing was similar to *On the Road* but not the same. We had the freedom, the same rapture at the world, the same restless desire to savour or to 'dig' the details and the panorama. Yet for us there was an extra privilege – we were able to give something back. Not just digging but planting also. Something both fragile and sturdy, our beloved Hamlet, with his unique capacity to break hearts and open minds. Each journey, each leg, was an inhale of sensation and culture, and an exhale of Hamlet. There was hardly ever a better exhale than in Lima.

★ ★ ★

Happy hour isn't just about cocktails. Out on the street, that hour between six and seven bristles with happiness all the world over, but nowhere as vibrantly as in South America. The long day done, the evening ahead, the work may have been hard, and the glass may be less than half full, but at that moment the promise of the evening ahead begins to fill the glass. At that moment, our lives are a blend of fact and imagination, the fact of the day past, and the imagining of the night ahead as we wonder how good the show will be, how tasty the dinner, how fierce the fight, how sweet the kiss.

The Peruvians were working up a frenzy of potential. It was not only our show opening that night, but also a festival. We were doing TV interviews on the balcony outside their theatre, and were comprehensively upstaged by what unfurled in the street behind us. A team of circus performers were doing impossible acts. There appeared to be trapezes and tightropes emanating from bicycles on which ludicrously lithe people hurled themselves around. Beyond their mid-air tumbling, large abstract shapes made from paper went up in spectacular flames. It was gravity defying and jaw-droppingly exciting. As a way of getting an audience ready for a production of *Hamlet*, it set the bar a little high. The theatre was a nineteenth-century proscenium palace, beautifully proportioned and all decked out in cream and gold. The tickets were free and the crush to get in severe. All of Lima seemed to be trying to cram in, and their excitement and their pleasure at being with each other was intoxicating. Ladi was out early in the pre-show and flirting with half the audience, and Keith gave the Mayor a flower, which was a good start. At the top of the show, when Tommy did his speech of greeting, he simply said hello, and the audience erupted into three minutes of greeting and applause, Amanda had a grin to split her face; the rest were slack-jawed in amazement. It was so warm-hearted as to be over-whelming – 'as a stranger give it welcome'. With fireworks.

The show that followed was everything you could want it to be. I had seen a couple of pale and disaffected shows in Bogotá, a very strong one in Quito, and this was a step-change. Strong, muscular, clear, carved out of space, definite, funny when it needed to be, private when it needed to be, epic when it needed to be. A thrilling story, a joyride of thought and language. The adrenalin rush that we hoped for. There was a sense at the interval that they didn't want it to stop. But the excitement picked up in the second half, and the committed attention to each word was breathtaking. Each word seemed to matter to that room as it passed by, and to add to the continuing life of this unlimited poem. The roar at the end matched and exceeded the roar at the beginning, and we floated off to dinner full of bubbling joy. We talked of all we had seen: the crowds of people, the great bustle of the earth, and how it didn't fill us with terror or gloom; it filled us with a great feeling of the sweetness of humanity. We straggled back to the hotel in twos and threes, walking through the dark of Lima, and all full of, well . . . fullness. Replete.

* * *

Hamlet, and indeed most Shakespeare, happily qualifies to share space within the magical-realist tradition. There is no shortage of levels. You've got a Ghost, who pops up on three occasions; you have streams of consciousness and songs of confusion and need expressed through blank verse; you have politics, both in the regime change which precedes the play and the revolution that continually threatens it; you have the ludic shifting of different realities with the play within the play; you have the classical backdrop with the speeches on the fall of Troy; there's a bit of broad clowning humour with the Gravediggers, which actually manages on occasion to be funny; you have a love story, both domestic and epic; there's family politics; there's fabulism and stories folding into other stories; there's even a generational saga element with the Fortinbrases and the Hamlets fighting it out through time. It's hard to imagine a García Márquez or a Vargas Llosa or an Allende that manages to stuff in more, or that takes greater pleasure in the telling. We often get so obsessed with the darkness and the gloom and the existential pain of *Hamlet*, we lose sight of the pleasure of telling a story.

As with the greatest magical realism, this is not just about setting up a checklist of different levels; it is about creating a story and a world where they can easily coexist. This is not about arranging a hierarchy of bits that are very important, those which are less important and those which don't really matter, with serious anguish at the top and low comedy at the bottom. This is about everything, every colour, every trope, every mode, sharing the same space. Whether it is a ghost or a small and deftly drawn moment of naturalism, whether some light-hearted advice to actors or a rejected lover's tears – all exist together. Each moment is strange and new, each moment welcomes the next in. In all Shakespeare's plays, each detail within the picture matters as greatly as each grand horizon.

As with physical detail, so with each moment, so with time passing. Hamlet welcomes every stranger, just as his author did. Each moment within time is as significant as every other. The philosophical space he arrives at towards the end, and which he articulates with:

There's a special providence in the fall of a sparrow. If it
be now, 'tis not to come; if it be not to come, it will be
now; if it be not now, yet it will come: the readiness is
all. Since no man has aught of what he leaves, what is't
to leave betimes? Let be.

is often taken, by me at first as well, as being about a calm, a
Zen plateau, and an acceptance of all. There is some of that, but
it is also about relish, about being alive to everything, and to each
moment you walk through. Before you recognise the providence
in the fall of the sparrow, you have to see it clearly. Before you
let the moments go as they wish to go, you have to try to make
sure you are fully alive in each. Readiness is not just about sitting
back passively and waiting for whatever cruel blows the world
wants to chuck at you. It is also readiness for life, for joy, for
excitement, for every goddamned sandwich.

This is the same appetite for life that Kerouac celebrated in
On the Road. Yet that book is about more, and if there is one
thing it fetishises as greatly as movement and experience, it is
friendship. The book is a hymn to the not quite love story between
Sal Paradise and Dean Moriarty – they drive together, they listen
to music, they share a love for a girl, they drink gallons of bad
wine, they watch the sunrise, they taste the sweetness of the world.
It is the dream writ large of every adolescent who wants a
companion to burn bright with. The final words of *On the Road*
are about friendship. As the sun goes down, the narrator tells us
that when 'nobody, nobody knows what's going to happen to
anybody besides the forlorn rags of growing old, I think of Dean
Moriarty, I even think of Old Dean Moriarty the father we never
found, I think of Dean Moriarty'.

Hamlet concerns itself with friendship as searchingly as do any of Shakespeare's plays. It is clear that Hamlet himself was a fizzing and ebullient friend before the roof fell in. Rosencrantz and Guildenstern's first encounter with him is full of a buoyant intellectual banter which sounds like a group with a shared rhythm and a long history of shared riffing. Hamlet's enthusiasm for seeing them, 'My excellent good friends! . . . good lads', is instantaneous, instinctive and thus trustworthy, as well as touching. Here and earlier with Horatio, Hamlet has a capacity to drop out of a glum mood at the sight of a friend, with the puppyish enthusiasm of the natural optimist. It is clear that there is a pre-existing friendship with Laertes of some depth, there is a courtesy towards Marcellus, and a long and heartfelt compan-ionship with Horatio. When Hamlet welcomes Horatio with 'We'll teach you to drink deep ere you depart', you imagine that Hamlet was once the life and the soul. The fizz of these pre-existing relationships makes the poisoning of them all the more sour. Shortly after Hamlet has welcomed Rosencrantz and Guildenstern with delirious spirits, he senses something odd, and questions them:

> HAMLET But, in the beaten way of friendship, what make you at Elsinore?
> ROSENCRANTZ To visit you, my lord; no other occa-sion.
> HAMLET Beggar that I am, I am even poor in thanks; but I thank you. Were you not sent for? Is it your own inclining? A free visitation? Come, deal justly with me: come, come; nay, speak.
> GUILDENSTERN What should we say, my lord?

HAMLET Why, any thing, but to the purpose. You were
sent for.
ROSENCRANTZ To what end, my lord?
HAMLET That you must teach me. But let me conjure
you, by the rights of our fellowship, and by the obligation
of our ever-preserved love, were you sent for, or no?
GUILDENSTERN My lord, we were sent for.
HAMLET I will tell you why . . .

Hamlet conceals his genuine hurt, having too much kindness and
dignity to belabour it, by flying off into 'what a piece of work
is a man'. His call on 'the obligation of our ever-preserved love'
is a heartbreaking call on trust, which makes it all the more
upsetting that that trust is broken, though it is to his friends'
credit that they do fess up. Hamlet bides his time to speak his
mind in full with reference to this breach of trust. It comes after
the disruption of the play within the play:

HAMLET O, the recorders! let me see one. Will you play
upon this pipe?
GUILDENSTERN My lord, I cannot.
HAMLET I pray you.
GUILDENSTERN Believe me, I cannot.
HAMLET I do beseech you.
GUILDENSTERN I know no touch of it, my lord.
HAMLET 'Tis as easy as lying: govern these ventages
with your fingers and thumb, give it breath with your
mouth, and it will discourse most eloquent music. Look
you, these are the stops.
GUILDENSTERN But these cannot I command; I have
not the skill.

HAMLET Why, look you now, how unworthy a thing you make of me! You would play upon me; you would seem to know my stops; you would pluck out the heart of my mystery. 'Sblood, do you think I am easier to be played on than a pipe? Call me what instrument you will, though you can fret me, yet you cannot play upon me.
ROSENCRANTZ My lord, you once did love me.

This is brilliantly set as a trap by Hamlet, and is crushing for Rosencrantz. Much as you admire Hamlet for the brilliance of the conceit and the elegance of the set-up, and though we are on his side, it does seem brutal as a public humiliation. Though not as brutal as his next action towards them, which is to send them to their deaths. When Hamlet is questioned about this by Horatio, his response is terse: 'Why, man, they did make love to this employment; / They are not near my conscience.' We have travelled a long way from the enthusiastic friend of the opening acts. But trust and truth are pivotal in the play, and to Hamlet particularly. Break trust once and you break trust always. They are rare commodities in Hamlet's world, and that puts a higher price on them.

There are two environments in which trust is an absolute: the military and the theatre. I would venture to suggest the theatre might have the better record. Theatre depends on an infinitely complex collection of moves, thoughts, shades and energies coming together at a particular moment and staying in some sort of pattern for the duration of a play. For that to be achieved, as a participant you have to have an absolute trust that your colleague will turn up, know what he or she is doing, and work with you throughout the course of a show. You have to cover their back if they are in trouble, and you expect them to cover yours. Beyond that trust are a complicated collection of etiquettes – not giving notes to your fellow actors unless invited to, not upstaging another actor, not crossing in front of another, and many more – which amount to a new code of friendship, at the heart of which is trust. Break that trust, as Rosencrantz and Guidenstern do with Hamlet, and the shut-out is immediate and complete. As it would be with any theatre company.

All that is true for a week of playing a thriller in Frinton-on-Sea. If you factor in all the other elements of trust involved in a tour on the scale this company achieved – the number of dates to hit, the difficulties of the venues, the tension in some of the places, the frequency of physical illness, the awkward relationships encountered – trust becomes both more testing and more essential. No one made scout-master speeches about it (the moment you start making those, you know you have already lost); everyone knew from their training that it was an absolute, that they had to have each other's backs or the whole ship went down. The way they rose to that task – looking after each other when ill, covering for each other on stage, ignoring some idiosyncrasies, keeping each other afloat and committed, being generous to each other with who played what where – was an example of not only trust, but also of how to be human. I have never seen it paralleled.

The saint of friendship within the play, and by example elsewhere and everywhere, is Horatio. He is the paragon of all the virtues we wrap together in a friend: loyal, discreet, sensitive, self-sacrificing, a good laugher, generous with listening, trustworthy. Hamlet says of him with a sparkling accuracy and a deep love:

Since my dear soul was mistress of her choice
And could of men distinguish her election,
Sh'hath sealed thee for herself. And best are those
Whose blood and judgement are so well commingled
That they are not a pipe for fortune's finger
To sound what stop she please. Give me that man
That is not passion's slave, and I will wear him
In my heart's core, ay, in my heart of heart,
As I do thee – something too much of this.

That last 'something too much of this' is deft observation – both
Hamlet and Horatio are embarrassed by the weight of feeling in
the moment and have to brush it off.

With Hamlet's laser-like acuity, he identifies the quintessence
of what we pray for in a friend – steadiness, lightness when the
world is heavy, feeling but not excess. It is what we prayed for
when we were picking our company, and by some miracle it is
what we got. People who were ready to support each other, who
could take the piss out of each other, who kept calm in testing
conditions, and who felt strongly for each other but not to the
degree that it was a burden. They were virtuosi of space, knowing
just the right distance to keep – close enough to care, not so
close that they suffocated. Always with an eye on each other,
never watching obsessively. There were moments when they
infuriated each other, moments when tempers were strained and
temperaments clashed, but they found their own way back to an
even keel, and all collectively worked to make sure that all others
were well.

Somehow, while carrying this whole goody-bag of virtues
on his back, Horatio manages to remain a credible individual.

That is another measure of Shakespeare's genius. All the actors loved playing him; six of them eventually shared the role. And when we hit the final run of performances, it seemed to be the role that they found the most upsetting to say goodbye to. Horatio's last gestures are heartbreaking, and a testament to his undying friendship. He tries to drink some of the remaining poison from the cup and to join his adored friend in death with the lines:

> Never believe it:
> I am more an antique Roman than a Dane:
> Here's yet some liquor left.

which always bring tears to my eyes – loyalty at the death. Hamlet forbids him with the injunction that he must stay and remember him correctly to the world, a final task that Horatio accepts. After his friend dies in his arms, he is in receipt of history and fiction's most heartfelt and most tender words of farewell:

> Now cracks a noble heart. Good night sweet prince:
> And flights of angels sing thee to thy rest!

Over the last few shows, the actor carrying this speech would find it hard to hold it together. It was, of course, largely because of saying goodbye to Hamlet, but something about playing Horatio, about the depth of care in it, became emblematic of all that they were to each other and to those they met. The moment spoke of all that the tour was: an adventure of friendship, a test of loyalty and steadiness, a journey into the goodness of the world. They were Horatios to each other, to the play, and to the world they travelled through.

★ ★ ★

I travelled back from South America to the UK via Los Angeles to check in on our production of *Lear* which was playing there. I had always been a fan of LA, but after the joys and excitements of Colombia, Ecuador and Peru, it offered a brutal lesson in deflation. I thought of Walter Benjamin and his concerns over the lessening of aura in any work of art in the age of mass repro- duction. LA suddenly looked like a manufactured version of South America, with all the concomitant dilution of effect and reduction of charisma. It may have been my own hangover from the vitality I had been sharing in, but it felt feeble in spirit and, as a way of disguising that, aggressive in attitude. It wasn't helped by the fact that Santa Monica, where we were, was full of displaced flat-faced Brits there for the American Film Market, their accents drearying the atmosphere. It looked like all the angry and desperate of Soho had been scooped up and tipped into LA, everyone shaven-headed with pilot sunglasses and stubbling away like amateur Jason Stathams. With nice girls from Surrey trying to look like Russian molls.

But as ever in LA, there was the ocean to redeem it, the waves consistent and repetitive in their soft crash like a mantra. Walking through the forest of leaning wooden struts which hold up Santa Monica pier as the sun went down into the Pacific was a strong way to calm the spirit, almost as effective as churchgoing in South America. The ceaselessly alternating white staining of the sea's edge by the froth, whitening, bulling away, whitening again. And the headmistressy scurry of the minuscule sandpipers, rushing with feathering tread ahead of the surf, is one of the world's great consoling natural comedies.

I think of Dean Moriarty, and Kerouac, and of our company; of the endless renewal and refreshment of touring, and the purity of movement. I remember hearing Peter Brook on a radio show with his *Midsummer Night's Dream* company, talking about the delight of touring, saying 'it gives one a reason for starting again as each new day breaks'. I think of the sheer, unadulterated joy I have experienced moving through the world with this company, and how illicit it feels, and how we sometimes seem to have misplaced the ability to put our courage into happiness, reserving it for seriousness and sorrow; how we often seem to have forgotten how to take pleasure from the world, and how to see the sweet, beautiful good in it. How we have turned Hamlet into this icon of glumness, when his spirit spills so much light into the world. And I think of a friar who came in to talk to us when rehearsing *Measure for Measure*. A lovely, sweet, open man, he was honest with us about every inch of his life, the disappointments and the failings and the rewards, and how testing and how extraordinary it was to be always out in the world, always meeting the worst and sometimes the best of what the world has to offer. When I asked him how he coped without the cloister that a monk enjoys, without that place of peace, he said as if surprised and without hesitation, 'The road is the cloister, and the cloister is the road.'

* * *

I flew back to London, and when I arrived back in Paddington, my way was blocked by an enormous, sad and tattered Pudsey Bear. It did not look like cultural vitality. As I drove through

London, along Buckingham Palace Road, hussars on horses pulled highly polished, antique machine guns in preparation for ceremonies for the war dead.

16

CAESAR IN ZAATARI

HAMLET *'Imperious Caesar, dead and turn'd to clay,*
Might stop a hole to keep the wind away' –

Act 5, Scene 1

IT WAS THE CHANGE IN the light that first tipped us off. The window frames, wood against tin, had been tapping nervously for a while, and looking out of one window I could see the canvas outside had begun to billow before starting to snap and slap the sides of the hall. Then, as the frames began to clatter and bang rather than tap and rattle, the light began to shift. There was no electricity in the camp – the UN having refused permission to turn the generator on – so the hard white light coming through the windows of the functional hall was all we had. That light turned from white to yellow, and then a deeper honey yellow, and just as that happened, the air itself started to thicken. The actors and the audience were enshrouded in a hazy miasma, as if the world had gone sepia. Then the light turned a heavy orange, and as the banging and clattering crescendoed into a load roar, the light disappeared altogether, and we were plunged into black. A biblical sandstorm engulfed us.

The children in the audience screamed, and their mothers with them. Not a panicky scream, but a bottom-of-the-stomach wail. This was fear of God, of the end of days, not of a weather event. They leapt up and all rushed for the stage, some to cling to the actors, some just to stand there. It was as if where the play had been taking place, a makeshift space built only two hours before, was now invested with the power to rescue and save, as if the make-believe of the play could ward off the evil. The actors looked bamboozled – the dark, the haze, the screaming, the play all colliding. They stumbled on for a while, then gave up and sat down. As the audience stormed the doors, worried for other family members outside, the UN officials stepped forward and told them all to sit down. Everyone appealed for calm, and we knew that our tour, stopped by a sandstorm, had reached a new zenith of craziness.

I rushed outside. Since a child, an electrical storm had always tempted me to run out and dance happily within the bang, crash and wallop. A wall of wind tractored into me, sand strafed mouth and face and forced its way into my eyes. Wrapping a scarf around my mouth, I leant happily into the wall. The visibility reduced to two or three metres, other figures would suddenly appear from the swirling cloud, criss-crossing through the storm. Actors loomed up, cackling merrily within the madness. One slow step after another, hair sticking out behind me as stiff as my scarf, I was framed in a cartoon which defined the tour, bent almost double and walking steadily into a sand-blasting wind.

★ ★ ★

At dawn the day before, hoping to snatch a couple of hours of sleep in transit through Beirut airport on the way to Jordan, I went to charge my phone. Beside the sofa I was attempting to crash out on were two twin plug sockets sitting primly side by side, one French, one British: the modern reminder of the continuing influence of the Sykes–Picot Agreement. This moment of colonial self-confidence, enacted by a British and a French diplomat in 1916 – Sir Mark Sykes and François Georges-Picot – carved up the Middle East with a ruler into a collection of nation states. Straight lines cut through ancient religious, tribal, national, gangster and family ties, with a pathological blithe self-confidence. The collapse of the Ottoman Empire was never going to be a pretty business – empires don't break up in a shower of rose petals and messages of love and understanding – but it's hard to believe that its end was assisted by men looking at a map, intent on competing spheres of interest, with all the local understanding and emotional intelligence of a geometry set.

History was everywhere around me – the airport was decked out with huge photographs of Roman ruins, archaeological artefacts sat here and there on plinths, blocks of broken marble hinted at great narratives of the risen and the fallen. The bookshop in Beirut was light on sensationalism and heavy on history. Having flown on to Jordan in the morning light over the mountains of Lebanon and the Syrian desert, as I drove in from Amman airport towards my hotel, my driver, a third-generation Palestinian, was generous with his knowledge of the long story of the city.

Amman has been continuously inhabited for almost 10,000 years. Built around seven interlocking steep hills, it was an important stop on the caravan routes which slowly transported people and goods from East to West and back again. Homes and towers from the Stone Age have been found there; in the time of the Trojan wars, it had become the Ammonite capital, Rabbath Ammon, from where the inhabitants went into battle against Saul and David; in the Ptolemaic time, it was renamed Philadelphia; under Seleucus, a successor of Alexander the Great, it came under Hellenistic rule for a couple of centuries; then a brief moment under Nabatean rule; then King Herod, a Judean king under a Roman mandate, ruled it as part of the Decapolis, a league of Roman affiliated cities, when it blossomed into full Roman grandiosity. It declined during the Byzantine period and was overrun by Sassanians in the seventh century until they were thrown out by the Arab armies of Islam only twenty years later in about AD 635. The story, as told to me by my taxi driver, was dizzying, a wild game of 'Who's the king of the castle' across millennia. And studded by names from Sunday-school picture books – Saul, David, Ptolemy, Alexander, Herod, Mohamed. These were figures from myth systems, tumbling out of brightly coloured educational books, and here I was in their back yard. The sense of contact with history was vertiginous.

The more recent history was no less disorienting, though its shapes were latterly defined against the television news rather than illustrated Bibles. After the Great Arab Revolt of 1916–18 Emir Abdullah bin Al-Hussein made Amman his capital in 1921. The city grew rapidly as a result of the wars of 1948 and 1967, when successive waves of Palestinian refugees were driven towards Amman; a further influx followed the 1990 Gulf War, and the continuing chaos in the region has drawn more lost people towards its towering hills. From a distance, it often seems that the Middle East (so named by the West, which claims naming rights over everything) is the research and development laboratory of human history, the place where conflicts, ideas and tensions are grown in petri dishes, only to be later marketed over time to the rest of the world. The earliest human stories grew here and have now expanded into myth. To be here within the fact of it was exhilarating, everything one saw bearing a crushing weight of imparted imagination.

Driving through the city to the theatre felt like a roller-coaster ride through the history of civilisation. You turned a corner and saw precipitate hills, all stacked with houses from different eras, each hill brought to sharp life by the lowering sun, each sliding in and out of view one against another, like movable scenery in a giant Pollock's toy theatre. Each hill was covered in a clambering Lego set of construction, all in various shades of cream and buff stone. Almost half of each mountain of buildings was left unfinished, one or two floors completed before a halt was called, leaving metal foundation spikes sticking cheerlessly up into the air. All those promises of home standing half-achieved and tenantless had a steadily lowering effect. Monolithic outcrops of rock burst out of the ranks of human habitation like some primordial trapped giant within each hill trying to stretch its limbs.

The theatre itself was magical, and when the company arrived to play in it, we were all flattered by a sense of privilege. Named the Odeon, it was built in the second century AD, in the reign of Antoninus Pius, and had been in continuous use as a theatre for almost 2,000 years. Surprisingly, it was right in the middle of the city, at the bottom of a steep hill, and was part of what must be one of the first theatre complexes. Beside it, stretching a third of the way up the hill, was a Roman amphitheatre, carved into the rock, built for spectacle and able to seat 6,000 people. The Odeon, a perfectly proportioned arena around a thrust playing space, seated only 600. We are accustomed in the present day to seeing big theatres spawning smaller studio spaces alongside, but I had no idea the practice went back 2,000 years. We started reblocking the show for this space but realised there was no time, so everyone determined to busk it and appear wherever and whenever their legs would carry them. The city honked and beeped cantankerously outside, but as the day dissolved leaving an inky black above, the residue of the day's light seemed to settle into the creamy marble of the theatre, emitting a soft reciprocal glow. The heat of the city dropped into and trapped itself within this encircled space, and as the audience filled it with noisy anticipation, the sense of event was thrilling.

The show was electrifying. The thrust space was a dynamic arena for the cast to move and swirl about in, and for human dilemmas to shape themselves across thrilling diagonals or triangles freighted with tension. The acoustic was perfect. Every word landed crisp and clear, and every character stood sharp and proud. Later, a student said to an academic travelling with us, 'I was worried that the noise of the traffic outside would spoil the show, but it soon disappeared, and after watching Ophelia die, I just felt sad that the world was going on outside as normal, and no one knew that this young girl had died.'

When Hamlet returns from his aborted trip to England, he engages with the Gravedigger. He has his iconic moment with the skull of Yorrick, the court clown on whose shoulders he had played and laughed as child. In that moment he stares death, actual and bony and hollow-eyed, straight in its fleshless face, and he feels not fear, but peace and understanding. It is a peace that is accessed through history. He holds the skull and asks:

HAMLET Prithee, Horatio, tell me one thing.
HORATIO What's that, my lord?

HAMLET Dost thou think Alexander looked o' this
fashion i' the earth?
HORATIO E'en so.
HAMLET And smelt so? Pah!
Puts down the skull.
HORATIO E'en so, my lord.
HAMLET To what base uses we may return, Horatio!
Why may not imagination trace thus. Alexander died,
Alexander was buried, Alexander returneth into dust; the
dust is earth; of earth we make loam; and why of that
loam, whereto he was converted, might they not stop a
beer-barrel?
'Imperious Caesar, dead and turn'd to clay,
Might stop a hole to keep the wind away' –

Here we sat, in a city which Alexander might have passed through
and Caesar visited, that Jesus might have drunk water in, and in
which Muhammad might have broken fast, a city right at the
crossroads of the human story, and these words twisted in the
night air, looking backwards and forwards through time.

Shakespeare, across his work, uses time and history as a portal
to calm. Much has been written and worried over as to what his
religious inclinations were, if any. It has always seemed to me that
he found in history itself, in its processes, its narratives, its crushing
roll forwards, something terrifying and yet capable of affording a
perverse transcendence. He writes of time as the ultimate arbiter,
a force which crushes human struggles and renders them meaningless, and yet within the appreciation of that fact there is a
liberation. To know that time passes inexorably beside us, or
without us, and that like a hapless swimmer of the seas our task
is to find the right pace of stroke to suit the waves which lift

and drop, to know that and to keep ploughing gently forwards, footling but steady, small within the billow and the surge, yet able occasionally to sink happily into the ride; to know that, and to do that, is a sort of peace.

It is not a Californian prescription for mental health, and no one achieves it perfectly, of course. Hamlet, with his adventurous and experimental capacity, gets as close as anyone, but his achievement is prone to turbulence. No one, least of all Shakespeare, is saying that you can learn this stuff on a three-day course.

This is also transcendentalism with political bite. It is not Everyman who is finding his or her place in history here, it is the two most iconic figures from the ancient world, Alexander and Caesar, both humiliated by the wrangle of time. The greatest warrior of all time turns to dust which is remoulded to block a hole in a barrel of booze; the greatest politician is used to keep the draught out. This is an extension of the intellectual freedom Hamlet discovers earlier in challenging Claudius before he is sent away. Having killed Polonius in a surge of fury, his 'antic disposition' having led him far from his own calm place, he is quizzed by Claudius as to where Polonius is and replies:

> HAMLET Not where he eats, but where he is eaten: a certain convocation of politic worms are e'en at him. Your worm is your only emperor for diet: we fat all creatures else to fat us, and we fat ourselves for maggots: Look you, a man may fish with the worm that hath eaten of a king, and a beggar eat that fish, which that worm hath caught.
> CLAUDIUS What dost you mean by this?
> HAMLET Nothing father, but to show you how a king may go a progress through the guts of a beggar.

This is a flash of illumination within a disordered mind: the later passage mentioning Alexander and Caesar the same thought handled with gentle bemusement. But within both is an anger at the ridiculousness of status, of baubles, of grandiosity and show, in the face of inevitable oblivion. The liberation here is realising the comedy of humanity's farcical attempts to look significant and to set up hierarchies of importance. Since everyone ends up 'going a progress through the guts of a beggar' (and how vicious a phrase that is – not just being eaten by a beggar, but passing right through him), then to what end is the hopeless search for distinctions?

It's a radical statement now, and must have been yet more radical for its audience in 1603, when social distinction was delineated with painful precision, right down to the fabrics you and your class were allowed to wear. It's radical to hear, yet more liberating to think and to say. Whatever the age, there is always an inclination for individuals to mythologise themselves, and often a social pressure to collaborate in their self-mythification. We are suckered into it, and join in the act of excess promotion, and end up frightened by those we have collaborated in glorifying. So it is always good to remember, and refreshing to say out loud, that Vladimir Putin, and Donald Trump will be sent by history through the sphincter of a beggar.

There is also a sharp tweak of the Renaissance nose at work within Hamlet's graceful humbling of Alexander and Caesar. Neither Hamlet nor Shakespeare had any idea that they were within anything called a Renaissance, yet they lived in an age with a rediscovered passion for the classical world. The idea that the Renaissance was about something being reborn has largely been forgotten. Many associate it with an aimless modernity involving Leonardo inventing helicopters; others just with funny trousers and swords. But it was a rebirth of classical thought and learning which drove it, and for a radical purpose. That thought was used to contextualise, and to subvert, the Christian hegemony of the day. The reverence for these figures within intellectual circles was freshly minted, so in reducing Alexander and Caesar to the status of dust, Hamlet is taking potshots at the fashion of his day, and its intellectual underpinning.

Sitting there, under the stars, surrounded by the hills of Amman, in a beautifully enclosed Roman arena theatre, unable to exclude the barking noise or the orange light of a modern city, but able to transport the historical imagination, sitting there in a city which for many millennia had witnessed the merry-go-round of human striving, as Babylonians, Assyrians, Persians, Greeks, Romans, Muslims, Ottomans, French, British and Arabs had all staked their petty claim against the shift of time, sitting there, it was not hard to appreciate and sympathise with Hamlet's cosmic joking at the grand comedy of human enterprise, against the backdrop of history and change. At that moment, all endeavours, including our tour, seemed something of a whisper in the wind.

★ ★ ★

The next morning, we were up at five, shovelling breakfast into our mouths before setting off to the north of Jordan. Our destination was Zaatari, a UN refugee camp created to house almost 120,000 displaced Syrians. There was no way we could play in Syria itself, and this expedition, playing to Syrian people, appeared to us the best substitute. Further sleep was attempted, the company tangled into the funny shapes which minibuses prompt in order to find comfort, but the landscape proved too vivid to allow much shut-eye. The edge of town was a broken and busted scrapheap, scrags of old metal leaning against busted-car graveyards. Beyond the edge of town, the long roll of ochre desert began, the continuing sweep of dust shading slowly from terracotta to yellow. Occasionally it was broken by a gathered rise to a small plateau of rock, before flattening out again to its long continuum of nothing. Small settlements pockmarked the landscape, homes with stockade fences enclosing minimal numbers of desultory goats or camels, whose ability to eke something out of this barren land beggared the imagination.

How has this tough landscape been so endlessly fought over, and why does it continue to act as the nodal point of so many of the world's antagonisms? Oil, yes, but there is something more as well. How did the three great monotheisms, Judaism, Christianity and Islam, which have had such a powerful hand on the historical steering wheel, get birthed out of this tough, scrubby land? Does the austerity of the landscape, its harsh blast to the spirit, provoke a need for a world elsewhere, for a religion beyond? Does God come from rocks not grass? I thought of a play about Farinelli we had recently played at the Globe. Written by a friend, Claire van Kampen, she merrily stole one gag from an email I had sent her, and exuberantly delivered by Mark Rylance it proved irresistible: 'Many gods are fun. One is a nightmare!' Does this barrenness lead inevitably to one god, and does woodland and running water lead to Panic fun? And how has the rest of the world been so bullied by the martyrdom of rocks, deserts and big skies? Why has this self-punishing monotheism, this determined pushing of the human away from its own body and its own physical world, so often won? And why does it keep winning, bullying the not-so-bothered-about-eternity majority with its bombs and its aggressive staring-eyed dumbness?

Why did it feel, stuttering along in a rickety minibus, like there was violence stored in the dust and the rock? Was that all projection? It didn't feel like the result of spilt blood; it felt like something geologically inherent within the striated red of the rock and written into the desert dust. The violence felt necessary. It seemed to be pulling the muscles tight in every taut held body you came across. How can you sit in a peace conference in Vienna and talk all that away?

The refugee camp sat on a low-lying level plain, which made it impossible to perceive from a distance and rendered its size impossible to gauge from close up. This was an effective means of concealing the awfulness of the fact of its existence. We halted at various outposts, where bored fat men in military costumes from bad theatre productions sat smoking, looking at papers, and looking to slow time down to their pace. There were two armoured personnel carriers at the entrance, but the sense of threat was low level. An earth rampart further concealed the camp, again seemingly for disguise. Once beyond that, we entered a small city of white boxes. We were confronted with an endless vista of low white prefab units, all a similar shape, laid out in serried ranks intersected by avenues, in an endless de-personalised parody of a communal living space. Every box, rather depressingly, seemed to have a satellite dish.

Beside the numbing brokenness of everyone living in a uniform white container, the atmosphere was surprisingly normal. It was a Sunday, and the feeling was Sunday bright. We glimpsed a public meeting between several boxes; there were boys show-boating on their bikes, looking for trouble; there were kids charging around looking for excitement, infants wandering about looking lost, mothers carrying their babies. Several of the boxes had shop-fronts pulled up to make awnings, which provided shade for rudimentary cafes and sweet shops. There was a distinct impression of people in their Sunday best, and a few highly blinged-up women walked past, clearly on their way to a party. A young bicyclist scooted past us, riding high on his pedals. I looked at the seat of his bike. It was rigged out with a complicated wrap of casually elegant embroidery which covered some of the frame as well. Beyond it, whooshed up by the pace of the bike, a section of purple tassels frilled up into the air. There was a confounding flair about this small detail.

We arrived at the small UNHCR stockade in the middle of the camp, where we were to present the play. It was a fenced-in collection of buildings built for education, around an open yard, with a meeting place in the middle shaded by a tin roof. We spent much of the next few hours trying to get out of the yard and to wander around the camp. Promises were made, people were sent for, permissions were sought, release was pending, but it never happened. A crowd quickly gathered to gawp at us. The company with their easy guileless charm approached the crowd and started uncomprehending conversations. A band of hopelessly cheerful youth crowded on the other side of the fence, and the names of football stars were bandied back and forth. Miranda let them play her mandolin, Keith astonished them with some magic tricks, and the international language of double-jointed finger-bending was indulged in. We were under strict instructions not to give them anything, but they seemed to have too much dignity to ask, and the play of laughter and mock insult and mock outrage passed freely to and fro through the mesh. The company gathered to practise their songs and musical cues in the shade, and the familiar tunes in the alien setting further nurtured a sense of dreaminess.

I wandered around the other buildings. In one prefab school-room, there were six models which had been constructed as group projects to bring the class together. Designs and drawings for each plastered the walls, and the constructions from paper, card, wood and anything that can be scraped together were impressive. They were all of ancient Syrian monuments, relics from old civilisations. The sense of these shapes, of Ozymandias-like broken grandiosities, was hard-wired into these people's genetic code, and displacement made them keener to recreate them. Articulating these shapes, recording them, making them real again, even with matchsticks and cardboard, seems to give security in a world that moves like a whirlwind. As IS charges round obliterating all traces of history, and of the world before Islam, this attachment to the ancient past in young minds was strangely fortifying. Of the six models, three of them were of ancient theatres. The impertinence of bringing theatre to a culture that was making uniquely sophisticated theatre when the British were still hurling cowpats at each other was underlined.

A small tin library was filled with women chattering in burqas. I asked if I could come in, they assented, and I wandered awkwardly amongst the books, my presence halting their chatter. The sheer tinpot courage of this – a tiny library for refugees in a desert – I wanted to lock in to my scrapheap of images as a symbol of hope. But alongside a few sensational bestsellers, and a few books about understanding civil war, the majority of the titles were given over to accountancy. There was a whole shelf for volumes on pension reform. The absurdity of this in this context almost had a sweet poetry to it. We are living in a Price Waterhouse world.

The show was supposed to begin soon, but there was a worrying lack of that vital ingredient: an audience. The start time was 12 p.m., and about five people had shown up. No one seemed worried, so we kicked around in the backstage area. By quarter past there were about twenty people. Alarmingly, at 12.30 the audience seemed to have shrunk back to about fifteen. The gag went around, 'This show's so crap, we couldn't get an audience in a refugee camp', and 'Everyone's got something better to do.' The laughter was a little nervous. The speed of motion and the early rise was catching up with me, so I sneaked into a small space between a curtain and a wall, lay down and tried to sleep. A hazy doze shuffled in to my brain, murmured into by noises of nervous actors and audience bustle, the shut-eyed blackness perforated by the images of the last few hours which spiralled into the void then careered out again. Then a gentle surprise, a face looming out of the blackness, a shape forming out of the pool of ink, and then, reluctant to be too present, falling gently back into it. It was a face that I had dimly glimpsed in a similar trance years before. The same qualities I remembered – warmth, shyness, sensitivity, a discreet sensuality – then an ebbing away. A long way from a sighting, but if you're going to get a sudden and strong sense of Shakespeare, why not in Zaatari . . .?

With alarming suddenness, I was kicked out of my slumber and took my seat in a packed and excited hall. This lot may have been late, but they certainly brought a party when they arrived. About 300 people crowded the hall, dressed for a carnival, mobiles out; the chatter was high and happy, and had the vivid animation of a group of people who were not going to shut up however hard you tried. There was a cheeringly large minority of kids, who charged around the place, shouting, yabbering, leaping on strangers' laps, laughter and happiness spilling out of them like water. The show started, and the animation didn't decrease in the slightest. The kids continued charging about, and the actors joyously accommodated it. At one moment, when Hamlet got out his notebook to record the words of the Ghost, 'My tables –

Meet it is I set it down', two young girls ran up and stood by his shoulder to see what he had written down. The Ghost went down a treat, a bit of white make-up, some staring eyes, and some rumble and thunder in the voice scaring the audience into silence. Ghosts felt real here. The story was clear, and a bit of explicit gesture in the acting gave much pleasure. There was a running commentary from everybody on everything – the stories, the actors' gestures, the characters. The audience segregated into women on one side – bright, excited and engaged – and men on the other – either lazily disaffiliate if young, or gravely austere if old. Everything was filmed on mobiles, most from a single position, though one young man, in an insanely bright-pink jumper, moved around the audience, standing on a chair, hanging from a pillar, lying on the floor, all to get the best angle.

Then the sand came, and an already strange event flipped out into something else. The night before, in Amman, history flattened us into inconsequence; today it was nature's turn to show us a glimpse of oblivion. Here we were, with the walls shaking, the sky filled with a thick haze, and the sun well and truly shut out. The reaction of the audience was a Shakespearean one: this was a properly ominous event. Heaven knows what fears passed through their heads, but for us it was another sign of our vainglorious irrelevance. In the middle of the storm, in a moment where it was hard to believe it would stop, the image of an enormous shift of sand burying us and all our silly gestures flitted through the mind. It was hard not to feel an appropriateness, that our endeavour would end up as a remnant in the dust.

What would be, what will be left of us? It is a question that exercises Shakespeare vividly and actively throughout his sonnets but rarely in his plays. Sonnet after sonnet recounts the power of time, its ability to crush kings and monuments, statues and the statuesque. But in each one, Shakespeare asserts the power of his words to survive, to endure beyond any destruction. There is a perversity in his faith in the indestructibility of words, beside the frailty of stone and power, even poetic words in delicate love poems. Shakespeare, as with many a great artist, always understood that strength is made of glass, and that tenderness is made of steel. The purest expression of this is in a sonnet:

> Not marble, nor the gilded monuments
> Of princes, shall outlive this powerful rhyme;
> But you shall shine more bright in these contents
> Than unswept stone, besmear'd with sluttish time.
> When wasteful war shall statues overturn,
> And broils root out the work of masonry,
> Nor Mars his sword nor war's quick fire shall burn
> The living record of your memory.
> 'Gainst death and all-oblivious enmity
> Shall you pace forth; your praise shall still find room
> Even in the eyes of all posterity
> That wear this world out to the ending doom.
> So, till the judgment that yourself arise,
> You live in this, and dwell in lovers' eyes.

All that is substantial will dissolve, and words, frail floaty words, endure. Strangely the plays rarely enter into the same discussion. Cleopatra shows an awareness of and a fear about posterity, and how she might be represented by subsequent generations. She and her paramour are ever eager to remind us that they are peerless, in their own moment and in the annals. But largely the plays live in the fury of their own present moment. They find their own perspective and their own context within time, but they do not strain to assert their power to defeat it. Shakespeare took little or no care to present these plays to the world or to posterity – unlike the sonnets. For him, the plays seem to have been disposable and simply for the moment of performance.

So here in the ultimate land of the blasted monument, ground down by history, or covered inexorably in the swift or slow shifts of the desert, it was an honour for us to be asserting, however feebly, the enduring clout of these words. Here in Zaatari, the audience may not all have been listening, the stage may have been beyond makeshift, the context may have been bigger and more tragic than we could ever hope to match, and nature itself may have been trying to call a halt, but here we were merrily tossing out these gorgeous words into the void. However words survive, on stone, on paper, in books, in mouths and ears, in the air itself somehow, and even in the minds of young children who have come to hear a play presented by some batty foreigners, somehow we were contributing to that ineffable daisy chain in the ether.

The show resumed, with a peculiar calm, after the light returned. The world seemed to have shifted on its axis a little. The audience, at first, were chastened and attentive, as if God had told them to hush a little. Some words still acquired an extra resonance. When the Player King arrived and told of the death of Priam, the fall of Troy and the great grief of Hecuba, the air got sharper. Not only was this more from ancient history, and an ancient history that wasn't too far away, but it was also a tale of a fallen kingdom and of the chaos which followed. It couldn't help but ripple in the air before a room full of refugees. The boys were over excited by the violence against the women. When Hamlet got a little rough-house with first Ophelia and then Gertrude, they squawked with an awkward excitement. The women looked properly alarmed. The young man in the obscenely bright-pink jumper was now taking his film-making even further. He frequently encroached onto the stage to get an extreme close-up of an actor. Then rather disconcertingly he stepped onto the stage, ignored the actors and started filming the audience. As the end approached, and the swords came out, and death accelerated towards the stage, everyone crowded round and got their cameras out. At the front, there was a small group who had taken so heavily against Claudius that when he was finally killed, they burst into spontaneous applause and jumped up and down with pleasure. Killing bad kings, even in show, still clearly caused much delight.

The show finished, and the audience and the energy that had filled the room both melted away. Some had clearly found it mystifying, some a little ridiculous, some had relished a great story, and some seemed to have eaten up every moment. I did a ridiculous interview with a film crew, which was frequently interrupted by a precarious pop-up UN banner placed behind me that kept toppling and falling onto me. A small group remained to talk to the actors, and swapped stories and sang a song to us. They told us that they hoped we would come back, and next time to Syria. We were all too punch-drunk to absorb the surprise of the day, and most slept out the journey back. One further final detail of weird poetry had silenced me . . .

As Hamlet died, at that exact moment, another noise softly filled the room, a gentle and percussive thap-thappity-thap on the roof. As Hamlet died, the rains came.

17

EMBATTLED THEATRE NEAR
THE GREAT RIFT VALLEY

HAMLET *What a piece of work is a man!*

Act 2, Scene 2

IN A SURPRISINGLY DOMESTIC MOMENT of betrayal, a small hill
in a play full of high mountains and sheer cliffs, Hamlet is let
down by his two university friends Rosencrantz and Guildenstern.
They have arrived to holiday with him, yet after a brief passage
of interrogation reveal that their presence, at the behest of Claudius,
is to spy on Hamlet. Out of this uncomfortable moment, Hamlet,
with characteristic perversity, forges from his mind the most
astonishing passage of prose ever written for the stage:

> I have of late, but wherefore I know not, lost all my
> mirth, forgone all custom of exercises; and indeed it goes
> so heavily with my disposition that this goodly frame, the
> earth, seems to me a sterile promontory, this most excel-
> lent canopy, the air, look you, this brave o'erhanging
> firmament, this majestical roof fretted with golden fire,

why, it appears no other thing to me than a foul and
pestilent congregation of vapours. What a piece of work
is a man! How noble in reason, how infinite in faculty,
in form and moving how express and admirable, in action
how like an angel! in apprehension how like a god! the
beauty of the world! the paragon of animals! And yet, to
me, what is this quintessence of dust? Man delights not
me . . .

The spice in the soup here is a pinch of play-acting. Hamlet is
lying ('wherefore I know not') – he does know, all too well, the
cause of his own grief. A little of his feigned 'antic disposition'
stirs some manic freedom into his invention. But the lie, and the
acted mania, liberate mind and tongue to pour out truth like
water from the tap of his melancholic soul. It is a paean to the
potential of the world for beauty and the human for grace, and
a heart-sore critique of the disappointments when that potential
is so rarely fulfilled. It is the hymn spoken with joy at dawn and
with sadness at dusk by every melancholic since. It is a proof of
soul. It says that you can see the glories of the world, and can
see through them at the same time. For many it is now a pose;
for Hamlet it was fresh as a daisy and dangerous as a petrol bomb.
This is the human claiming new space for himself, new Renaissance
capabilities, claiming equivalence with God and the angels, and
at the same moment seeing the futility within such claims.

★ ★ ★

Somaliland was our toughest gig to that point, an independent
republic carved out of the north of Somalia twenty-three years
earlier and still not recognised as a state by the African Union

or the UN. It was dangerous – not quite Mogadishu, but not far off. Before we set off, we gathered in a hotel room in Addis Ababa and were given a security briefing by stage management. The atmosphere was unsensational but tense. When we arrived in Hargeisa, we were shuffled into a private room as they arranged the armed convoy to ferry us around. John and I sneaked back onto the airstrip for a cigarette. Our bags and sixteen flight cases scooted past on a trailer tugged by a tractor. It was driven by one of the happiest men I have ever seen. He revved his engine, toot-tooted his horn with reckless abandon and waved to us. Just witnessing him bucked the spirit. We smoked in silence for a while. Then the little tractor, barely bigger than a sit-down lawn-mower, passed back the other way, its elation seemingly increased, now zig-zagging merrily to compound the pleasure of the revving and the toot-tooting and the waving. We remained in silence for a while, until John said, '*That* is exactly the sort of job you dream of having half an hour before a press night.'

We were shepherded together by Ayen, an elegant Somali woman and one of our chief hosts. Part resident in London and part in Hargeisa, Ayen had come into our offices early in the process of the tour and had moved heaven and earth to get us there. Behind heavy gates, we climbed into three black-windowed Land Cruisers and set off. Beyond the gates were two pick-up trucks, crammed with boy soldiers loosely holding Kalashnikovs, one of which preceded us, the other followed. This was a long way from a genteel tour of the Home Counties. We drove to our hotel and weaved our way through a long series of crash barriers, metal grates and industrial lumps of concrete.

The sense of forbidding didn't stop once the gates had been passed. Each room displayed a prominent set of house rules. These included an edict against any gatherings, gambling or playing of games of chance. It was Keith's birthday and, as Chief Spielmeister, this interdiction was going to hit his plans very hard. It also said that no women were allowed in boys' rooms or vice versa. This immediately prompted Amanda to charge into Beruce's room and display herself in a less than devout manner. A similar spirit prompted us later to tell the hotel that we were holding a prayer meeting in Ladi's room, where we gathered to play a desultory game of poker. It was hard to work up a spirit of Runyonesque shadiness under strip lights, drinking Coca-Cola and with guards with machine guns patrolling the quiet night streets outside.

The next morning, our youthful escort of AK47s returned, and we headed off into town to visit the Cultural Center whose founders had organised our visit. The streets were a technicolour riot, the most startling combinations of primary colours decking out each shopfront, some in abstract shapes, some just happy clashes of pigment punching into each other. Elsewhere the sun had blanched some of the earlier vibrancy into pastel shades. Shop painting felt like high-street art, pinging image and life out into dust and sand. For a while we lost our escort in the bustle and the chaos, and started to feel nervous, then it rattled up beside us, young arms merrily holding death in their grip, and we moved on.

The Cultural Center had a high red-clay wall around it. We walked through the gates to discover a barrage of cameras and reporters and microphones. They all shyly backed away, staring at us as if we were aliens. This brought home how rare cultural visits were. We were the first company to visit in the history of the republic. The respect was excessive and disorienting, and we stepped forward quickly to shake hands and say hello and defuse specialness. A Foreign Office young bubble of enthusiasm stepped forward and introduced herself.

'Hello, I'm —— ——, and I'm not here!'

'Ah, hello, where are you?'

'I'm in Addis Ababa. I'm not allowed to be here, because the country is not officially recognised yet.'

'Ah, how often are you not here?'

'Four days a week.'

She introduced us to the Ambassador, who had flown up from Mogadishu. He was very much here and surrounded by a terrifying security detail, all ex-SAS, all scrawny, grizzled, lean statements of violence and intent.

The whole group of us were led around the centre. We were shown a library, a small room with high shelves of books surrounding a plain table, and an exhibition gallery full of art wrought from horrendous pain – lost souls piling on top of each other on boats, and women twisted in metal chains of entrapment. Rape, hunger and flight breathed through the oil of the paint with a directness which made most art seem frivolous. And a theatre, which was a glory. A tiny oblong, it was built from wood strips, some boards and a load of crude mats formed by weaving wool through reeds. Seating about a hundred, something about its simplicity of construction and its focused shape felt perfect. A space for rough and sustainable magic. A ghetto blaster pumped out disco music, and we were treated to a display of local dancing. The company, being too generous to spend too long receiving, got up and joined in the dance.

A table was laid out on a dais in the open air for a press conference. A crowd of journalists attended, and their excitement seemed disproportionate. One of them asked, 'How are you so brave?', and when we asked him to explain, he said, 'How are you so brave to come here when no one else will come here?' This was in some ways embarrassingly gratifying, and in more others embarrassingly wrong. All the courage was theirs in inviting us here, in creating a cultural centre, in keeping going. We were fly-by-nights, passing through. I tried to reply but got it wrong, and my answer landed too heavily on the air and took some of the magic out of the event. Unsurprisingly, the inevitable question about North Korea came up. 'Everyone is entitled to a story,' Amanda said, and I locked that away as a good line.

Ayen was our introduction to Somalia. Our official host, and the man behind the Cultural Center, was Jama, a genial, bustling soul, whose energy was more that of a deal-maker than an aesthete. All the better for it – Lord save us from the aesthetes. Creating this centre was clearly a miracle of adamantine will and polygonal appeasement. The thought police didn't want it, the real police were reluctant, the government muted, even those who most wanted it were frightened to ask, given the opposition of all the others. This was not the sort of opposition who write a tart paragraph in the latest Shakespeare quarterly; this was the type to lob a mortar. That was the reason we couldn't play in the Cultural Center itself and were going to have to play in the hotel. There were insufficient defences against mortar attack.

Hargeisa had built itself a proud national theatre in the 1970s, a cement lump like our own National. It was the pride of the city. When the occupying Somali power left in 1992, just before they departed they placed mines under that theatre and blew it to rubble, just to ensure that all that happy nonsense of laughter and thought and insight could never be enjoyed again. There is still something stubbornly subversive about the nature of theatre. Even now the power of words on stage reaching ears open to democratic thought sends a shiver down the spines of the powerful.

We tried and tried and tried to get into North Korea, in spite of all the lambasting and mockery from the press and pundits.

We were in briefly, and then our trip was cancelled because of a brouhaha at the UN. We picked up the pieces and tried again, and eventually manoeuvred their UK representative onto the sofa in my office. A delightful man, if guarded, he told us about North Korea's cultural contact. This seemed to comprise the New York Philharmonic, Dennis Rodman, a tribute band called the Beijing Beatles, an enthusiasm for the film *Bend it Like Beckham*, and visits from the Middlesbrough Ladies football team. Middlesbrough featured very large in their cultural mythology – North Korea's defeat of Italy there in the 1966 World Cup was probably their greatest moment as a nation. The meeting went well, and we were hopeful. The word came back that we could come, but only if the performance consisted solely of 'music, dance and acrobatics'. No words could be spoken. No play had been enacted there since the beginning of the nation, and they weren't going to start now. We declined. Extraordinary how words, even in a foreign language, pose a challenge that little else does.

Jama told me how various religious and cultural authorities, both within and without, had turned theatre itself into a sin. He remembered Hargeisa, his hometown, as progressive and relaxed and free when he was young, a place where all opinions could flourish. Now an unholy mix of those with the most money, their pet demagogues, and those with the least, were clawing back all such freedoms. They wanted societies based on simple and manipulatable hatreds. 'Shame on them,' Jama said, his outrage spilling out, 'and shame on the West for starving us of support and culture. Shame on the whole lot of them.'

In the midst of this fear, Ayen and Jama had formed their Cultural Center. All around there was chaos and mayhem, some venality, much needless suffering at the shitty end of the international stick, and in the middle of it all, a few educational books picked up here and there, some strikingly naïve art giving witness to pain, and a place for people to sing and dance and tell stories together. 'Those with the money [I think this vague expression was supposed to imply people outside Somaliland] dictate a culture of fear and hatred to us. Why should we not create a counter-culture? Tomorrow, after your *Hamlet*, Somaliland will be different.' The weight of responsibility was impossible, the reality – that our *Hamlet* would change nothing – was undeniable, but the sentiment was overwhelming.

We rumbled off over crumbling roads in convoy to lunch in a small tourist village. This featured a few reconstructed huts to show the lifestyle of the Somali nomad, and a couple of larger barns, built from the same combo of wood strips and matting. We were served a simple yet ornate feast of camel and goat and fish and corn, all appearing artlessly in wooden bowls. Jama told me at length about the poetic traditions of this region, a whole cornucopia of different verse forms each calibrated in tone and rhythm for their particular task – forms and songs for addressing goats and camels. Sitting in a big nomadic tent and finding out about camel song was one of those moments where you have to check if you're not dreaming.

It was then he told me of their national poet, Hadrawi. A figure as influential in this region as García Márquez in Latin America or Shakespeare in England, and towering above any politician. He was still alive and had wanted to come to *Hamlet* but had not been able. An irascible old man, he had refused to become state poet throughout his life, preferring to be chief state critic. For his troubles, he had been imprisoned under three different regimes, each occasion making him more popular with the general public. He now had something of the status of a living god. His poetry sounded, from Jama's description, like a sort of dynamic performance poetry, a blend of ancient form, modern politics and the inspiration of the moment. Somewhere between Homer and rap. To audiences of thousands, he launched himself into a microphone, seized the attention of the room and devastated everyone. The work was part improvised, part full of his own stock of phrasing, all full of his own wisdom.

I asked Jama to give me some of his favourite lines – he quoted me something packed with husky aspirant h's, and long swaying vowel sounds from which dust seemed to rise. The form is full of alliteration, a memory tool as well as a musical flourish, where the opening letter scatters itself through the sentence that follows, both at the beginning and within the words. He then translated the line for me as:

> I am bitter and sweet, both at the same time found in
> the same place . . .

In the cold light of day, that may look a trifle banal, but in a big nomad tent, with a mouth full of lemony camel, it more than passed muster. In that moment, it was sort of everything.

★ ★ ★

Hamlet's conundrum, as set out in 'what a piece of work . . .', seemed out of place here in Hargeisa, and yet, through a paradox, acutely appropriate. The lament of a fully privileged Renaissance prince could seem fey in such a toughened environment. Hamlet lived in a castle, Elsinore, where musicians sat all day long in solitary rooms playing their instruments so their lonely music could travel along interior pipes to rooms which could let in the music or stop it with the opening or closing of a soundproofing vent.

This was the most labour-intensive stereo system in history. Elsinore, when it was built towards the end of the sixteenth century, was one of the wealthiest and most impressive edifices in Europe. The Danish king, training his cannon on the straits which gave the world access to Russia, Sweden, Finland, Poland, the Baltics and northern Germany, and vice-versa, had one of the easiest and most profitable tax harvests of all time. He turned it into the magnificent heap of gloominess that is Elsinore. Hamlet had been educated to the highest standard at one of the most forward-thinking establishments of his day. All of the accomplishments and achievements of the Renaissance congregate together in this young man.

A small portion of his exultation at the glories of the universe comes as a result of royal privilege. A larger portion as a result of his education. The vastness of his knowledge, the opening up of classic texts, the liberation they offered from an identity-constricting Christian order of being, the thrill of being able to think, to express thought and to find new forms within which to express that thought – all has whisked him to the top of a tower of possibilities:

> How noble in reason, how infinite in faculty, in form
> and moving how express and admirable, in action how
> like an angel, in apprehension how like a god! The beauty
> of the world . . .

He is not only saying these things; he is claiming for himself the right to say them. And within that act of naming, the right to be them. These are assertions as well as statements. To say this is an act of self-enfranchisement. Claiming parity with angels and gods may seem like hubris, but in an age when travel and science were opening up whole new worlds both micro and macro to the all-seeing eye of man, there must have been something celebratory about them. To see the great beauty of the spreading universe, and to find the perfect words to express its expanse, is both an act of description and of appropriation. I invoke therefore I own. The view from the top of the tower is exhilarating, and might delude anyone into an impression of divine self-investment. But it is also vertiginous.

Clear sight exposes potential but also reality. Hamlet can see the great dance of being human, and at the same time the paltriness of human behaviour. Science enables but it also reveals. A telescope or a microscope can open up thrilling new details or vistas, but can also strip away mystery. It is exhilarating to see so much sky above, but terrifying to live over an abyss. Hamlet is one of the many journeymen, if not the prime one, on our lonely path away from our first selves and towards we know not what. Glorious but stupid us, and reaching further, frontiering and pioneering away, reaching and reaching too far, and forever losing our own base. Not good enough to be gods, and not good enough to be animals.

In the tent in Hargeisa, Jama quickly offered up another few lines from his national poet Hadrawi, in another swirl of rasping vowels, and again offered his own swift translation:

> The real victory comes when you put all things together
> Both the split and alienated self
> And the dissenting body politic
> Holding them all in one place is the victory, not one side
> beating the other . . .

The explicit intent here is political, but the binding together of the broken self, together with the collapsed polity, seems to offer Hamletian solutions, however impermanent. In Hargeisa, we saw the inverse of Hamlet's speech. Here there was no Renaissance luxury, little dizzying sense of new potentials; here there was toughness and brutality, here far too much of the insolence of office, enforced with bullets and knives. But alongside that harshness, you saw acts of commitment, all the more remarkable for their context. A bright splash of shopfront art, a desire to enable others to understand more through a library, a need to bear witness to horrors through painting – these may not be Hamlet's Renaissance ideas of dizzying potentiality, but they were as great an expression of what it is to be human, and to reach for more. Given the courage it took to make them, it is hard to sum up the totality of their grace.

'What a piece of work is a man!' summons up brilliance when we say it in the comfort of the West, where we think of Michelangelo, Shakespeare or Mozart as being at the summit of human endeavour. But when you see life at the rawer end of experience, it is modest acts of courage and human ambition that summon the spirit of Hamlet's hope.

Then, just in case we over-sentimentalise Jama, he gave us his last bit of poetry, a man's song to his camel. Giggling throughout his recital, he translated it and apologised for its chauvinism:

> When you die, the people will go hungry,
> When a man dies, society will collapse . . .
> When a woman dies a man prepares to go out and find
> another wife . . .

Jama hooted with delight at the disapproving faces of the women on our team.

★ ★ ★

The performance that evening was tough. We were playing in a low-ceilinged ballroom at the hotel, with the least-sexy flat-white (with a shade of green) lighting in the history of luminescence. Pre-show there was the usual front-of-house chaos, though happily the room was packed, and with people who we would want to be there – students, actors, local people – whose excitement was palpable. There were riots going on in town, different gangs were rumbling, and everyone arrived late. The Minister of Planning got stoned on his way to the play, his car was a write-off, and he was lucky to escape with his life. The Ambassador's detail were all jiggling around looking indiscreet.

The show flickered and faded, within a very mobile audience, who were either on the move or using their mobiles as a complement to the show. But from many there was a fascinated attention as if they were looking at something rare and odd. Laughter erupted with easy abandon, and at the end when the swords were out, and when people started dying at an express rate, the audience got up and crowded down to the front, all pulling out their cameras to record it, chattering away with excitement. It was like a group of people witnessing a street brawl. Then a standing ovation, which was customary, and after that, one of the most moving events in the course of the whole tour. When the clapping stopped, the audience all sat back down, folded their arms and stared at the space where the show had been. They looked at the vacuum, so recently filled with swirl and event, with an expecting silence. They didn't want to leave; they wanted the storytelling to go on. They wanted the empty space to be filled with more serious nonsense. The silence was embarrassing but beautiful.

Something had to spoil it, and in the context it had to be me, so I was dragged down to the front and made a brief speech in praise of Jama and Ayen. There was more applause, and then the stage management appeared to do their lightning-fast striptease of the set, and everyone drifted away into the Somali night.

A young woman had attached herself to us like a limpet throughout the trip. The next day she sat and talked with us, and accompanied us to the airport. She wanted to be a playwright, an international playwright she said, the next William Shakespeare. She told us that she liked the trust in our group, that we had made her proud, and that more groups like us should visit. She said that we were good food. We promised to put her in touch with theatres in London who are interested in international writing, which we did. We left her with sadness, and with the guilt of knowing how easy it was for us to move on.

A young baggage handler at the airport shouted out to us all how much he loved the show. He leant in to Naeem, who was Hamlet, and whispered, 'But you were the best!' A guy who served us coffee told us that his best friend had seen the show and thought it was 'Top!' The young woman who was the last stop in immigration had also seen the show, and announced that her father was a famous poet, and wanted to talk about Shakespeare's poetry. The length of the conversation almost made two of us miss the plane. Clouds covered the landscape on the journey back to Addis, unlike on the flight out.

* * *

When we flew from Addis to Hargeisa, the words 'what a piece of work is a man' popped into my head like a puffball in a spring field as I looked out of the window of our plane. Below us was the Great Rift Valley, the landscape that has had the longest relationship between human and Earth of any in the world. Though interrupted by the occasional boob-like swelling of mountain inclining out of it, and though some vertebrate spines of rock jag out of the evenness, the vast majority is a flat plain, riddled with inlay and crevices, like a woodcut of early civilisation. A landscape of grinding hardness, it is in permanent and dynamic conversation with wind and rain, where once a year brown gives way to green, and desiccation to life. A patchwork quilt of endlessly farmed land, a long history of cultivation has created a detailed check of reddish mud browns, shit browns, yellows and fauns. Weaving it together is a complex irrigation system worked out by nature and man, dark etches of tree-lined waterways varicose veining their way through the dryness, creaks and streams snaking through the earth, which has softly crumbled down into them.

Communities have gathered around nodal points of water. Ancient drove roads trace patterns across the landscape, pathways which nomads have driven livestock along for tens of thousands of years, towards bare circular clearings older than Stonehenge. From a height, the old nomad routes spread like raggedy spokes of a giant wheel, in starlight rays, away from the biggest gathering points. Routes like these, made from the feet of centuries, have a shifting poetry which roads and motorways cannot hold a candle to. Small stockades dot the view, wooden fences surrounding communities of huts. Organically circular, they look from the sky like cells or amoeba, some on their own, some clinging together to make more complex hydrocarbons.

But dipping further back into the past than agriculture, for many this is where the human story began, in this Great Rift Valley. Up the creeks that cut their way through the blasted earth, the stardust surprise that was Mitochondrial Eve herself, and her followers, the originators of *homo sapiens*, dragged their genetic inheritance. Woman and man began walking north alongside the watery tendrils which cut the plain, the human story beginning hiding in the crevices and folds of a great earth blanket, tucking into the small traces of green. Cradled by shade and water, she and we migrated up towards the same Nile all these creeks flow into, and on and out into the rest of the world.

What better name than Rift to describe the beginning of our human story. For Mitochondrial Eve, bearing that genetic uniqueness, that staining originality, it was a rift from all that was before. It introduced her and her kind to a long history of separation and aloneness. Always and ever since, arising out of the dust to be dazzlingly unique like Hamlet, but never amounting to any more than the dust itself. The difference hard-wired into her and us, the first and enduring alienation we have never found a way of overcoming. Cast out for ever from the Eden of simplicity, Eve, glared at and excluded, but soldiering on. Like the Earth and the Moon – separated at birth, yet still clinging to each other – the human and the world from which she grew. Eve and her descendants, feeling like a wound the distance and the difference, yet knowing like a comfort that all ends the same. A paragon, and a quintessence of dust.

Here spread out below, the land where the human experiment began its inane and beautiful flourishing almost 50,000 years before, and here above, a group of actors flying in an aeroplane, bearing amongst many other 400-year-old insights: 'What a piece of work is a man . . .' Another adventure in newness, another futile attempt to escape the dust.

And then the plane landed with the ugly efficiency of rubber hitting tarmac.

171 **Belgium**, Brussels   11 February 2016
    Théâtre Saint-Michel

172 **Mauritania**, Nouakchott   16 February
    Maison des Jeunes

173 **Greece**, Megaron–Athens   27 February
    The Athens Concert Hall

174 **Monaco**, Monte Carlo   29 February
    Columbus Hotel

175 **Andorra**, Sant Julià de Lòria   4 March
    Centre Cultural i de congressos Laurèdia

176 **Liberia**, Monrovia   7 March
    RLJ Kendeja Resort

177 **Sierra Leone**, Freetown   9 March
    British Council Auditorium

178 **Guinea**, Conakry   12 March
    Centre Culturel Franco-Guineen

179 **Morocco**, Rabat   14 March
    Théâtre National Mohammed

180 **Luxembourg**, Luxembourg   16 March
    Grand Theatre de Luxembourg

181 **Liechtenstein**, Lichtenstein   18 March
    Saal am Lindaplatz (SAL) Auditorium

182 **Switzerland**, Geneva   19 March
    Le BFM

183–5 **Mali, Burkina Faso and Niger (France)**,   28 March
    Paris *UNESCO Headquarters*

186 **Israel**, Tel Aviv   30 March
    Cameri Theatre

187 **Pakistan**, Lahore   1 April
    Perin Boga Amphitheatre, Kinnaird College for Women

188 **Iraq**, Erbil   5 April
    Saad Palace

189 **Iran**, Tehran   7 April
    Tamashakhaneh Iranshahr-Nazerzade Kermani

190 **Afghanistan**, Kabul   10 April
    British Embassy

18

THE REST IS SILENCE

THE LAST WEEKEND WAS ALWAYS going to be tough. A collection of endings and beginnings, greetings and farewells, had been concatenated around the day when we celebrated both Shakespeare's birth and his death: 23 April. It was the end of my ten years at the Globe; it was the 400th anniversary of Shakespeare's death; we finished our season of the four late plays in our indoor theatre; we were unveiling a huge public project – thirty-seven short films capturing some of the essence of each of Shakespeare's plays shown on thirty-seven large screens up and down the Southbank; a whole day of broadcasting for a new pop-up BBC channel from the Globe; in the morning a big service in Southwark Cathedral with Prince Philip; and most rending of all, the end of the Hamlet tour. Hamlet was coming home, and then dissolving to nothing. The rock that we had struggled to push uphill for two years, and which we had taken to 190 countries and several refugee camps, was simply going to disappear.

Four days before it had begun, tangled in absurd logistics, an extra level of complication had of course been added by the visit of President Obama. As curve balls go, that was the curviest. The

President doesn't just drop in. For days, armies of visitors checked the place out – security, and press, and protocol organisers. When he did arrive, police and homeland security shut down the whole of Southwark. Robocop-like figures crowded every doorway of the Globe, the brutal modernity of their firepower and protective clothing clashing weirdly with the oak and the plaster.

An hour before he arrived, we were rehearsing a quick omelette of music and soliloquies to present for him. A helicopter appeared overhead and drowned out all noise (the Globe's lack of a roof makes it ever vulnerable to curious helicopters). 'We can't have that,' I shouted over the noise of the blades towards a White House aide. 'Hold on,' she said, 'I'll get the head of security.' She came back instantly with a man who was extremely civil and taller than Goliath. I craned upwards and repeated, 'We can't have that', civilly but loudly. 'I'm sorry, sir, but you have to have the helicopter; we need the coverage.' 'Fine,' I said. 'We won't do the show then.' He looked at me briefly, muttered something into his collar, and the helicopter flew smartly away.

Three days before, I had spoken to the company, all gathered around a mobile phone in Vienna airport. I had been told not to name our visitor, so simply said that the least-disappointing man in the world was showing up. Even though I was in London, I could hear the hyper-ventilation and suppressed joy as the news passed through the group. They were flying on to do two shows at Elsinore before coming home to London. They played in the Great Ballroom of Kronborg castle, the same austere palace of marble and wood that several members of Shakespeare's own company would have played in in the 1580s. They played before Queen Christina of Denmark, just as George Bryan and Thomas Pope would have played before King Frederick II. Various circles were being brought to a close. The Danish audience loved the teasing way the company dealt with the Danish royal, and treated the play very much as their own.

On the Saturday morning, we all had to come in at 7.30 and pass through airport security in the foyer. After our rehearsal, we were ushered into the wigs and wardrobe space backstage to await the arrival. It felt odd and a little resistible that this army was moving into our house, forcing us to live in our own corridors. As the world's least-disappointing man moved through the backstage area, we shadowed him, chaperoned by his staff. We were full of giggles and silliness, and kept being told to shush by aides various. As we were about to go out and meet him, I turned to the group and said, 'April Fool!', and they burst into big laughter. More shushing, and then we were out and off.

The company did great. The music relaxed the air and made the presentation less formal. Obama stood in the yard on one side, almost a hundred press on the other, the actors in the middle, and Matt, Ladi and Naeem steered us through the major speeches. They were crisp and clear and precise and spoke with feeling, and the President was attentive and alert. I invited him to come and join us on stage, and he did, shaking everyone's hand. We chatted of this and that, his honesty and his warmth disarming. At the end, he was told that I was leaving my post the next day. 'What are you going to do?' he asked. 'I have no idea,' I said. 'Well, maybe you can come and hang out on the beach with me.' That just about made my year. We did a photo together, shaking hands. Involuntarily a noise came out of my gut, which could just about be discerned as me saying, 'Thank you, sir. You have been an inspiration to me and to my daughters.' He looked alarmed at first, since the gruff noise sounded more like someone making a discreet pass than a message of gratitude, but he settled, said an uncertain 'Thank you', and was then ushered away. 'That was better than the whole tour,' Ladi said.

Activity was frantic as we tried to kick our public event into life and force the company which was mounting the big screens up and down the Southbank to agree with us that turning them on might be advantageous. This was a big free giveaway event which would play over the weekend to a couple of hundred thousand people, some dedicated Shakespeareans, some casual passers-by. Simultaneously I had to rush to Southwark Cathedral, the community that Shakespeare and his company would have worshipped in, the place where his younger brother is buried, to attend a service which Prince Philip was attending. This combination – playing to a huge public audience being given culture for little or for free, while simultaneously playing to a queen, a president and a prince in the space of two days – was very Globe, both then and now. The service was slow (why is the Church so fond of pauses?), so I had to leave early to rush back to do a BBC live broadcast. The fiction of this was that they were filming the moment when the *Hamlet* company comes home, whereas the company had already been back for twenty-four hours. No matter, they entered the Globe through one of the vomitoria, and we all whooped and cheered, though our hammy acting of amazement had to be seen to be believed. We did a ceremony of greeting, which bordered on the hysterical, and then everyone prepared for the first of four shows that weekend. We still had real business to do.

When the first matinee was about to start, I nipped into the theatre to see the show up. Above the stage we had placed a screen on which, during the preshow, as the actors milled around and greeted the audience, we were showing a series of images from the tour. They triggered a rush of memories and feelings: Ladi standing in the Zaatari refugee camp soliloquising to a room of Syrians; a group of kids in a sports hall on a Pacific Island;

the company jigging on the sands of Djibouti to a gathering of Yemeni refugees; the assembled ambassadors of the UN (that picture raised a laugh); the improvised space in Cameroon; the wide courtyard in Latvia; many more of the actors caught in the articulate whirl of storytelling, and the audience attending with the stopped breath of excitement; in all of them the generous faces of the actors and the shining faces of the audience. The photos stopped, the actors began the music for the opening, Tommy stepped forward and said, 'Good afternoon', and the audience roared and roared and roared. And roared. The affection shown to the company, for their efforts, for their steadiness, for their achievement, for all that mileage, was overwhelming.

★ ★ ★

There are a host of ironies running through Hamlet's last words, 'The rest is silence.' Peter O'Toole used to tell a story of when he played the part at the Old Vic. At the end of his first day of doing the complete text in two shows, an eight-hour marathon, he said, 'The rest is silence', then muttered loudly for the benefit of the company, 'And thank fuck for that!' His fellow actors got such terrible giggles that when they had to hoist his corpse up on their shoulders, the whole caravan shook uncontrollably, and they almost dropped him. Not least of the ironies is the wrongness of it. If there is one thing that Hamlet has not been since his first death in 1601, it is silent. He has reincarnated, and his words have been quoted and requoted more often than any dramatic character. He may die in one place, but he springs back to life instantaneously somewhere else in the world, questioning, answering, talking.

The last scene is a whirlwind, and a bugger to stage. I think we only got close to bringing it off two or three times in the hundred or so iterations that I saw over the tour's many performances. There is so much plotting to cover – the fight, the sword that is tipped with poison, the goblet within which Claudius drops a poisoned pearl and its movement around the stage, the multiple betrayals. It is a hard enough technical achievement to tell the simple story, let alone cover the relationships: Hamlet's reconciliation with Laertes; Claudius's parting from Gertrude; Gertrude's reach-out towards her son; Hamlet's conclusion with Claudius; his farewell to Horatio; and his final farewell to his greatest love and his greatest adversary: life. All happens in only about five minutes of stage time. It is hard within that typhoon to keep gracefully on top of the action and to give each moment its appropriate weight. Within that chaos, we have to watch Hamlet die. Whether we love or loathe Hamlet, whether we admire or disapprove of the actor playing Hamlet, the mechanics of the play have compelled us to feel intimate with him, and watching an intimate die is always a blend of compulsion and abiding sorrow.

From the moment the court enter the scene to join Hamlet, he knows in his bones that the end is approaching. He makes peace of a sort with Laertes, he leaves his mother and the court in no doubt as to the nature of the mental disturbance he has been through, then enters with spirit into the fencing duel. There is an astonishing Hamletian moment of civility in the middle of the frenzy. He makes a compliment to Laertes:

HAMLET I'll be your foil, Laertes: in mine ignorance
Your skill shall, like a star i' the darkest night,
Stick fiery off indeed.
LAERTES You mock me, sir.
HAMLET No, by this hand.

Even at this moment of extremity, with Laertes working himself up to murder, Hamlet swears that he is not mocking Laertes, nor would he. He is hurt at the suggestion that he might – even though he has killed Laertes' father and been the cause of his sister's death. In this instant, he can't bear that he might be thought to be rude. It is one of Shakespeare's contrary and all-too-true grace notes. True to Hamlet, and to human nature. It is remarkable how an intense politeness and civility about the tiniest things overcomes many on the point of death.

In short order thereafter, Hamlet bests Laertes in two of their three fencing bouts; Laertes stabs Hamlet outside the competition with a stroke that means his eventual death; Gertrude swallows the poison intended for her son; Hamlet stabs Laertes with the poisoned sword; then Claudius too, whom he also forces to drink from the poisoned cup. After a lot of chat, a lot of mayhem, Hamlet, having procrastinated and delayed action for several months of life, several hours of drama, suddenly becomes a hurricane of action. This is partly psychological: Hamlet proves himself a creature of impulse, and when backed into a corner he lashes out, and effectively. But also it is a choice of dramatic rhythm: as a counterweight to the dreamy philosophical stasis before, a maelstrom of action. It is a just balance. It is also right that a swirl of activity surrounds Hamlet, that he is the still central point of a viciously spinning top. It is part of the nature of the play, a circularity of action, like the corridors that ring the central courtyard of Kronborg, a swirl of spinning atomic activity, which turns and spins the bright shining light at its nucleus.

Within all that centrifugal mayhem, there is something effortlessly light about Hamlet in the middle. After the nature of Laertes' and Claudius's plot has been made clear to him, he forgives Laertes for his involvement before he dies, then pivots and announces, 'I

am dead, Horatio.' The baldness and the simplicity of that statement is overwhelming. It is possible to imagine it said with a
gentle smile. He stops Horatio from killing himself, to protect
his friend and his own reputation. His plea that his friend stay
alive to tell his story and protect his name for posterity is a serious
one. Upholding honour matters, as does maintaining the truth in
a world that likes to blur it. Most vital is that the story is told
with grace and dignity, not cheapened or made simple. This is a
frequent concern of Shakespeare's characters (Cleopatra is the
most worried), as it was no doubt for the author in terms of how
he wanted his work produced.

He hears that Fortinbras is approaching, announced by cannon.
He makes a last supreme effort to act the Prince, and to tidy
everything up. What he is saying at the end matters, but it is not
everything; what matters is the courage and the ebbing resources
which go into keeping going, keeping talking. At the end, he is
almost talking banalities (for the first time in the play) . . . before
finally he gives in:

> HAMLET O, I die, Horatio;
> The potent poison quite o'er-crows my spirit.
> I cannot live to hear the news from England,
> But I do prophesy the election lights
> On Fortinbras: he has my dying voice.
> So tell him, with the occurrents, more and less,
> Which have solicited. The rest is silence.

We see a spirit, the brightest, pass out of the room before our
eyes. For a moment, we and the world are diminished. That bright
boy who fought so hard and so brilliantly against the entropy of
the world, who listened and looked so eagerly and so haplessly

for virtue and love, who tried so hard to halt the endless shrinking and falling and wasting away of all around him, and who seemed to protect us from the same, whoever we are and wherever we are in the world, that bright Prince is stolen from us by death.

* * *

For the very final performance on the evening of 24 April, I stand at the end in the middle gallery and watch as Naeem and the company play out the last moments of the play, their good taste and their fortitude pushing them through one of the best renditions they have given, despite the excitement and the sorrow swirling within them. This simple, simple show is telling itself one final time. The packed crowd is full of old friends and public all willing them through it. As the dead rise to dance their final jig, the crowd erupts, the groundlings with hands over their heads applauding, the galleries standing to acclaim. I rush back to the tiring house, then after their second call I step out to join them, as is the habit at the Globe, to say a few words. I am worried that I will collapse into tears, but the company around me look exhausted and liberated and free, and the Globe at these moments has such energy in it, such generous blessed health, as you look out in the shared light to see face on face, that I get through it. It is hard to feel sorrow when held within such an embrace of life. I thank the audience, I thank the creative team, I thank our mission control and everyone who has helped to hold the project together, and then finally the company themselves. Then I step back to let the company take their final call. As is the Globe habit on a final show, they throw roses out into the sky and the crowd, and roses are hurled back at them. I look back from the central doors and see the lit-up company standing and moving within a rain of roses falling from above, with a carpet of roses spreading around their feet and a storm of noisy goodwill landing around them.

Eventually, they make their way back to the tiring house, where I await them. We fall immediately into greedy clutching, and tears flow freely. Partners are swapped in a carousel, a daisy-chain of bear-hugging, clinging to each other as if to stay upright, as if to stop from falling. The tightness of the squeezing, the unembarrassed need in it, tells its own story. Beyond this room wait lovers and family and friends, to reclaim each of these people for themselves and for the future. Within the room, still with make-up on and still dressed funny, this small company, who have shared the last two years as if they were one body, say without words, and just with their holding of each other, thank you, and sorry, and I forgive you, and I will miss you so much, and wasn't that something, and, because of the cruel ephemeral nature of our game, goodbye. We have travelled all the way round one world, and now we are all going back into another. And into a long silence.

CONCLUSION

THE COMPANY WERE PLAYING IN St Lucia, in the West Indies, and they had been told to expect a rowdy house. A little talking back and a little spontaneous collaboration from the audience was part of the culture here. There was a hum of natter throughout, and a constant sense of characters and choices being dissected, but it was far from intrusive. That is until Hamlet, by mistake, lashed out at the arras with his sword and pulled it back to reveal the mortally wounded Polonius. Hamlet left a pregnant pause here, probably over-pregnant, since it was interrupted by a woman's voice from the second row, drawling out with relief, 'Fiiiiinally, somebody dying' . . .

They were performing in the west of Cameroon in a refugee camp set up for displaced people from the Central African Republic. They arrived on a bus in the morning with no idea where or how they were going to do the show. Tom Bird was with them and managed to secure a space outside a bar and, after an interview with the camp's head policeman, permission to perform. However, the licence was conditional on the policeman's desire to 'be a presence there', as he put it. 'Fine,' said Tom. Shortly before they started performing, two junior policemen were seen crossing a square towards the space they had created, bearing a large desk. They set it down, dominating a third of the space. The chief policeman arrived shortly after and sat at his desk, from where he observed the show as it swirled around him, with a suitably stern expression . . .

Two stories picked out from a barrel containing thousands, from a tour which took a story for a walk, which listened to many of the stories of the world, and which generated a fair few itself. Every corner of the globe we live in is packed with tales, it is a world of proliferating narratives, all equally worthy of respect. The aim of our tour wasn't to present one story as exemplary, or to say that certain stories should rule. Unification under one banner or creating hierarchies is not the Shakespeare way. The aim was to unearth other stories, and to spur more to come into the light. The tour was a provocation not a definition.

'Why do it?' was a question asked often. If I was feeling flip, I'd shoot back, 'Why not?' If not, I think I came to an understanding of sorts, though I think only a partial one. First and foremost, it was to prove that it can be done. That anything you set your mind to can be done. We live in an age full of limits, boundaries defined by tribes of people not wanting others to achieve anything. Nothing is allowed to step outside a set of norms, definitions of possibility set as an act of self-definition by the tribes themselves. The internet and social media sometimes seem like a howling scream of denial of pretension and ambition. Yet what would we have without pretension and ambition?

Growing up in the 1960s, the space programme was always there in front of you as an impossibly daft, and chivalric, bit of dreaming. Tom Wolfe wrote about the contest between the Soviets and the Americans as a return to jousting. There are a million ways in which you can be cynical about it (and rightly), but there was a purity of romance, something properly Earl-of-Essex-daffy, about sending people 250,000 miles away to collect a bit of rock and bring it home. That size of dreaming, which the space programme so eloquently exemplified, we seem to have lost, terrified by this tribe of begrudgers on the left and this bunch of exploiters on the right. We seem to have resigned big projects to the corporations who seem more intent on controlling the dreams we have than opening out new ones.

To compare what we achieved to the space programme is nutty aggrandisement, but it was a little push in that direction. All my working life, I have tried to push back against whatever is proscribed, and at the Globe, happily because it lived outside conventional ideas of what a theatre should be, there was no one to say no. An international festival, yes; thirty-seven short films, OK; a new theatre, why not?; and a tour to every country in the world, I suppose so. We were blessed with an outstanding set of colleagues who thirsted for higher and higher challenges. They worked with the conviction, as expressed by one, that if hands were held tightly enough together over mad enough ravines, and if there were enough hours in the day, then anything was possible.

There was a substantial element of taking an old classic out to the world as well. Being a play, it was not an edifice; it was an ever-shifting artefact as re-understood in each moment that it was performed. But it had gained some of the authority which accrues to anything that has had four centuries of use and life. Many in the bizarre world we live in would point at that as something to be ashamed of. That is an idiocy which we have to combat if we are to retain a grown-up international culture. We skirted around Syria in several countries as we toured the crescent that surrounds it – Turkey, Iraq, Jordan, Palestine, Israel and Lebanon. We were taking our old play around, and at the same time IS were circling within that crescent, intent on the wholesale destruction of anything ancient which didn't fit their world-view. There was horror and outrage at these acts of Year Zero destruction, but not enough, and not enough resolution to stop it. We sometimes seem to be witnessing the erosion of a benevolent internationalism within which I grew up, the idea that people talking to people, and culture talking to culture, often through the ancient artefacts which in part define them, was one of the best hopes that we had.

I remember from my play-going life the LIFT festival run by the formidable Rose Fenton and Lucy Neal, and regular arrivals at the Almeida, the National and the RSC of companies from abroad. LIFT survives and does great work, and shows pop up here and there, but with little of the focus, acclaim and éclat they used to. At one point when we were stumped for a theatre in Japan, we leant on the good offices of that mischievous angel of cultural internationalism Thelma Holt, a woman who for decades brought new voices and new cultures to this country. She secured us a date at the Saitama Arts Theatre, the home of the late great Ninagawa in Tokyo. She travelled out to see the show and sent me this note afterwards:

Dear Dominic,

I am writing to you from Tokyo as I am just back from the performance in Saitama. The 'Hamlet' was splendid and beautifully received. I don't give standing ovations in theatres as I think it is a rather vulgar American custom, but I was on my feet at the end, and sharply told the British Council to get to her feet too.

What they are doing is magnificent. This is not a 'Hamlet' in the West End and it is not a 'Hamlet' on Broadway. You know what it is: it is the UK at its best, when we really have turned our gaggle of actors into an ensemble. Their energy is controlled by them, and it is very seductive. What a hell of a tour they are doing.

I feel this week as if I have been firmly corseted, but from the beginning of 'Ha mlet' my stays were unloosened.

Thelma

At the heart of that cultural conversation is and always has been those historical artefacts, be they ruins or churches or snatches of song or paintings or plays, that teach us who we are and about the otherness of others.

We were touring in the name of a brilliant and beautiful young man, Hamlet, who sees doubt as a duty, and whose natural inclination at any moment is to stop and think, to place a pause of thought between intention and action. Who reminds us that procrastination is a virtue, not a vice. Within a play that feints at making an argument about human nature, but it is only a drop of the shoulder to deceive defenders. Finally, Hamlet works against all smokescreen certainties and painted cloth morals. I began this Hamlet journey in the belief that there was a journey through the play, and attempted to shoehorn the play into that shape. I learnt, as we all have to learn and learn again, that journey and the greatest art don't go together. Hamlet, finally, just is. The play is about a life lived, and a life lived more fiercely and more alive than most.

People have wasted long hours looking into fires for many millennia: it was the evening entertainment of choice for aeons. Until television came along (though isn't television essentially the fireplace in the corner, with its flickering, insensible images?). Or they have stared for hours into candlelight. Isn't that the compulsive element within Shakespeare's Hamlet – this example of light and life stumbling towards death – and isn't the simplicity of that what brings us back and back? Staring into the light.

Shakespeare wanted to justify his art to life not to logic. The whole structure of *Hamlet* has no satisfying logic or perfection, but it is right and true to the chaos of a life. Fucked up by parents and sinister uncles, heartbroken by the cynical cruelty of the world, saddened by the cynicism and the shabbiness of the political estate, cruelly abused by the optimism of love, and then predictably run over by its disappointment, putting off our biggest decisions with too much thought and discussion, striking out at the wrong targets, let down by friends, and perennially uncertain about where we go when we die (for all the mad bluffing certainty of the religious, and the mad bluffing certainty of the irreligious) – isn't that all of us? All around the world, I have seen audiences compelled by this figure, many without understanding a word he has said. Looking at Hamlet, aren't we just watching ourselves naked?

The other great fallacy from the start of the tour, beyond seeing a journey within the play, was that we would be having a benevolent effect on the world. Madness. The two fallacies probably feed into each other, seeing Hamlet as someone travelling towards a greater good, and the idea that he can effect it in the world. But maybe the greater good is different from the one I first imagined, maybe Hamlet is there to make things uncertain, and less easy, to scuff up a little trouble in the world. Hamlet is not there to turn us all into little Buddhas, or to represent Swift's Houyhnhnms, creatures of perfect reason, but to remind us that we are imperfect, restless, reaching humans. And that we should stay restless and keep reaching.

Of all the moments in the tour, possibly the strangest was the biblical sandstorm in the Syrian refugee camp. When the storm struck, and the light disappeared, and the wind bashed at the tin hut, the wailing children and their screaming mothers ran to the stage and grabbed the actors. They allowed the audience to grab them, and stood there in bewilderment and confusion. Though we were performing on a knocked-together set, in a beaten-up UNHCR hall, the actors were still invested with authority.

My father has spoken to me about being an evacuee in North Wales during the Second World War and seeing Lewis Casson and Sybil Thorndike turn up with a rickety production of *Macbeth* in the local village hall. They also seemed to have the power to thicken the air around them, and seemed to be exemplarily human. For my father, they were an aid to understanding the world at that deranging moment. Within Shakespeare's theatre, those actors whose names grace the First Folio, dishing out that singing beautiful verse to 360-degree theatres in a shared light, would have had an extraordinary authority, not from shouting or hamming it up, but from being human and modest and true, and helping the audience to understand themselves better in a world that was turning corners at electrifying speed. In Zaatari, we got a small impression of what that meant.

Probably the most frequently asked question of all my time at the Globe was, why is Shakespeare so popular? I habitually trotted out some blah about his unique capacity to bring together the public and the private, which was true but became a little formulaic. In the middle of the tour, I was dwelling on this question as I walked a circuit of hills in Normandy, two of my daughters trailing behind me. They were just close enough for me to pick up traces of their conversation, which was a leisurely pass through their friends – who was getting off with who, who was having growing problems, who was having trouble with their mother, who was using their boyfriend to fill the gap left by their parents

– a conversation filled with examples, anecdotes and gentle analysis. Stories about people – that simple. One of the great pleasures of life, and the principal way in which we understand the world around us – we tell each other stories about people. Some of those stories are able to gather together around a central magnetising crystal a range of exemplary factors – political, psychological, magical – which when they grow organically together become a work of art, which can talk to everyone and help us to understand each other, across any boundaries. That is what we were testing when we took *Hamlet* to every country on Earth: how far a group of people could get, telling a story about people. We made it all the way round.

The telling is an act of connection, we tell others to entertain, we listen to understand more. Within the act of telling or listening, we are learning and reminding ourselves that we are not alone, and that our lives are not entirely our own. The *Hamlet* tour was a small act of binding, a modest attempt to pull geography and history into a shared light, the light shed by an old play. It was a reminder of belonging, a reminder that although overwhelmingly and refreshingly different one from another as societies and as individuals, that our links define us as capably as our loneliness. That from the warm attachment of the womb through to the final separation of the tomb, we are bound to others, to those long gone, to those here now, and to those still to be. And that in every small act, of breaking or of building, we birth a future for ourselves and for each other.

ACKNOWLEDGEMENTS

THERE ARE TWO SEPARATE BUT confluent streams of gratitude: one for the book, and one for the tour. Since there would be no book without the tour, I'll start with the theatrical achievement. My first and most obvious debt of thanks extends to the sixteen people who actually did it. Without their trust in taking it on, their courage in setting forth, and their endurance in bringing it home, there would have been no story. This is much more their story than mine, and I hope that they all get to tell their own. One evening in Bogotá, dining around a restaurant table, I asked the question, 'Who's writing a book then?' The question floated around the table, and the answers came, 'Yep', 'Yes', 'I think so', 'Well, a book of photos', 'A sort of journal', 'Yes, a book'. It turned out everyone was writing one, until we got to Rawiri, who said proudly, 'No, I'm not writing one', and then after a pause, 'I'm getting someone else to write one for me.' I hope they have all persisted, and their books find a way into the light.

The veteran's award goes to Tom Lawrence, who toured the first manifestation in 2011, then re-joined it in 2012, then did the full two years. That is dedication. Tom is a witty comedian, a great dancer, and a beautiful naturalistic actor. I had little thought he would want to play again, but, an ardent traveller and a great theatre man, from the first he was lobbying to come. After four years of playing everything but Hamlet, he did eventually deliver his prince in New Zealand, which was by all accounts a blinder, and then chose, rather poetically, to leave it there. Another veteran of the 2012 tour was Matt Romain. Our small-scale tours were set up partly to find a way of bringing more young actors into the family. Matt was a find – a sympathetic actor, great with the verse and with a direct truth, as well as a great musician, and mature beyond his years. He is also deeply caring with others and keeps a weather eye out for the mood of all. After the first year, he became our third Hamlet.

The third actor from the 2012 tour was Miranda Foster, our Gertrude. An experienced actress in the West End and the National, she is a classic thoroughbred, though she carries alongside her old-school glamour a streak of anarchy and of innocent generosity, which makes her as much flower child as Dame. She proved a gold standard in terms of setting a high bar of quality, whether in a gilded theatre or on a dusty roundabout. So too would John Dougall, who is the closest thing to pure actor you can find. John travelled the world with the English Shakespeare Company in the late 1980s, the first British company that realised the full potentials of air travel and Shakespeare. They flew hither and thither leaving chaos and children and fun in their wake, the old Comedians of England written large. John likes to dive whole-heartedly into the night of a town but will always be ready to play the next day, with a theatrical verve, a lightly held truth, and a sharpness of wit that wakens the room.

Rawiri Paratene is a king of the Maori acting community, and the star of the film *Whale Rider*. He joined our International Actors Fellowship in 2009, returned the following year to play Friar Laurence, and in 2012 brought a company to play *Troilus and Cressida* in Maori for our international festival, one of its many highlights. A father and grandfather to many, and in ways to his whole community, he is an actor of open heart and irresistible fun, and the equal as a man. Keith Bartlett, an actor of long distinction with the RSC and the National and with the Globe, and a man of insatiable curiosity about the world and its workings, was another old friend who came on board. A great actor, he was so struck by the disparities and injustices of what he saw that he has temporarily parked his acting career to raise money for a charity he chanced upon in Malawi. He is working tirelessly to raise money for Mary's Meals, who feed over a million hungry children per day worldwide in their local school using local labour. All this for £13.90 per year. Check them out at marysmeals.org.uk.

Amanda Wilkin had been in the *Tempest* and a new play, *Gabriel*, at the Globe the year before we set off. A statuesque Amazon of a woman of Jamaican heritage, she startled us that year with the quality of her acting; she was also a figure of shining goodwill with a smile for the ages, and it was noticeable how companies arranged themselves around her good-heartedness. Jennifer Leong was recommended to us by a brilliant Cantonese company we had worked with from Hong Kong. Jen is at the opposite end of the statuesque spectrum from Amanda, but is a whirligig of nature, an actress of great grace, and as tough as teak. She is also the most befriended person in the world, and barely a country went by where a friend did not appear. Phoebe Fildes had worked in our department as the music assistant for a while, though a trained actress. We knew her as a bundle of fun and warmth, and had no idea of her quality. She left us to go and join the musical *Once*, and worked her way up from being an understudy to playing the lead in the West End, and, in contemporary parlance, smashed it. Beruce Khan is a lovely man, of puppy-doggish enthusiasm and good cheer. A fine actor, he, like Amanda, was one of those people that groups organise themselves around. They come to rely on their unflagging energy and brightness to give themselves the life they need. A demented Sunderland supporter, he resolved to have his photo taken in his Sunderland shirt in every country in the world, an ambition he achieved.

For both Ladi Emeruwa and Naeem Hayat, the tour, and shouldering the happy burden of Hamlet, was a huge ask. Something about taking on the role implies that you take responsibility for the whole evening, and hence the tour. We operated a complete ensemble ethic, where everyone was treated equally, but the weight of it flitted through their heads. For advance publicity they had to do the photocalls holding skulls, and the early round of press. I went along to do a television news story with them before we left, and they were both tongue-tied with terror and shaking afterwards. (By the end of the tour they were as practised as old politicians.) They were both too gracious to burden others with their fears, and wore them as lightly as they were able, but the gravity of the job was clearly felt. What was most remarkable was their generosity with each other: they watched each other's performance, supported each other, discussed the part and grew together. Their Hamlets were different, as different as they are as human beings, but in some way they were brothers.

The four stage managers completed the company. One, Adam Moore, an absurdly able man, had been with the previous two tours and wanted to carry on further. As well as stage-managing, he was acting, dancing and playing three instruments in the show. Two, Dave McEvoy and Carrie Burnham, had worked on previous tours for a while. Carrie is a bustle of energy and willpower; Dave takes the word phlegmatic to whole new places of levelness.

Finally, Becky Austin, who had been a stage manager with us for a long time, couldn't resist the opportunity to get her boots on and go on the road again. A tower of strength and patience, within a system which was not very hierarchical she became a natural leader.

These sixteen (plus an honourable mention to David Tarkenter and Dickon Tyrell, who did a little covering when numbers got thinned) achieved something extraordinary. When we set out, we spoke of finding astronauts – people who could cope with floating around in the space of the world for a couple of years, keep their heads and their hearts steady, and remain focused on their craft. This group exceeded all expectations. They were loyal friends to each other, calm in the face of ridiculous demands, always working to bring the show alive, and always warm and courteous to everyone they met. The hats of the world are raised to them.

For the creation of the show, I have to thank, and copiously, my creative collaborators, Bill Buckhurst, Jonathan Fensom, Laura Forrest-Hay, Bill Barclay, Siân Williams, Kevin McCurdy, Giles Block, Glynn MacDonald, Martin McKellan, Tatty Hennessy and Alex Thorpe. We all shared a bright, sunshiny day at the Globe, where we worked hard at what we did with simplicity and honesty and humility. No one raised factitious arguments about why, or showed off about how, or wondered whether. We simply did. Great bliss it was.

Beyond that was our whole Globe theatre family, a group of people who glad-heartedly made the impossible possible and did it with an insouciant shrug. I have celebrated those specifically attached to the tour, but they all made it work together, and all share in the quiet inner achievement it offers to those close to it. Whatever anyone else may say about us, we did take *Hamlet* around the world. They are in no informed order: Tom Bird,

Lotte Buchan, Helen Hillman, Paul Russell, Wills, Fay Powell-Thomas, Bryan Paterson, Matilda James, Karishma Balani, Jess Lusk, Sarah Murray, Lottie Newth, James Maloney, Tamsin Mehta, Claire Godden, Malú Ansaldo, Helena Miscioscia, Kate Rayner, Kate Ellis, Holly Blaxill, Illaria Pizzichemi, Emily Benson, Rosie Townshend, Chui-Yee Cheung, Elena Krysova, Andrei Manta, Alexandra Breede, Richard Gravett, Marion Marrs, Harry Niland, Megan Cassidy, Pam Humpage. Great friends all. And in the time in which we shared the great privilege of the Globe, all splashed with happiness at being alive and being allowed to make things, and pleased as punch to share that happiness with others.

We were lucky as always to enjoy support and enthusiasm from other areas of the Globe. The research department led by Dr Farah Karim-Cooper were good guides for us as we set out and great companions on the road, particularly Dr Malcolm Cocks, Dr Will Tosh and Dr Penelope Woods. We should also thank Anthony Hewitt and his team for dogged pursuit of money against frustrating odds; Mark Sullivan and team for spreading the word; and a large thank you to Neil Constable, our Chief Exec, for staunch support and unremitting enthusiasm. It would be churlish to exclude the Globe's beleaguered Board of Trustees from gratitude for backing and continuing to back an impossible venture.

And finally there was, of course, the unspeakable generosity of the world itself – its limitless and mountain-moving curiosity. We finished the tour greatly indebted to several thousand new friends across the globe, whose enthusiasm to join us in this escapade made it achievable. I mention a few – Jerzy, Ekaterina, Ayen, Jama – but they are only representative of individuals in each country who prepared a welcome for us and made the show possible and then special. They made our journey a joyous adventure into the heart of much of the goodness of the world.

For the book, in place of a conventional bibliography, which I'm not sure the scholarship of the book merits, I should state gratitude for much stimulating reading. Christine Schmidle, a former textual assistant at the Globe, allowed me to read and use her hugely thought-provoking thesis on the Comedians of England; Tony Howard is illuminating on huge amounts of performance history, and his *Women as Hamlet* is a great eye-opener; and we are lucky always for the depth and the brilliance of so much writing on Shakespeare, a field of study interesting for itself, but also as a passport to thinking about so much else. In that field I am indebted to many, but the stimulation provided by James Shapiro, Jonathan Bate and Stephen Greenblatt should be transparent from the text.

Canongate, led by Jamie Byng, have been an invigorating and buccaneer publisher, and I am hugely grateful for the energy with which they have pushed this book into the world. As I am to Patrick Walsh for helping to pull it all together. I have also been honoured by the enthusiasm of Jamison Stoltz of Grove Atlantic in the US. Emma Draper looked at early drafts and helped gracefully as she has done with much of my writing. Bill Swainson edited the work he was handed with a scrupulousness and a rigour for which I am hugely grateful, and did it with a tact and a gentle strength which was exemplary. Ailsa Bathgate has refined it and helped to pull all of the disparate elements together. Jo Dingley carefully shepherded the book through the whole publishing process. I am permanently struck with surprise that such distinguished people bother with my writing.

Much of this was written when I was in a punch-drunk haze shortly before I left the Globe, and in the two months of confusion after. For keeping me on an even keel, and inspiring me to keep going while at the Globe, I have to thank my assistant Jess.

ACKNOWLEDGEMENTS

For the softest and gentlest cushioned comedown after the Globe in Glasgow, I have to thank my daughter Siofra. For the perfect writing boltaway in Somerset, and for the care shown for my Globe grieving, I have to thank my old friends Quentin and Rowena. For further writing adventures in Madrid, my daughter Grainne. And finally, after many silly wanderings, for the stupidly predictable and needlessly neglected joy of going nowhere, I have to thank my love Sasha, and my daughter Cara. We walk a long way, and then we come home.

INDEX

INDEX